400 AT 5:30

WITH NANNIES

INSIDE THE LOST WORLD OF SPORTS JOURNALISM

PETER BILLS

FOREWORD BY SIR GARETH EDWARDS

For Averil, who has shared so much of the journey with me, and through kindness and generosity made so much of it possible.

And for Serge, who has redefined for me the real meaning of friendship.

———

400 words at 5.30pm was a standard order from a newspaper for someone covering a Saturday soccer or rugby match. 'With nannies' was cockney rhyming slang – nanny goats = quotes (from managers and/or players)

First published by Pitch Publishing, 2015

Pitch Publishing
A2 Yeoman Gate
Yeoman Way
Durrington
BN13 3QZ
www.pitchpublishing.co.uk

A CIP catalogue record is available for this book from the British Library.

ISBN 978-178531-032-4

Typesetting and origination by Pitch Publishing

Contents

Other books by Peter Bills:

Sports viewers Guide: Skiing (1983)
Sports viewers Guide: Darts (1983)
Sports viewers Guide: Wrestling (1983)
Sports viewers Guide: Snooker (1983)

Jean-Pierre Rives: A Modern Corinthian (1986)
"An excellent biography" Karl Johnston, *Irish Press*

A Peep at the Poms: Allan Border with Peter Bills (1987)

On a Wing & a Prayer: David Campese with Peter Bills (1991)

Will Carling: A Man Apart (1993)
2nd revised edition 1996
"An elegant, well-researched probe." *The Guardian*
"Revealing insight into the Carling behind the carefully carved mask."
Yorkshire Post

Deano: Dean Richards with Peter Bills (1995)

Passion in Exile: The Official History of London Irish RFC, by Peter Bills (1998)
"This is truly an excellent production" Louis Magee, President, Bective
Rangers RFC.
"Quite a magnificent effort" Colin Gibson, ex-London Irish

Gareth Edwards: The Autobiography, with Peter Bills (1999)
"Combines... charm with forthright views on rugby" *Daily Express*

Tackling Rugby: The changing world of professional rugby.
Gareth Edwards with Peter Bills (2002)
"There is a lot here to make rugby administrators sit up and take notice, but
will they?" *Sunday Times*

Willie John McBride: The story of my life, with Peter Bills (2004)
Re-printed 2005

Bill McLaren: My Autobiography, with Peter Bills (2005)

The right place at the wrong time: The autobiography of Corne Krige with Peter
Bills (2005)

Rucking & Rolling: 60 years of international rugby by Peter Bills (2007)
Updated editions 2011 and 2015.
"Peter Bills has succeeded, probably because of his own standing in the game,
to elicit strong views from players. He has done the game and its players proud
in a work that zips along. He has straddled the difficult divide of writing a
history full of scholarship that remains entertaining." George Hook, Irish
rugby analyst for *Irish Independent* & RTE TV

Sporting Great Britain: The 100 Most Famous Photos (Getty) 2015
Captions by Peter Bills

Awards for the author:
Peter Bills was highly commended in the 1992 *British Sports Journalism Awards*
for "the clarity and authority" of his writing on rugby union. He then won
the 1993 *Magazine Sports Writer of the Year* award

Acknowledgements

A LOT of people helped me with this book, in a variety of ways. Some read particular sections of it for critical comment on that part of the book, others offered general advice and some helped with a few specific details.

It is impossible to name every single one of them here, but I want to mention a few while thanking everyone who played a part. Your time and efforts have been greatly appreciated.

In no particular order, Michael Lynagh helped with the Australian section, David Mayhew, a true Kiwi, with the New Zealand chapter. Martin Lindsay was an enormous help and encouragement to me in Northern Ireland and in the south, Tony Ward gave valuable assistance and encouragement. Likewise in South Africa, Stephen Nel contributed to the process.

In France, Serge Manificat gave me much worthy advice and helpful comments.

Others read individual sections and gave their own opinions, like Joan Reason, a wonderfully vibrant lady with extensive Fleet Street knowledge and experience, Norman Howell, who worked for many years for the *Sunday Times*, Mark Baldwin who is a regular contributor to the sporting pages of *The Times* in London and Tim Arlott.

Paul Camillin, Jane Camillin, Graham Hales, Duncan Olner and Dean Rockett, all of whom were instrumental in putting this book together. My grateful thanks to all of them.

Thanks, too, to Tom Clarke, the best, most motivational and professional sports editor I ever came across during my days working for Fleet Street. Non-journalistic comments came from Kris and Erle Kelly, Grahame Thorne and assorted others.

Finally, thanks also to Sir Gareth Edwards for contributing the foreword.

When you become immersed in a project such as this, it can become increasingly difficult to remain objective in certain areas. That is why I have so valued the views and comments of all those listed here and others unmentioned.

Foreword by Sir Gareth Edwards

I KNOW from personal experience, a rugby dressing room can contain a wonderful mix of characters and personalities. I imagine the same thing can be said of a newspaper office's reporters' room.

In the dressing rooms I knew, admittedly a long time ago now, there were people who could make you laugh, cry, tear your hair out in frustration or encourage you to great deeds. To see this amazing collection of people thrust together with the same purpose in mind could be a very inspiring experience.

I assume the same goes for newspaper offices, although they too have changed considerably over the years. Whenever I am in Cardiff these days and I pass the site in the heart of the city where the famous *Western Mail* was faithfully produced every night at Thomson House, I feel a little twinge of sadness that it is no longer there.

As kids, we used to scan the pages of our local paper to find the latest news about our favourite players and when matches would be played. We were like kids all over the world, keen to follow the fortunes of our local team and country through the pages of the newspapers.

When, as a young man, I began to play rugby, certainly at international level, we would be hugely interested in the views of leading writers such as J.B.G. Thomas of the *Western Mail*.

If you discover a writer you particularly like and who can inspire you, then he is worth reading at regular intervals. There were some great stalwarts of the game writing in newspapers in those days, the likes of Cliff Morgan, Bleddyn Williams and Vivian Jenkins. Those guys were synonymous with the game. You felt if you had been complimented by them it was a real badge of honour. Any criticism you took as a statement of fact. And if you didn't get mentioned at all, you took that as a little criticism!

Of course, the big difference today in media terms is the march of technology. Social media has arrived and that has transformed the way everything is reported.

But whenever we toured, in the late 1960s and through most of the 1970s, with Wales and the Lions, the reporters were welcome members of the touring party. In fact, such was the trust on those tours, especially with the Lions, that some journalists were invited into the team room, the inner sanctum. But as the game expanded and the media mouth needed more feeding, things started being written which spoilt that. And the thing that used to annoy players most of all was when things were written which were just not true.

But in my day just as much as today, there were some writers you knew you could trust implicitly, while you had to be guarded with others.

Too many people think that journalism is about criticism. It is not, it is about writing the facts of a certain situation. Some people may be good writers but they don't have the emotion of the game to find a way of saying it. Sometimes their words are too clinical and calculating and that leaves you cold reading it.

But overall, I always felt I had a good working relationship with the media. I understood they had a job to do and if I could help with some thoughts or opinions, I was only too pleased to try. I am proud, too, that many of those relationships have stood the test of time.

It is, of course, a great bonus if you get on really well with a writer. That can be the basis for a thoroughly valuable working relationship.

I have now worked with Peter Bills for a considerable period of time. We wrote two very successful books together and what has stood out for me is his understanding of the game. In my view, it is not necessarily important to have played the game at the highest level. But what is vital for anyone writing about the game and wanting to be respected is that they have a real understanding of the sport and an appreciation of its spirit. Peter certainly has that.

I enjoy working with him because he puts a huge amount of time into a project. He is not only very knowledgeable about rugby but much involved with the game, not just in writing. Others have perhaps not got the same emotion, that same feel for rugby. He cares for the game and what he writes about it, and that is a sign of a good journalist in my opinion.

Things have got to be said but there is a way of putting them. Players always have time for a writer of that kind and the fact that Peter has had access to the best players in many sports throughout his career, says something.

What I enjoyed most about the books we wrote was the amount of time we spent together. Sure, it was a liaison between two people who enjoy rugby and the sport itself. But we talked about so many other things, great tales that roamed far from sport, to life itself.

I am certain you will enjoy the story of Peter's career with all the highs and lows, fun, scrapes and characters he has met along the way.

Introduction

SO you want to be a freelance sports writer, eh?

Enticed by the international travel, the free press passes to world events like Rugby World Cups, Olympic Games and The Masters at Augusta National? Reckon you could handle the business-class flights and working with leading sportsmen and women?

Can I ask you two questions? Have you taken leave of your senses? When did you last see a doctor?

You see, you'd need to be sure you were of sound mind to embark upon the freelance sports writer's life. Images of dining out under the stars on a warm night in Durban or swimming off Bondi on an Australian summer's morning may well be alluring. But they're a mirage. Most times they don't exist.

Take the night of 22 November 2003: the night of the Rugby World Cup Final in Sydney. Fantastic. England have won the cup. I'm an Englishman and I'm in Sydney. Someone has paid me to be here and write about it. How good is that?

It was a hectic, dramatic final with England requiring extra time to edge home. Jonny Wilkinson's dramatic drop goal sealed the deal. So you head straight out to a celebratory dinner and get legless, yes? Er, no.

We formulate in our minds a straight match report and/or analysis piece for our respective papers. Then we encamp to the press conferences and take our notes. This takes much time and with good reason. One team has lifted the World Cup and they want to preserve the moment with their mates in the privacy of the dressing room. The other lot have lost and the last people they want to face are the inquisitive media.

Given, too, this was a night match, the clock has long since passed midnight. And Telstra Stadium at Homebush is miles out in the suburbs of Sydney.

When we've finished the official press conferences, we need to talk to the players. This, too, takes time.

It's past 1.15am when I get out of the stadium, my notebook with enough quotes to include in the many reports I need to file in the next few hours. It's pouring with rain but I'm in luck. Without much waiting, I find a train to get me back to central Sydney. But it's too late for a connecting bus to Coogee, where I'm staying, and the taxis are in huge demand as the rain teems down.

Again, I get lucky. I grab a cab and direct him towards the eastern suburbs. We get to Coogee sometime after 2am. It's still pouring and I'm soaked.

So I make a hot coffee, get out the computer and start writing...for newspapers all around the world. There are the titles I work for in Ireland and England, then there are the South African papers. There is one in New Zealand. And I also have a couple of radio interviews to do.

Remember, there is one intrinsic difference between the freelance writer and the staff reporter. The latter works for one paper. I might be working for eight or nine at a major event such as tonight.

There are evening papers in Cape Town, Dublin and Belfast which need my stories by the time they first come in at around 6am. Then there are the morning papers in Auckland, London, Dublin, Belfast, Johannesburg, Durban, Pretoria and Cape Town that want to have a look at the analysis or comment pieces I have written by about mid-afternoon in their offices. Then there are the follow-up features to consider for the Sunday papers in the group. You need to think of an angle and try to keep it back for them.

All the while, you need to have in mind the time of day or night it is where your newspapers are based. Can you say instantly, what time it is in Johannesburg, Auckland and Dublin when it's 2am in Sydney?

So I tackle the list of orders. Outside, the rain continues to fall as I hammer away on the computer. You can't write one story and hope to get away with it – almost certainly, you'll need to tailor it to a particular market with a local angle somewhere in the piece. So you have to write a different one for the papers in each country.

Eventually, my fingers almost bruised by the thousands of collisions with the keys, I finish my last piece and press the SEND button. I yawn. I'm weary.

It's past 5am and I've gone through the night. But hey, England have won the Rugby World Cup. Where's the party? To find it, at the England team hotel across the harbour in Manly, I'd have to drive for about an hour, either myself or in a taxi. And it's still chucking it down outside.

To hell with it. I'm tired out, written out (until the morning when I'll have to settle down and do some more analytical, reflective pieces) and I head for one place. Bed. I haven't had a single drink all night. Just too busy. So this was my night when England won the Rugby World Cup.

So now you've got a clue, a small idea about this freelance life. Now you should realise it isn't all about swigging from bottles of champagne and frequenting clubs into the small hours. Not if you're doing the job properly.

As a freelance, you'll have made all your own travel arrangements, made the bookings yourself and checked out hotel availability in the cities where you will be working. The staff guy has all this done for him. He just has to collect his airline passes, hotel vouchers and such like and he's away. To write for just one paper.

So why would anyone freelance? They're doubling, tripling, quadrupling their workload in the blink of an eye. Must be mad, surely? Well yes, but why did Daley Thompson become a decathlete and tackle ten disciplines in his sport? He could have specialised in just one of those events. Why did Jessica Ennis take up the heptathlon with its seven disciplines? The same reason,

I suspect. It's much tougher to succeed that way so there is an inherent challenge. You have to work so much harder and longer hours. But if you make it, it is very satisfying.

Freelancing requires certain qualities. You need to learn to operate, to duck and dive. 'No' doesn't mean no, it means 'find another way to do it'. And if that doesn't work, discover a third. Of course, these are the fundamentals of journalism in general.

But a freelance life is lived on the edge: thinking on your feet, thinking out of the box and very often just thinking about how to get the story others can't. For that's how you live. You sell your stories only if the staff guys can't get them. So they've got to be good and they've got to be plentiful for you to make a decent living.

Let me give you an example. On the morning of Wednesday 12 January 1983, the *Daily Mirror* sports desk in London called my office. The hot sporting topic of the week, not just in the UK but worldwide, concerned an imminent rebel cricket tour of apartheid South Africa by a West Indian squad. This was dynamite in the sporting world.

Cricket, unlike rugby union, had long since banned all sporting contact with the South Africans. For a West Indies squad in particular to have agreed to tour, was a sporting sensation.

The party had slipped out of the Caribbean like fugitives from the law. They caught a flight from Miami to London and had all day UK time before their flight to Johannesburg that night. Trouble was, no-one in the British media knew where they were spending that day.

'Can you track them down for us,' was the request from the desk. It wasn't quite needle-in-the-haystack time but not far short. I made one decision straightaway, based on pure logic. It was unlikely they had gone far from Heathrow, where they'd flown into early that morning. But there are a lot of hotels in and around Heathrow airport.

My working partner and I drew up a list of about 20 hotels. We didn't have a clue whether they were at any of them but knew one thing. The hotel wasn't likely to be forthcoming.

We each called ten of them and offered a name or two of the rebels. No-one answered in exultant terms, like, 'They are here just waiting for you to come and do an exclusive interview with them. They have rooms on the ninth floor.'

Doesn't work like that, unfortunately. I drew a blank on my first half-dozen calls. But the reply I got on the next raised eyebrows.

'Do you have a Mr Richard Austin staying with you?' I asked.

The reply was so fast I smelled a rat. 'He isn't here,' I was told. But there was something in the voice that made me doubt it and anyway, how did they know the name so well?

I jumped into the car and headed for Heathrow.

When I got there, I had to find someone behind the desk who looked as though he or she might be willing to help, not erect a brick wall. And I didn't want to sound desperate, either. For sure, that would have alerted them given the fact that front desk reception had almost certainly been warned not to give out any information, especially to the media.

So after a few minutes watching the staff handle queries, I sidled up to the one I thought might be the most cooperative.

'I need a room number for my friend, Richard Austin.'

He checked a sheet of paper with a list of names on it.

'He's in 417. Would you like me to call him, Sir?'

What? And alert him the media were downstairs? I think not.

I went up to the fourth floor, took out my notebook and scribbled a short note. It said that I needed to see him for just a few minutes, there was no hidden agenda and I certainly wasn't from the anti-apartheid movement, which had condemned the tour. I slipped the note under the door and took a chance he was there.

In two minutes, the door was opened. On the chain.

'What you want?' said the voice.

I figured I had no more than ten seconds to make my case. Then the door would slam shut and that would be it.

So I told him everyone else had had their say. He should have his, make his case and defend his views if he was going.

The door closed, but then I heard the chain being undone. It was opened furtively and I was admitted.

I had half an hour with Richard Austin and also spoke to his room-mate and fellow rebel, Everton Mattis. And the next morning's back page lead story on the *Daily Mirror*, Thursday 13 January, said, '"Why I'm going to land of race hate. I cannot feed my family on principles" says Tour rebel Richard Austin: Exclusive by Peter Bills.'

It was the story no-one else got that day. And that night, their lips sealed, the players boarded their flight to Johannesburg.

But the story ended in tragedy. Richard Austin, who was so versatile a player that West Indies cricket enthusiasts once labelled him 'the right-handed Gary Sobers', was paid about £60,000 for each year of a two-year contract. But it ruined his life. He was ostracised thereafter back in the Caribbean and died, homeless and abandoned, as a drug addict at 60.

Now, do you reckon you could handle challenges like that, most days of the week? Oh yes, it's pretty much a 24/7 job freelancing. While the staff guys are out on the golf course on their couple of days off a week, you're on the phone trying to line up an interview or writing an article for someone within the hour. Always, you need to come up with something different to sell it to a paper.

And if you manage all that, if you do actually make it work as a freelance, what are the advantages of such a life? In a word, fun.

It is my belief that Australians know a thing or two about that particular commodity. Somehow, they seem to possess a sixth sense in such matters.

One of my closest mates from that part of the world, Australia's 1991 Rugby World Cup-winning coach Bob Dwyer, is a man certainly in tune with this topic. Dwyer has such fantastic connections to the Almighty that when he had a heart attack a few years ago, he just happened to be in a hospital's examination room when it occurred.

Clearly, he'd been tipped off about it by someone.

Dwyer emerged from that little brush with his maker in a reflective mood. 'Mate,' he once told me during one of our many long discourses about life, 'there are very few men who get on their deathbed and wish they'd spent more time at the office.'

Very true.

What Dwyer was saying was that if you don't have fun and enjoy life while you have the chance, it's going to be too late when your maker picks your number out of the black bag of balls and calls you up for tea.

Thus, FUN is the word that is the core element of this book about freelance sports writing.

Life can be viewed through a prism of varying colours. On one side it might seem dark and grey, on the other, bright and blue, even on a dark and grey day. It just depends how you perceive it.

Now I accept that some jobs hardly lend themselves to humour. If you're sitting trapped in an office, doing a boring job that never changes and you are counting down the days of the last 19 years before you can retire and flee the place, humour might seem a touch misplaced.

But a multitude of people aren't fettered by such chains. Many possess riches beyond the imagination of their forefathers. Yet how do they look? Bloody miserable.

I mean, is it an ingrowing toenail that's troubling them? Or do they actually enjoy looking about as friendly and happy as Gordon Brown on a bad day?

The point is, humour is omnipresent. But you need eyes and minds tuned to the correct wavelength to see it. Some people wear a 24/7 expression of happiness and contentment, not to mention an eye that twinkles with humour. Then you find out later they're suffering from cancer or they have lost a wife or child in a car crash.

If you spend the better part of 40 years in any single profession, chances are you're going to encounter some lean times, periods when the gambling chips seem stacked forbiddingly against you. It's at times like that, you have a choice. Shrug, order up a beer and raise it to 'a bloody sight better tomorrow than today', or let the grim statistics overwhelm you.

Once again, I got lucky. I met many great people in my years as a journalist. And they gave me so many reasons to smile, to enjoy their company.

Great? Some were, literally. In that rarified category, I'd include Nelson Mandela, who once gave me an exclusive one-on-one interview at his home. Mandela had more reason than almost any other human being to be downcast and miserable at his lot. The vile apartheid system in his country had robbed him of 27 of the best years of his life. By the time he emerged from his incarceration, he was an old man, his life almost done. What man could ever forget that?

Deep inside, I doubt Mandela ever did. But outwardly, if you judged him by his demeanour, it was as though he'd just been away on a cruise for a few years. And, crucially, that sense of joy at being alive was infectious. Others in his company caught it and left feeling uplifted.

But great does not just fit a world statesman as renowned as Mandela. Others, like a friend of mine, a writer for years, fit comfortably into such a category.

He worked for decades establishing his reputation. Then he got a highly debilitating illness that wrecked his career and his paper eventually fired him. He had to go to court with all the associated trauma of that process to claim what was rightly his. Then he got cancer. Then his sister revealed she had it too.

For most people, the sun would never have brushed his features again. But not this guy. He has endured his treatment, brutal as it has been, with a philosophical grace. And whenever you meet him or spend time with him, he remains the roaring great host he has always been.

He would never allow your fun and pleasure to be affected by his illness. To him, that is a no-go zone. Even when he doubtless feels lousy, he'll pour you a glass, chat and share some fun with you. If it is an act, it is in the Oscar class. But it isn't.

The point is, people like him are an inspiration to others. In the case of Mandela, he inspired a whole nation; actually, much of the entire world. As for my friend, he just earned the deep admiration of his friends who knew his story but would never have guessed had they not been told.

I remove myself rapidly and completely from such esteemed company. I am not fit, as they say in sporting parlance, to lace the boots of such men.

But when I set out on this journalistic odyssey what seems like about 200 years ago, I was determined about one thing. Whether the idea soared or crash-landed, I was going to have some fun along the way. And that was one of the main reasons why I became a freelance.

Thus, what you will read in this book are not long essays as to the merits of the *Guardian*'s change in paper size, arguments over the moral issues wrapped up in *The Sun*'s Page 3 girls or revamped, boring reports of matches played long ago.

In my career as a freelance writer, I worked for most of the London daily and Sunday newspapers, the UK provincial press and newspapers all around the world. Some elicited fun and excitement, others drudgery and boredom.

But in many cases, there were funny things to see, brilliant times to share. And this is what this book purports to be about.

So don, if you will dear reader, your special glasses marked 'Humorous times, happy events and wild, mad, dangerous escapades' and join me on the road that rambles across most of the world to enjoy some of the stories.

They are, I have to confess, all completely true.

Prologue

Diary Notes: To Paris, 4 October 1989

An odd time to be going to Paris.

Husbands, wives, lovers, sweethearts; they all head to Paris for Le Dirty Weekend in autumn. But rugby writers from the UK? We don't indulge in such things. The November internationals haven't yet begun and the Five Nations Championship games won't be starting until the New Year.

Yet along comes an oddity. France v Les Lions Britanniques. The Lions play Australia, New Zealand and South Africa. They had never played France before but to celebrate what the French called Le Bicentenaire de la Republique, the 200th anniversary of the Revolution, they arranged this game.

Mind you, you never mind going to the Parc des Princes. It's a bear pit of a stadium, more like the Coliseum in Rome. And when the president general of the FFR (French Federation de Rugby), Albert Ferrasse, a man built like a bull and as unsmiling as one of those beasts denied his lady love for the night, was sitting high up in the best seats of the committee box imperiously surveying the scene below, you had to look twice to check it wasn't the Emperor Nero.

Anyway, these matches are always a bit of a joke because at the end of the day, they don't mean anything. And that's not just my view. The excellent *Rothmans Rugby Union Yearbook*, the guidebook for the game for so many years before it became un-PC to have anything sponsored by a tobacco company, didn't even bother to record the result of this match a year later. For the statistically obsessed of the world, the unofficial Lions lost 29-27 but they didn't have their captain from the Lions tour to Australia earlier that year, the Scot Finlay Calder. So taking it all with a pinch of salt was justified.

THE fist started somewhere behind my right shoulder and standing right in front of it was a senior French police officer. Luckily for him, it smashed down on a bench with a metal covering. A pot with a few pens standing in it jumped a little way into the air, as if momentarily startled by the blow.

Certainly the French officer on the other side of the bench looked shocked. Which was the intended purpose.

I'd had a long, relaxing lunch with a pal in Paris on the day after the Lions match. No rush to hurry off back to Calais and the coast because the boat wasn't due to leave until 8pm. So I drove slowly north, for once not scrambling to make the ferry.

By the time I reached Calais, it was dark. But then a strange sight loomed as I followed the car ahead into the dockyard, to join the queue for the boat home. A gendarme was waving a torch and directing us to some dark, lonely corner. We came to a halt far away from the usual lines where cars assemble for boarding. The guy in front and myself jumped out of our cars.

'What on earth are we doing over here?' I asked him, with an exasperated air.

'Look,' he replied, his arm steering my gaze across the darkened dockyard to the normal point of entry for cars heading for the boats.

Our eyes froze upon an alarming sight. Perhaps 700, 800 or more cars were lined up, as if new models straight out of the factory and awaiting delivery on to the boat heading for the UK market.

'What on earth,' I began to ask, but his response cut in.

'I heard about this on the radio. The French police are on go-slow. They're taking 20 minutes to examine each car before they allow it on to a boat. We're going to be here all night.'

Going to be here all night. The words stuck in my throat like some fishbone. I'd had an extremely pleasant lunch, the journey to Calais had been calm and I was contemplating a gentle sea crossing and short drive home from Dover. Instead, the dire prospect of a night in the car in Calais dockyard, watching a succession of boats sail away, hove into view.

Ye Gods, what on earth to do? They don't teach you how to get out of these situations at journalism training college, do they? They prattle on about the importance of learning the libel laws, developing your shorthand speed and such matters.

But what about cunning, innovation and a sense of how to operate? None of that was on the agenda of the college I attended.

There is a phrase that might be useful here; necessity is the mother of invention. Well, I had the necessity all right. Now the invention was the tricky bit. I walked away to a wall beside the sea, sat down and thought. Very, very deeply.

Gradually, what Baldrick would later term 'a cunning plan' came to mind. Over lunch, my pal and I had discussed the qualities of the con artist. Separately, we had both been the victim of con men in Paris at some point in previous years. Of course, afterwards, in the calm light of day, we lamented our naivety. We beat ourselves up frequently along the lines of, 'Thought you were much travelled, a veteran of the game. How the hell could you have fallen for that old ruse?'

But what emerged from both experiences was the utterly convincing element of the con, right down to the frazzled appearance of the alleged victim.

In other words, to succeed, such a con would need outrageous thespian skills worthy of the finest stage. Anything less than convincing stood no chance of success.

But to put yourself into that state of mind takes preparation. To start with, it required a specific appearance. I grabbed my tie, undid the top button and tugged it halfway around my neck so the tie draped down untidily over my jacket lapel.

Next came the toughest part, psyching myself up into a lather of anger, frustration, fear and excitement. Not easy to throw a mental switch and create all those emotions. So the process began with a physical battering. Yes, a proper punching session. I landed a series of well-aimed blows which struck me on the forehead, on both cheeks and around the eyes. After half a dozen or so decent hits, some of which plainly hurt, I reckoned my face would start to show the evidence of trauma.

Honestly, the men in white coats would have had a field day. Here was a bloke in a suit, shirt and tie, bashing himself up at 7pm in a lonely corner of a French port. 'Oui, oui Monsieur, I'm sure it will all be all right in ze end, don't you worry, just come along with us.'

Restricting your breath is another way to get the body pretty excited. Although I couldn't see it, and didn't want to anyway because I was by now deep into the world of acting, I imagined my face was getting redder and redder. That was promising. But what I had to do was co-ordinate this performance, like the conductor of an orchestra. A little more emphasis here, a dramatic intervention there, a sudden, startling movement or sound, it all had to play its part.

They say you know when the time is right for action in a certain situation. And by now, I was halfway down the road to being permanently sectioned. So it seemed like as good a time as any to unleash the con.

Heart pumping and sweat starting to trickle down my temples, I strode angrily across the dockyard. As I neared the logjam of vehicles, I saw the sign I needed – POLICE. I barged my way into a bland, sparsely furnished Portakabin type construction. Long, strip electric lights lit up a cheerless scene of whitewashed colour walls and a few items of functional office furniture.

Standing beside a largely empty table with a metal top was a bored-looking gendarme. Perhaps in his mid-30s and dressed neatly in his blue uniform with cap, he looked mild and inoffensive, as if he were mentally counting down the hours to the end of his shift. Maybe to the end of his career. But he was about to have his dull Thursday night shift greatly enlivened.

I walked up to him and grabbed him by the lapels of his jacket. You couldn't quite say I had him pinned up against the wall, but it was a major risk and I knew it. Few policemen take kindly to being detained in such a fashion by some irate motorist.

The words of explanation came pouring out of my mouth like machine gun fire. And very, very loudly. So loudly in fact that everyone in the shed turned to see what the commotion was all about. I blurted out in a booming tone full of panic, fright and fear, 'Monsieur, monsieur, you must help me.'

He managed to extricate himself sufficiently from my grip to free an arm and pat it reassuringly against my side. At least that was an encouraging sign.

'Monsieur, calmez-vous. What 'ees the problem.'

'Monsieur, it is my wife, she is having a baby. TONIGHT.' You couldn't say I spoke the last word. Shouted it was a whole lot closer to the truth.

He listened carefully and I thought I detected a sort of paternal expression appear on his face. He patted my arm this time.

'Un moment, Monsieur, un moment.'

I had kept my focus rigidly on his face throughout this extraordinary saga. But I'd managed to spot out of the corner of an eye a gathering of senior police officers at the back of the shed, their attention diverted by the rumpus at the front.

The officer joined them to explain the commotion, while I tried to look consumed with grief and angst. He was obviously explaining the details to more senior men. Presently, a tall, somewhat stooping man with what appeared to be a dark cube of meat for a moustache and whose shoulders seemed almost perceptibly to be sagging under the weight of white braid on each epaulette, not to mention a vibrant streak of white on the front of his cap, began to approach me.

He was probably in his late 50s, the face sketched by deep lines which ran east and west across his forehead and by his weary gait he gave the firm impression that the last thing he wanted to encounter was an imbecilic Englishman having his mid-life crisis on an autumn Thursday night in a French dockyard.

But for me, this was the acid test, the climax to the show. I'd either be busted for wasting police time and probably spend the rest of the night in some Calais cell, or I'd be as free as a bird within the hour. My chances? Maybe 80-20 against, I'd reckoned at the start.

'What 'ees the problem, Monsieur?' he repeated, as if to try and wind me up still further. And hey presto, he succeeded. The decibel level cranked up another few notches.

'It is my wife, my wife. She is having a baby. TONIGHT.' I just about screamed the last word at him, as if he was some dim halfwit who couldn't grasp it in ordinary terms.

Perhaps the outburst pulled him from his state of semi-torpor, I don't know. But his reply presented me with another wondrous opportunity to make the point.

'Where is your wife, Monsieur? In your car?'

The fist swung in an arc and landed flush on the table. I thought that might at least catch his attention.

'No, no, not here; in London, in London. I must go to London to be with her,' I shouted, the sweat by now running off my face. Whether it was nature losing the plot and laughing at me so much, I didn't stop to think. But I figured the sweat couldn't do any harm.

He looked me up and down, as if to say, 'What have I done to deserve this crackpot on my shift?' And then he, too, invoked the 'calmez-vous' routine. 'Un moment, Monsieur, un moment.'

His heavy footsteps made their way down to the back of the shed where his colleagues awaited. Some muttering ensued among them. I suspected eyes were studying me and felt another example of the West End stage routine was required. Quietly stopping any more breathing for a short time and then wiping my forehead with an exasperated, desperate flourish of the arm, I kept my head down and temperature up.

Presently, almost disbelievingly, I heard a single word used amid the huddle. The word was 'humanitaire'.

Eventually, the chief left his huddle and walked down the shed towards me to deliver his verdict. For the first time, he peered forward with a modicum of concern upon his face.

'Monsieur,' he said carefully, 'you must say nuthin'. But you take your car, you go back around 'ere, down zees road and through 'ere. We will show you.'

Quite honestly, I wasn't far short of crying myself by this stage. Whether they were tears of laughter, joy or sheer relief I never knew. But I felt Laurence Olivier never finished one of his virtuoso performances without some flourish, so I put both hands on the French police officer's shoulders, looked deep into his eyes and said weakly, 'Monsieur, I thank you so much.'

Outside the shed, my mind was instantly plotting the next step. 'Now don't go whooping and hollering back across the dockyard like an idiot because that will ruin your chances of the Oscar,' I told myself. So I plodded, wiped away imaginary tears from each eye (just in case they were looking) and slowly made my way back to the car.

Extricating my vehicle from the mess, I steered my way slowly back out of the blocked dockyard and on to the side road which was solely for police vehicles. Eventually, I came to a barrier with a metal arm blocking my path.

Magically, the arm lifted and as I drove through, the loveliest sight in all France greeted me. No, not Brigitte Bardot stepping naked out of a fur coat to welcome me; not even a case of Cristal champagne awaiting my arrival. But there stood a plain and simple gendarme. And joy of joys, what did he do? He SALUTED me.

If I hadn't still been strictly in acting mode, I would have burst out laughing. But I offered a sort of serious, well-meaning Presidential wave in return and continued on my way.

The chaos around the police checkpoint meant they had to force a path open for me. No security check, nothing. I drove unhindered past more lines of waiting cars, up on to the ramp and down into the bowels of the boat.

I hadn't been on board five minutes when the giant doors began to close, readying the ship for sea. If there were 50 other cars loaded by that time, it would have been a surprise.

So where do you go to celebrate such a trick? Why, where all gentlemen go, of course. The gentlemen's room.

I faced the wall and pondered the scam. Beside me, an elderly gentleman attended to nature's needs and let out a long sigh that I somehow detected might not be altogether to do with the passage of liquid waste.

'It's a disgrace,' he stormed. 'We have been here seven hours waiting for a boat. How long were you there?'

'Oh, I suppose about 25 minutes in all,' I replied, matter-of-factly.

I never actually looked to check but I had the sense that his hands fell to his side and a little trickle of water missed its intended target and dropped on to the floor.

Part 1

SOME go to journalism colleges, some to university. I went to church to become a sports writer.

I should declare my true motives at this point. And that muttering you hear is no Gregorian chant, just formal apologies to the ecclesiastical brethren. For all my cherubic expressions from the choir stalls each week, I had devious, ulterior motives.

Every Sunday morning at our local church, a few pages of scruffy notes were always stuffed inside my prayer book. They came out just as the vicar was settling to his weekly task of explaining some part of the Bible and relating it to modern life.

'And the Lord said' read his notes.

'Blackheath 6 Swansea 3' read my notes.

We parted company in terms of attention very early in his oration.

'It was the Lord's wish that...'

'It was the Blackheath forwards that...'

I would soldier on quite oblivious to his words. I had a list of scorers from the day before. And on a clean sheet of paper, I gradually filled in what I considered was a far more important lesson.

'The Swansea half-backs could not break down an efficient Blackheath defence.'

Nor was this simply a vainglorious exercise in filling time while the vicar droned on. I knew he talked for about 20 minutes. That was my deadline. I would aim to get down about 150 words by then.

My first ever deadline. I was seven years old.

It was either something extraordinary or very sad. I've never been quite sure which.

℔ ℔ ℔ ℔ ℔

I never had a hope of making school work. The crucial year when I took my senior exams was 1966. That should give you a clue. The whole period of the examinations coincided with the World Cup which Bobby Moore's England would win. I mean, what chance did a sports-mad youngster have? Which idiot could possibly have scheduled school examinations for roughly the same time as the World Cup finals?

Honestly, which would you have chosen to study – Bobby Charlton's searing shots that threatened to tear the roof out of the Wembley net, or some algebraic formula? Not even history, a subject I would come to adore all my adult life, had much of a chance.

The only history I was interested in that month concerned previous World Cups. I could tell you about 1962 and the South American World Cup. And, clever boy that I was, I knew there were two Koreas although only one, the North, featured in those 1966 finals.

So the ecstasy of England's triumph was cruelly terminated when a grim-faced father walked into the bedroom one morning with my results. It was like a prison sentence about to be read out. Not even the replay of a Bobby Charlton goal could put a smile on my face at that moment.

But I had a 'Get out of Jail' card. And now was the time to play it.

After all, I'd known nine years earlier what I wanted to do. In the winter gloaming at Blackheath's Rectory Field ground in south-east London, we kids would wait eagerly for the end of the game. Blackheath v Swansea, Blackheath v Harlequins, Blackheath v Oxford University, it didn't matter which game it was.

Almost the moment the match was over, piles of glutinous mud all over the ground, we'd dash on, grab one of those old heavy, mud-caked leather balls and immediately start to pass or kick it. Mind you, they often seemed heavier than a couple of us put together.

As the crowd drifted away and the light began to fail, the November winter fog settling like a blanket, we'd line up crucial penalties or drop kicks at goal. Within no time, we were covered in mud and grime. Pigs in shit might be the best analogy.

We were out there in all weathers, all seasons. Even Boxing Day. Especially Boxing Day.

Boxing Day lunch, using up all the turkey left from the giant emu-sized bird we had only partly devoured the previous day, plus half the mountain of uneaten vegetables, had to be on the table by 1pm. Otherwise, Grandfather was in a condition far removed from the Christmas spirit.

We, the male members of the family, would wolf down our meal and gather our coats. Then we'd set off across the heath to The Rectory Field, home of Blackheath, said to be the oldest rugby club in the world.

In those days, Blackheath always played a home Boxing Day match, against the renowned Racing Club de France. This was about 1957 so it's unlikely the visitors would have nipped over from Paris on Eurostar on the morning of the game.

Spying rugby men from what seemed to me at that time like a distant, foreign land was a mouth-watering spectacle. They ran on in their chic soft blue and white striped jerseys, pristine white shorts. And the rough, gruff men of the Blackheath pack usually treated them like a clove of garlic in the crusher. Still, the *entente cordiale* somehow seemed to survive.

And then, late one winter's afternoon after we had kicked the grossly heavy, muddy ball around for a while, it struck me. Not the ball, but a career choice. Peering through the gloom, I spied a naked, single light bulb at the front of the big, old, decrepit double-decker stand on the ground. Alongside it, sat a reporter. He was telephoning his report of the match to a newspaper.

That's what I'll do when I'm older, I thought.

There, decision made without a bloody careers advice officer anywhere in sight.

Simples, as they say in that advert.

٪ ٪ ٪ ٪ ٪

IF 1966 was a landmark year in the lives of footballers such as Bobby Moore, the Charlton brothers and Nobby Stiles, alas, I could hardly say the same.

Poor Dad. My abysmal results meant a visit to the headmaster for him. He approached it with the foreboding of Sir Thomas More heading for the scaffold.

W.R. Hecker, headmaster of the Senior School, was a patrician figure carved from the mould of Victorian institutions. Tall, balding, and, by then into his early 60s, he examined the pieces of paper in front of him that told of my failure with the displeasure of someone who had stepped into something foul on the footpath.

'He will, of course,' came the deep, booming voice, 'stay down in the fifth year and take his exams again.' It wasn't a comment; rather, an order.

Father shuffled his feet uncomfortably.

'The problem is, headmaster, I am not sure that would make much difference. You see, he has decided he wants to be a sports journalist.'

The headmaster's explosion of incredulity was akin to Mr Bumble, the beadle's response to Oliver Twist's request for more food.

'A journalist?' came the roar from the headmaster's guns. 'We do not train boys at this school to become journalists.'

The word was spat out like gone-off milk.

Tacitly, Father decided retreat was the order of the day. Besides, the headmaster was quite wrong, he was talking nonsense. The school had prepared me immaculately for a career of ducking and diving, thinking laterally and at times downright disingenuously. Amid some of those malcontents and no-gooders, you learned quickly that rules and regulations were for others, not yourself.

How else to explain the day I nearly got run over by a train at Catford Bridge, a London suburban railway station? The school was still playing soldiers in those days in the form of a junior military section. You'd get dressed up in army uniform (there were also a few sailors, I seem to remember, but the less said about them, the better).

Drill parade involved marching around the school playground for an hour or two once a week, in enormous heavy boots and wearing a uniform of coarse, itchy brown material. And there was the occasional afternoon parade. It was as farcical as *Dad's Army*, just a younger version of the species.

Luckily, I got a tip-off from a pal to clamber on board the great skive. We joined the band. True, we had to polish our bugles every week. But as the other poor suckers marched around the playground, often under a hot sun, we would lounge around in the covered playground, most of us taking a furtive drag on a fag, waiting for the band leader, a sixth-former, to turn up. He was always late.

In fact, he was almost as big an idiot as the rest of us. After one madcap plot, the details of which I forget, he was hauled in front of a senior teacher and admonished.

'I expect it from that lot but not from you,' he was told. We sniggered and went back to deafening the neighbourhood by blowing our bugles out of tune.

One day a year, the whole school – well, those in military uniform which meant about 95 per cent – decamped to Chelsea Barracks in London to march around a new bit of tarmac and be inspected by some top wallah of the real army.

But before we could get there, the school's fighting force nearly suffered its first casualty. We'd been told to meet at the local railway station. But I was late, disastrously late. Coming from where the bus dropped me, I had to go over the bridge to the far side where you boarded trains for London. Then you had to walk up a long approach road before you finally reached the station entrance and platform.

Alas, as I started going over the bridge, I saw to my horror the London-bound train was already in. Worse still, our apology for the British Army was pouring into the carriages. I knew I'd never catch it if I went down the other side and had to run up that lengthy approach road.

So a brilliant plan came to mind. I could nip down some stairs which took me on to the Down platform, jump on to the tracks and climb up through a door or window of the train that was sitting waiting to leave for London.

I am not sure whether you have ever tried to board a train while standing on the tracks. I accept it is not the conventional method but I thought I'd just ask. If you haven't, my advice is don't. Let me tell you how difficult it is, especially when you are clad in army gear with heavy boots and an equally heavy kitbag slung over your shoulder.

I might have been all right but for the noise this rag-tag army was making inside the carriages. Clearly, they couldn't hear me banging on the carriage door as I tried to jump up level with it, all the while making sure I didn't slip on to the live rail.

The difficulty was then enhanced by the sight of a train coming around the bend and heading straight for me on the Down line. This did pose a problem.

The banging on the train door became increasingly urgent as the other train got closer. Even worse, judging from the speed, it didn't look as if it was planning to stop.

A few hundred yards away might seem a safe distance. But it was closing seriously quickly and my options were diminishing at about the same pace.

Eventually, someone inside the carriage did hear. They wound down the window, saw me, looked up the line and saw the train approaching. There were shouts of alarm.

The door was opened on the track side (they must have been mad, there could have been a terrible accident) and two burly arms lifted me up into the train and deposited me on the floor of the carriage. They slammed the door shut and the other train rushed by.

'Nearly our first casualty of the war, Sir,' said some joker to the master in charge. I have to admit, he looked white with shock. But then, not all these army types are much good under the guns.

In my experience, journalists are far more reliable when the proverbial hits the fan.

※ ※ ※ ※ ※

THAT'S about it from school times. One story, that's your lot. You will gather from that it wasn't exactly a fun-filled time of my life. I'm sure there must have been some fun times but I can't remember them. Probably blotted everything out, good and bad.

In mid-winter, when the crystals of frost were thick in the lush grass on the rugby fields behind the vast, imposing school buildings, Saturday mornings were the highlight of my week. We would rush out of school at 12.30pm and when it was a Five Nations rugby weekend and England were at home, jump into my pal's dad's car and drive around the South Circular Road to Richmond and then Twickenham.

Those were the days when ordinary people could afford to buy tickets, even four of them in our case, as opposed to today when the corporate, prawn sandwich brigade hoover up most of them. The closest many genuine rugby supporters get to a Twickenham international these days is a chair in front of the television at home.

Back then, the tickets were something like 30 shillings and the programmes four shillings. Find me the deviant who thought up decimalisation and I'll hand you back a corpse.

Mind you, one early Twickenham adventure might have turned me off rugby forever. It was 1962 and England were playing Wales. It was the first international rugby match I ever attended. We filed on to the south stand terraces, got ourselves immersed in the middle of the Welsh lads and waited for the action. Trouble was, we waited and waited.

Oh, the game began all right. But it would be stretching the truth to say there was any action. In those days, most England teams were filled with chaps from Oxford and Cambridge, the Harlequins club and the City of London. Welsh teams were composed mainly of schoolteachers (the backs) plus steel workers and miners (the forwards) from clubs like Ebbw Vale, Newbridge and Pontypool.

Anyway, all the lot of them did that day was concede penalties that allowed the opposing team's kicker to line up kicks at goal. Copious numbers of them, I seem to remember.

I think England missed six, and Wales, five. And that was about it for the afternoon's entertainment.

Final score? England 0 Wales 0. To this day, 53 years later, there has never been another 0-0 draw between the old protagonists.

'Welcome to the sport, son. Cracking game, wasn't it?'

'Er, Dad, can we go to Charlton next time instead?'

But of course we didn't. Kept making the same faithful trek to Twickenham. And it did get better.

Naturally, Sod's Law decreed that I missed seeing one of the greatest ever tries scored on the ground. It was 1965 and England were hosting Scotland. The Scots led, 3-0, until the dying moments of a foul day when the England left wing got the ball and set off into the mist and rain, a la Oates leaving the tent, on the most unlikely prospect of reaching the Scottish line 90 metres away.

With conditions underfoot resembling a farmyard, Northampton's finest Andy Hancock side-stepped a couple of opponents yet somehow managed to keep his feet on the liquid mud. Opponents slipped and slithered as they tried to reach him but all failed. So the poor bloke had no choice but to keep going.

By the time he reached the Scottish line and flopped over it, he looked as though he'd just completed a route march across Britain from John O'Groats to Land's End. And then some idiot wondered why he hadn't run around behind the goal posts to make the conversion easier. Which part of the sentence 'I'm knackered' do you not understand?

So the kick was missed and it was a 3-3 draw. But it became known as Hancock's match.

I'd have seen it all, rather than avidly reading about it in the next day's papers and seeing it on the TV highlights, but for one thing. I had a music exam at 3pm that very day, just as they were kicking off at Twickenham.

I've always born a grudge against pianos for missing that try that day.

%%% %%% %%% %%% %%%

THREE pounds, seven shillings and sixpence. That was it. My first weekly wage in my first job, at Hayter's Sports Agency in London.

Outrageous exploitation? Well, not exactly given that I was one of the youngsters charged with making tea and phoning the stories written by the real reporters on the staff. We kids were only playing at it in those days. Charlatans, fraudsters, wannabes the lot of us.

We'd do shift hours – 9am–5pm, 12noon–8pm or the dreaded 2pm–10pm. And with the last, your final task of the day was to nip around Fleet Street and deliver to all the national newspapers an envelope of results from sports such as squash or real tennis which had been played that night, then telephoned into the office, printed and run off on the office copier by an old chap whose face was creased by the smoke drifting out of his strong Capstan cigarette, which seemed permanently attached to his lips.

And you'd curse *The Guardian* and *The Sun*. Their offices were way out, at Grays Inn Road, Holborn, and in the old Covent Garden at Endell Street.

If you were really late and in danger of missing the train home, you might inadvertently slip those last two envelopes into a nearby post box. Well, it was only the squash results, they probably wouldn't even use them that night.

Hayter's had a lofty office on the top floor of an old wartime-type building in Shoe Lane, off Fleet Street. For some of the senior staff trying to negotiate the steps after a long, tiring lunch it could be hazardous. It was an odd thing but I'd sometimes hear some of them singing to themselves as they made the ascent. Presumably to pass the time on the journey.

Our big excitement as kids came when they let us out on Saturdays to attend a game. Not to write anything, of course. It was far too premature for that. But we'd go as the telephonist, to telephone a proper reporter's copy or story to a newspaper.

I remember one foggy November night in the late 1960s down at Fulham beside the Thames. They were playing Manchester United in a League Cup replay. Sometimes, as the telephonist, you got a seat in the press box. Boy, you were lording it on those occasions. But if it was packed, you squatted down on the steps of the press box in the old wooden stand.

You would either phone the reporter's match report as the game progressed, or you had to be ready once the final whistle had blown.

I was told to phone for the guy from the *Manchester Guardian*. Didn't know who he was, but he'd find me, I was told.

Five minutes after the game ended, I heard a voice shout, 'Hayter's boy.' That was my cue. I crossed the press box and there stood a gentleman in a long trench coat with bushy eyebrows, thick jowls and a kindly smile.

'Would you be so kind,' he said in his gravelly voice, as he leant over the bench and slipped me the two typed pages of his match report. I looked at them but felt something underneath. It was a £5 note. I can tell you, in 1967, £5 was very definitely worth having. Especially when your weekly wage was £3, seven shillings and sixpence.

But then, that man always had style. He was different class, John Arlott.

%, %, %, %, %

YOU might have been just a kid, and there were no guarantees you'd ever make it as a journalist. Even so, you'd get to some smart places on the circuit: Arsenal, Chelsea, Tottenham and West Ham. If someone was in a foul mood in the office and really didn't like you, it'd be Millwall at the old Den.

At Highbury, the charismatic old Arsenal ground, they had the best half-time food and especially hot sausage rolls anywhere in London. It was calamitous if you had to phone someone's story during half-time. By the time you had done that and got downstairs, most of the food had gone.

In time, they even let us kids out for a real game. Not to cover Arsenal v Tottenham or Fulham v Manchester United, you understand. But maybe Crystal Palace Reserves v Plymouth Argyle Reserves. A 150-word report to be phoned at the end to the *Western Morning News* in Plymouth. Is it even still going?

And so it began. A life lived knee-deep in newspapers. This was Fleet Street in its pomp, the long trailer lorries blocking all the hooting traffic as they unloaded vast reels of paper to the *Daily Express* building, the so-called Black Lubyanka, just up the side of Fleet Street, and the bustling, rushing vans of Associated Newspapers darting off here, there and everywhere with the stacked early editions of the *Daily Mail*, *Daily Sketch* or, in the daytime, *London Evening News*. The hive of activity was as frenetic as the London docks.

At night, if you worked late, you'd nip into the printing room of the *Telegraph*, or *Mail* or *Express* and spy out a friendly, familiar figure checking the early editions. Amid the deafening roar of the presses, he'd always slip you a fresh copy to read on the journey home.

One day in 1968, there was great excitement in the office. Reg Hayter, the boss himself, came into the room where we kids, Fagan's gang you might say, were based with an item to phone to all the Fleet Street daily papers. It wasn't a story but something much more important.

It said, in essence, that the South African-born England cricketer Basil D'Oliveira, who had been left out of the original England squad to tour South Africa that winter but then included when another player cried off injured, would give an interview commenting on the decision of the South African apartheid Government to ban the tour rather than allow D'Oliveira, a Cape Coloured man, to return to his own country as a member of the England party.

The story had caused a crisis in the cricketing world and Hayter had shrewdly signed up D'Oliveira. To this day, I remember my eyes almost falling out of their sockets (and I wasn't alone) when I read, 'For this interview, we would propose a fee of 750 guineas.'

That was serious, serious money in those days. And which of the UK national papers could refuse? None.

✌ ✌ ✌ ✌ ✌

HAYTER'S was a breeding ground for future sports journalists. They turned them out as if some sort of manufacturing company and their record was exemplary. But after a couple of years, albeit a period in which I learned so much, I decided I wanted even closer exposure to a journalist's world. So I joined a newspaper. I also wanted experience as a news reporter if the sport idea didn't work out.

Of course, the confident kid from London Town thought he'd have no problems on that front. So he wrote to about 40 regional newspapers around England extolling his virtues and promising each and every one of them that another Hemingway was in the making and they'd be well advised to offer outstanding attractive terms.

Of the 40, three bothered to reply. Two said no. But a third said, in so many words, well, maybe. But only perhaps.

Thus, I found myself on a London Waterloo to Southampton train very early one morning, to see the editor of the evening paper in Southampton, the *Southern Evening Echo*.

I had a reason for the early start. I was beginning work at 2pm at Hayter's and needed to get back to London after the interview. But the sight of a keen young journalist knocking on his door at 8.10am was something the editor found hard to grasp.

Rodney Andrew peered up from his morning post, re-adjusted his spectacles and in a voice that told of the English shires and perhaps a military background, exclaimed, 'Good God laddie, what on earth are you doing here so early?'

'Well Sir, I'm very keen to get a job and join your paper,' I told him. Two questions later, he was asking me where I would live IF I was offered a position. The cat was in the bag.

So in 1968, I went to Southampton and became a junior reporter, tasked with writing, not sport, but news. It was a real eye-opener.

I quickly learned the value of adaptability. You would cover pretty much anything that came into the office. It might be wedding reports, 'the bride wore a taffeta dress laced with…', or an invitation to the Women's Institute Flower Show, the local beauty pageant (I managed to get off with the runner-up one year – she wasn't bad going) or some horrific road accident.

The docks were a key part of Southampton life and I got there just in time to see the final years of the great shipping liners. What a privilege. On a regular basis, you might see five P&O liners berthed in the Western Docks, one of the great Cunard ships, the *Queen Mary* or the *Queen Elizabeth*, coming in from New York to the Eastern Docks, the elegant SS *France* or one of the Union Castle liners like the *Windsor Castle* departing at 1pm every Monday for Cape Town from Western Dock 102.

Once, I suggested a feature to the news editor focusing on the customs service. They were tasked with trying to search the liners for contraband when they arrived in Southampton and my love of ships made it a dream job.

I spun the project out to last an entire week. The highlight was undoubtedly clambering into a rubber, outboard motor craft with the customs officers and whizzing down Southampton Water early one morning to wait off the Isle of Wight for the great American liner, the SS *United States*, which held the Blue Riband for the fastest crossing of the North Atlantic.

As we bobbed around in the swell, eventually we saw this giant shape loom up through the morning mist off the island. She was at Dead Slow and a long rope ladder was flung down the side of the ship by the crew.

Only problem was that by this time, the *Queen Mary*, outbound for New York, was gathering speed down the Solent. The wash from her bows made it a perilous task trying to jump out of the rubber launch on to the bottom rungs of the rope ladder.

One by one, we made it and climbed, ant like, up to the deck. From there, customs officers fanned out to begin their search of the ship. But before long, we were informed there was an invitation to attend the captain's cabin. There, we found the captain with his senior officers and a gargantuan spread of American cheesecakes, baked especially for their visitors.

After almost an hour of this feeding frenzy, someone asked what time we berthed. 'Did so 20 minutes ago,' answered the American drawl. So the cheesecake eat-in just carried on.

%% %% %% %% %%

YOU could meet a lot of interesting people in those days working for a paper like the *Echo*. By that time, a pop group called The Who were creating major waves with their brand of music, Mod clothes and Pete Townshend's violent guitar wrecking routine at the end of most acts. They looked, sounded and acted like the bad boys of the music scene, especially set alongside the perfectly coiffured, perfectly boring Beatles. Excellent. A challenging interview to do.

The Who were due to play some gig in Hampshire and the same plot was employed by yours truly. 'What about doing an in-depth feature on them?' I suggested. 'Great idea,' was the response. So I set off to join the band for their short tour of the north-east. They would play gigs in Middlesbrough and Sunderland and I'd snort (sorry, follow) along in their wake. It was classic 1960s stuff. If you were there, you could never remember much of it.

Now to someone who knew only really London and the south, driving north and getting out of the car in Middlesbrough High Street on a Sunday evening represented something of a culture shock. I stood there and gawped at the run-down buildings, closed-down shops and general grime. This definitely wasn't France's Cote d'Azur on a sunny day.

And on an early Sunday evening with the rain dropping steadily on the desolate scene, it was tempting to get back in the car and head south. I resisted the temptation and never regretted it.

A few hours later, at about 11pm, it's so hot in the club I have to remind myself I'm not actually in France on a summer's day. Roger Daltrey is stripped to the waist, sweat running down his body in little rivulets as he blasts out another anthem, 'I'm free, and freedom tastes of reality.' Immortal line.

Pete is swinging a guitar and Roger Daltrey a microphone perilously close to those of us at the front of the stage, where my pass enables me to shoot some photos for the article. Bass John Entwistle, rock-like at the back of the stage, looks half out of it. And behind him is an explosive human cocktail named Keith Moon.

Now to call Moon just the drummer would be absurd. Keith was a thousand things to The Who; madcap inspiration, demolisher-in-chief of convention, lunatic in charge of the asylum, experimenter like none other of any path to craziness. If Keith wasn't doing it, smoking it, screwing it or wrecking it, it wasn't worth knowing about.

Daltrey continues to roar out the famous lines. 'Hope I die before I get old,' from Townshend's fabulous songwriting. And it's all going off in an enclosed, underground cellar-type room where the smoke threatens to choke your lungs and the heat rises in waves off the musicians and the swaying, rocking kids in the audience.

You leave gigs like that with a ringing in your ears. The decibel levels would send today's EU Health & Safety tzars into a frenzy.

They might have been up most of the night, but the next afternoon, the caravan by now encamped in Sunderland, the guys seem in great form. They say Pete never made many friends at school, which could explain why we hit it off. Maybe he recognises a fellow individualist, in part a loner. He's friendly, helpful and provides some great quotes for the article.

As we talk, there are frequent outbursts of manic laughter from Moon. The guy never stops, the madness never abates. Nor the wacky baccy smoke that wafts across the room. But then, that'd be the mildest of things on offer in a room full of back-up men and a few hangers-on.

They're loud, brash, in your face and, especially in Townshend's case, supremely professional, this lot. It's no wonder a group he put together made it, big time. The guy always had a presence, there was never a doubt of that.

Course, they carried the madness to the grave. Keith Moon was dead at 32, after swallowing about a third of his 100-pill collection to help his alcoholism. Ironic, that, given some of the really lethal pills he'd consumed in his time. As Pete Townshend put it, 'He always took pills in handfuls. It was just a habit that he had.'

As for Entwistle, he would die what someone called a true rock-n-roller's death, suffering a heart attack induced by cocaine in a hotel bed in Las Vegas, the night before the latest Who tour was due to get underway. In bed with him was a local stripper or groupie who woke up alongside the guitarist to find him cold.

Incongruously, back in England, Entwistle lived the life of an English squire, with his partner, in a vast, rambling house overlooking the fields of the genteel Cotswolds. They mourned him at a funeral service held at St Edward's Church in Stow-on-the-Wold. He was 57.

There wasn't a whole lot of humour going around on the particular days when they were found dead. But then, if you think about it, both guys crammed a lifetime of living into their lives. And they played out Pete Townshend's words. They sure died before they got old.

%% %% %% %% %%

I'D covered enough major road accidents during my time as a news reporter with the *Echo* to know the horror of them. Once, while I was working at the paper's Basingstoke office, a call came through to get out to a site on the A30 bypass. This was in the days before the M3 motorway was built which meant that just about all the traffic from Devon, Cornwall and the south-west heading to London, came up the A30.

We found a dreadful mess and a major story when we reached the crash site. A car in which the then Liberal Party leader Jeremy Thorpe was travelling, had been in collision with a truck. His wife Caroline had been driving and was killed outright in the accident.

Not that long after, an inquest was opened at Basingstoke and I covered it. I just remember one awful, arresting image – an ashen-faced, mentally broken man, Thorpe, being helped by friends into the courtroom for the hearing. That is what death on the road to a family member or friend does to people and it is haunting.

Our office received another call one day of a similar kind. My colleague volunteered to do it, jumped in his car and raced out to the crash site, somewhere in the country outside Basingstoke. A car with four elderly people had turned from a side road straight on to a no-speed limit road on a fast downhill stretch. They had driven straight into a heavyweight truck. The carnage was appalling, bodies and blood littered the road.

All of which might incline you to the view that it wouldn't be any great shock to me if I were to end up in a major road accident one day. Let me tell you differently.

Firstly, hands up in confession. I hadn't been to bed for about three nights because of various parties. Then I'd driven with a bunch of pals to Portsmouth, left the car and boarded the ferry across to the Isle of Wight. It was 1971 and that year's pop festival had a very special performer. Bob Dylan. As a reporter on the *Echo*, somehow I managed to get passes for all of us.

So Dylan rasped in his distinctive tone and the place was as high and happy as could be. But we didn't get back to Portsmouth until 2am and I had to drive two hours back to south London with my pals, before setting out for Basingstoke and a day's work at 7am. Something had to give and it did.

After less than three hours' sleep, I set out by car for north Hampshire. It was a journey doomed to disaster. Somewhere near Bagshot on the old A30, not far from the prestigious Wentworth Golf Club, I lost it. Fell completely asleep.

Apparently, the car kept going for a short distance before it began to drift across the road. It was a dangerous road with a 70mph speed limit and no crash barrier. The explosion of metal against metal jarred me awake. What I saw was alarming. The car, one of those old VW beetles with the engine in the back and just a small, empty luggage compartment in front, had struck a lamp-post head-on which basically had cut the front part of the car in two, like a tin opener. Had anyone been in the front passenger seat, they would have been killed instantly. The car was a wreck, a total write-off.

Fearing an explosion of the petrol tank, I tried to climb out but found myself trapped, as well as covered in blood. Keep calm, keep cool, I remember thinking. I did, quite soon, extricate my trapped leg from the mess and crawled out and up on to a bank where I lay, half propped up against a tree.

I drifted in and out of consciousness. Yet, when a Jaguar stopped on the other side of the no-speed-limit road, something in my sixth sense foretold danger. That's not a safe place to stop, I thought.

Seconds later, there was an almighty bang. A car at full speed smashed into the back of the stopped vehicle and the impact threw both cars up into the air. The Jaguar turned over and came down on its roof.

In the ambulance heading for St Peter's Hospital at Chertsey, Surrey, were not only a young journalist, his face cut to pieces and his back damaged, but four older people who looked distinctly unamused.

As I lay in theatre, a Polish doctor inserted a needle into my face and I winced. 'If you move, you will lose your eye, it is that close,' he said. Funny, isn't it, how you suddenly forget the pain and just keep still.

He put 60 stitches into my face and I was ready to audition for a role in *The Munsters*, the American spoof horror show of the time. The hospital claimed an ambulance would take me home. But even then, the dear old NHS was coughing and spluttering like a patient on its death bed. I waited four hours, no ambulance came, so I got a lift to the local station and caught the train home.

The worst part of the journey came at the other end, when the damage to my back just about stopped me walking. I stopped a car, pushed my freshly stitched-up face close to the driver's window and moaned about the pain, asking him if he'd give me a lift down the road close to my home.

An expression of naked fear spread across his face, he quickly wound up the window and revved the engine. Maybe I looked too gruesome even for *The Munsters*.

※ ※ ※ ※ ※

BY 1971, I knew I wanted to return to London and work for myself. And as I soon discovered, when you worked in or for the Fleet Street papers of those days, boredom was never a part of the job.

Entertainment was close by, and I don't mean just along The Strand at Aldwych where London theatre land began. In truth, you didn't have to put a foot outside Fleet Street to get rip-roaring entertainment.

Some winter afternoon one year, I remember crossing Fleet Street and coming upon a quite extraordinary sight. It was around 4.30pm, an hour when you might expect most reporters to be in their offices hammering the keys to get out a story for the next day's paper.

Not so these two well-known gentlemen. Both lay in the gutter, bodies side by side flailing their fists at each other and trying to land some meaningful blows. I have to say, the only people in physical danger were not the two would-be pugilists but by-standers risking rupture by their groans of laughter at this side show.

There was every bit as much entertainment on offer at most of the newspaper offices. At *The Sun* in Bouverie Street one afternoon, the noise and clatter of a busy working newspaper office was silenced by a roared expletive that rebounded around the newsroom like a sonic boom.

'What the fuck do you think you're doing?' came the shout. Typewriters stopped dead, telephone conversations hushed. All eyes craned to see the editor berating some poor unfortunate.

Although by then I was a freelance, I once accepted an offer from one of the tabloid red tops to do a six-week stint as back-up soccer reporter, while one of their staff guys was away through illness. Frankly, the money they offered made it non-negotiable. Where do I sign, was the only sensible thing to think in response.

I asked what time they wanted me to go in the first day.

'Oh about 11 will do,' I was told.

So, drifted in at 11am, made a cup of coffee, read the morning papers and called a couple of contacts. At about 12.30, I received another offer.

'Want to come over to the pub?'

Ask an Eskimo if he fancies an ice bath.

So we headed for one of the Street's hostelries, ordered pints and began to sup. As you do. Or rather, as you did in those days.

Lunch? What do you mean? We were having it. The liquid variety.

And so it went on. To 1.30pm, then to 2.30pm, then to 3pm. At which point, after I have no idea how many pints we'd drunk, the landlord rang the bell for closing time and I began to drink up. An expression of bemusement crept across my colleagues' faces.

'What are you doing?' they asked, almost in unison.

'Well, drinking up. They rang the bell.'

Disdain replaced bemusement in their expressions.

'God, don't worry about that. It's only to empty the place. We can stay as long as we like.'

And we did. Until 20 to five. At which point, I stumbled back across Fleet Street, made my unsteady way back to my desk, made a couple of completely nonsensical calls and told them there didn't seem to be much going on.

'Oh that's all right. See you in the morning,' was the reply.

After a week of this, with just the occasional story to write, an even odder thing happened. One of the sub-editors who also happened to be an NUJ (National Union of Journalists) official, came ambling down the sports news desk table one afternoon.

'Got yer exes?' he said to me.

'What exes?' was my response. 'I haven't been out of the office all week.'

His face dropped a few notches and a cloak of frustration appeared upon it. 'Oh bleedin' heck, not annuver of 'em. Don't tell me I gotta do the 'ole bleeding lot for you too. Gawd, gimme that pen. Right, what yer do Monday?'

If I'd been honest, I'd have said something very close to, 'Stood in the pub for over four hours and got pissed.' But this didn't seem the time for honesty.

'Well, I rang someone at QPR and then spoke to someone up at Arsenal and...'

I'd almost finished the sentence, but not quite, when he cut in and began to fill in the form.

'Right. Taxi to Shepherd's Bush [where QPR were based]: £12.50. Lunch, west London: £15. Taxi to Highbury [Arsenal's then home] £14. Tea £5.50.'

So it went on. According to this weekly ledger, I'd taken enough taxi rides around London to keep half the Cockney drivers in employment for the next six months. Lunches? The café owners and restaurants must have been celebrating at the number of meals I had consumed.

Not far into Tuesday's list came that catch-all phrase. Drinks. I swallowed hard at the first amount he put down; £11.75. But what was a long session worth? I remember one amount; £24.50.

This fantasy existence (and associated expense) spread across every day of the working week. By the time he'd got to Friday, I reckoned he'd written a list longer than the invasion plans for the Normandy beaches in 1944. And there was not a receipt in sight.

The total was enough to make jaws drop. Remember, in the early 1970s, a sum of more than £130 a week in cash for expenses was something worth having.

'What do I do with this?' asked Mr Innocent.

'Gor blimey, what yer think yer gonna do wiv it? Eat it? I'll put a name on the top and you go upstairs and get it. Or do you want me to do that an' all for yer?' he asked.

I didn't even bother to check the name he wrote on the top. I thought I knew my name. How wrong can you be?

As we queued outside an office with a small glass window, a curious thing then occurred. The man behind the glass screen pulled it open and called a name.

'Dickens, C.'

Eh? I thought I'd misheard. But another guy from the sports desk pressed forward and scooped up an unknown amount of notes and coins into his hand. The window closed and we resumed our wait.

A couple of minutes later, the same voice called out.

'Shakespeare, W.'

I did a double take and turned around to share the joke with the guy behind me. He wasn't moving a muscle in his facial expression.

Just to be sure, I looked down at the name on my sheet, to check it was authentic. It was. Churchill, W.

And so eventually came my finest hour. Well, you'd have to say scooping up over £130 in cash for a week's expenses, when I had only left the office to have a series of liquid lunches, was some achievement. Perhaps with hindsight, it might even have been close to a Churchillian act.

%%% %%% %%% %%% %%%

IT wasn't quite like that when I resumed my real freelance working life in the early 1970s. You had to work for your money in my world.

But the system, if you could call it that, worked in your favour. For example, you wanted some quotes from a First Division footballer or an international rugby player? Well, you had most of their home numbers so you just rang them up. Or if you wanted a tape interview for a radio station, you drove to a club's training ground, parked up beside the multitude of Ford Cortinas and Ford Zephyrs of the day and waited.

When they finished training, you'd greet them in the clubhouse and tell them what you wanted. They would sit down and do the interview. Any time, any day of the week. You could walk in and pick whoever you liked. They were all there, most of them friendly and happy to help. Of course, it's all changed a little these days. In May 2015, Barcelona star Lionel Messi gave his first interview for TWO years.

I'd spend just about all my evenings on the phone, talking to players, getting quotes for some story or a preview of an up-coming match. Then I'd write up the stories I'd got and call the Fleet Street sports desks around 11am the next day.

'Hi, I've got this angle from the Arsenal keeper, the Chelsea striker says so-and-so and there's a yarn from West Ham.'

Nine times out of ten, they'd say 'bung it over'. And the next morning you'd often see three or four of your own stories in the sports pages of most national papers. All with the by-line of one of their staff reporters. I used to think, gee, he's had a busy day.

But who was complaining? Almost always, I filed by noon so they could read the stories and maybe alter them a little. Most times they didn't even do that. So by 1pm, they'd have a large chunk of the next morning's paper filled. Time to go over to the pub. As for me, I'd have a nice cheque in the post a few weeks later. It was happiness all round.

I wasn't the only freelance operating so I couldn't say they came to rely on what I'd send them. But I did wonder, especially one Christmas.

In those days, the national papers didn't publish on Christmas Day or Boxing Day. But the sports staff writers who would be in the office on Boxing Day morning, would be looking for stories for the next day. And they wanted them early.

One of them called me at home one Christmas night. 'What yer got?' said the Cockney voice.

'What have I got? Well, I got a cuddly toy, a box of golf balls, a new sponge bag and a book…'

'Nah, nah, don't mess about. What yer got for tomorrow mornin'? I'll be in early so send everything you've got.'

So I set about ringing around players from most of the London clubs. Okay, it was Christmas night, but none of them seemed to mind. They'd give me their thoughts on their team's form, upcoming opponents or whatever. And by midnight, I'd done four or five interviews and written stories from all of them.

Friday nights were frantic. You might think it was a down night after the rush of the week. In truth, it was usually one of the busiest.

I'd be in the car driving to London by 5pm or 6pm. Why? The clue was in the next day's fixtures. Arsenal v Manchester United, Chelsea v Liverpool, QPR v Hull City, Fulham v Sheffield Wednesday might be the games. It meant that you had a glut of footballers from all around the country, sitting bored in their London hotels most of Friday night. It was simple to do interviews with as many of them as you could manage, whether it was for magazines or newspapers. Like shooting into an open goal.

Manchester United usually stayed at the Europa Hotel in central London and you'd find players like George Best, Denis Law, Alex Stepney and others just killing time.

'George, got a minute?'

'Sure, what do you want? Sit down.'

I'd first met Best when I worked for the paper in Southampton and Manchester United were due to play them a few weeks later. 'Go up to Manchester and do an interview with him,' they said.

We sat in his clothing boutique, did the interview and then he asked me a question, 'Are you fit?'

'Sure, why?' I replied.

'Well we're going for lunch now but when we get outside we'll have to run for it. There'll be hundreds of them.'

We opened the door, saw about 200 young women and started racing down the road, followed by a screaming female army. I don't know about George but it was the only time in my life I've ever run AWAY from women.

He was lovely, pure gold that guy and years later, I would work with him, editing a World Cup guide magazine. A special bloke, and Denis Law was just the same.

On a typical Friday night, you'd then maybe drive on to the Royal Garden hotel at Kensington, to find someone like the then Hull City manager Ken Knighton or one of his players. Once, I got drinking port with a First Division manager until 2am or 3am on a Saturday. Long night, that.

Just about all of them were happy to chat, actually to do something. They couldn't leave the hotel so you had a captive audience.

Even on Saturday mornings, you could pick up a story or two or do a longer interview with a player or manager. Norwich City came to London to play West Ham one year, and I sat down for an interview with the Norwich manager Ron Saunders for half an hour over coffee. At 12noon, we hadn't quite finished, so he invited me into the private lounge for the pre-match lunch with himself and the players. It was like that in those days.

With rugby very much an amateur sport, football was where you made your money as a freelance. Especially if you worked for television.

The freelance business I'd started up in 1971 grew significantly. We'd cover matches all over London on Saturdays, both soccer and rugby. Then, one year, we picked up a contract to supply London Weekend Television with any stories, statistics, rumours, gossip about transfers or the like for its Saturday night highlights show which started at about 10.30pm.

That meant some serious work. Someone in my office might get a call at 5.30pm, saying the programme wanted a picture of a certain player with his wife or his son, or with his car, for some reason.

So you'd have to track down a home number for the guy and then you'd need to arrange a courier company to get to his home, collect the picture and rush it by bike to LWT's studios in South Bank, by Waterloo Bridge.

That process could contain some alarming hiccups. You'd think it was all arranged and head out for dinner yourself (having left your contact number wherever you were going to be, with the studio. Remember, this was in the days before mobile phones). Then you'd get a frantic call to the Italian restaurant where you were about to tuck into a plate of calamari.

'Where is he, the bike hasn't turned up,' you'd be told.

'Okay, leave it with me, I'll get back to you.'

So you'd put the phone down in the restaurant, pick it up again and call the courier company.

'Where the hell is your bloke? We're running out of time here. It's less than an hour to the programme.'

'Okay, we'll get back to you,' they would say.

You'd return to your table and long-suffering girlfriend, mumble apologies and take one mouthful of the by now half-cold dish. Then the phone would ring again.

You could tell the owners were getting tired of this game.

'Eet's for you, again,' they would scowl.

Part 1

'So where is he? Well, how far is that from the studio? Do you want me to send a taxi or something?'

In a world without mobiles, this nonsense would go on endlessly. I'd need to update the studio with what was happening. Then I'd have to check again with the courier company as to the bike's progress.

At one meal, I finally got back to the table as my girlfriend was just finishing her coffee. My dinner was by then stone cold so we paid up and went home.

※ ※ ※ ※ ※

IN many aspects, a freelance reporter's lifestyle resembled the whore's way out. Sell yourself to the highest bidder but aim to please all the customers all the time. And to extend the analogy, you get punters who want the usual, some who want the downright impossible and others who are just mixed-up, sad bastards.

Maybe that's why you can't expect to find many normal people being freelance journalists. The insecurities would kill off most logical types.

If you had a staff job in those days, it was all set up for you, you were in easy street. Airline tickets booked by the office secretary, telephones arranged and in working order when you turned up in the press box, hotels fixed, cash advanced. Biggest problem those guys had was trying to get 25 receipts for every meal they ever ate for their expenses chit. Oh, and persuading taxi drivers from Bucharest to Birmingham not to fill in the amount for the fare. Of course, that's the oldest trick in the book. Four guys share a cab to an airport from the city centre, get blank receipts and sign each other's chits for, well, what shall we say, £60? Or £80?

A nice little earner, as they say. Arthur Daly had nothing on those jokers.

If you're a freelance, life doesn't quite work as smoothly. You have to do it all yourself. Chase whoever you want for interviews, chase the people who employ you to pay you, find the funds in the meantime, book the hotel and plane yourself, talk your way into where you want to be. And most of the time you might have some mentally retarded, alcohol-craving lunatic back on the sports desk, just waiting to scream the vilest abuse down the phone at you because some prima donna you've gone to interview either hasn't bothered to turn up or doesn't want to give you more than one minute of his valuable time.

To survive all that you need a combination. Not of whisky, gin and rum, but wit, ingenuity and cunning. Wit, because you need to laugh, whenever you can. It keeps you half sane, at least. Ingenuity, because bucking the trend is what you are all about. You have to find ways to get stories, ways to operate and overcome barriers that others wouldn't think of. And cunning because sometimes you'll need to convince people that the porky pies which have just accidentally slipped from your lips are actually true.

It usually depended on which newspaper you worked for, what sort of treatment you got. In those days, the *Daily Express* had a male copy taker who was legendary in the business, the star of Fleet Street. Never mind getting out of bed the wrong side one particular morning. This guy was born on the wrong side.

Your heart sank when you phoned up to dictate a story and he picked up the call. First there was the obligatory clearing of his throat (and presumably stubbing out of a cigarette). Then there would be the brief, weary and distinctly irritated enquiry, 'Who is it? What yer got?'

Any article longer than about 49 words began to get the heavy sigh treatment early on. Then it got personal. 'You got much more of this?' he'd say in an exasperated tone.

'About another 400 words,' you'd reply.

'Oh my gawd, you're jokin', ain't yer? I can't take all that.'

You would give him another couple of paragraphs and he'd erupt. 'Look, this ain't fair, I can't take any more o' this bleedin' stuff.'

And with that, he'd put the headphones down on the desk, cough again and clear off. You had to wait for someone else to pick up the call to continue.

But joy oh joy. How absolutely lovely it was when you dictated a story or match report to a broadsheet paper of those days, like *The Times* or *The Guardian*. Here, intellectualism ruled, and equally so right throughout the newspaper offices.

You would get a copy taker who would smoothly type your words on to his or her machine and then stop for a moment at some word.

'Now,' they would say, rolling the word around their tongue for consideration. 'Do you think that is the right word? Or could we use something better. Let me see. What about…'.

Nine times out of ten, they would suggest a word far more suited to the sentence.

It was the same when you called the sports desk of *The Times* or *The Guardian* to check all was well with your story.

'Lovely stuff, old boy. But do you think you could possibly manage to give us another 75 words? We're a little short. As soon as you can, there's a good chap.'

The decency all but came down the telephone at you. Alas, while the heavyweight papers wanted YOUR opinions, the tabloids demanded those of managers and players. And you had to brave the rottweilers on the door to get to the latter.

Sometimes, the adrenaline would get the better of you when you faced some obtuse, downright objectionable idiot barring your path to a dressing room or players' lounge.

'If you weren't wearing those spectacles, I'd hammer your head into next week,' was one memorable over-reaction.

When the guy removed them, sense prevailed. 'Um, not a great idea to get into a punch-up here,' said a voice somewhere in the back of your brain. And you found another way. Always had to do that.

※ ※ ※ ※ ※

PEOPLE turning up late for interviews was par for the course. But a week late? The great West German footballer of the 1970s Franz Beckenbauer broke all known records in that respect.

I'd gone to Munich to interview him for a series of articles I wrote every Saturday in the *Manchester Evening News* sports edition, or *The Pink* as it was known. Writing on overseas football was interesting and it was a niche a top provincial paper like the *Manchester Evening News* was keen to fill. So they commissioned a weekly column from me and were usually willing to send me to some European destination to do a series of interviews.

They flew me to Madrid to interview Real's Dutch coach of the time, Leo Beenhakker. And on another trip, I went to Barcelona to spend three or four days doing interviews with that mercurial Dutch footballing artist Johan Cruyff, as well as some of his colleagues of that era at the Nou Camp like fellow Dutchman Johan Neeskens. Nice people to work with, too. Couldn't do enough for you.

So I went to Munich one winter to interview Beckenbauer. He'd agreed the time and place. Alas, when I got there, I was told he'd had to go on some trip unexpectedly. So I hung around Munich and he came back a week later. Not very apologetic.

Others were more helpful. I couldn't remember a more stimulating interview than with Paul Breitner, Beckenbauer's colleague for Bayern Munich and West Germany. Breitner was a Maoist and we spent most of an afternoon one day exchanging views on politics, the world, etc. I think we discussed a bit of football but not much. It wasn't Paul's idea of fun to spend hours analysing past soccer matches.

Breitner was a left-back for Bayern Munich from 1970 to 1974 and the club had another world-class full-back on the other side of their defence. Right-back Bertie Vogts. Now Vogts was quick, decidedly so. Especially in the white Porsche 911 he drove at that time.

I'd gone to the Bayern training ground and he'd agreed to do the interview. But not there, he wanted to go back to the club. 'Follow me,' he said. I did, and nearly died. But not as nearly as his friend who was in the car between Vogts's and mine.

I had a quick car of that era, a Renault 17 convertible which I'd bought second-hand from an Iranian and which had been specially made for him at the Gordini factory outside Paris. When the turbo was in sync and properly tuned, the thing flew. I remember doing Plymouth to West London, up the old A38 (M) motorway section to Bristol and then down the M4 to London, in 125 minutes very early one midweek morning. The things you did to get your girlfriend to work on time in London.

The problem in Munich this winter morning was that ice and fog were everywhere. Vogts set off at a decent pace but his pal following behind in a big BMW clearly thought the footballer wasn't going fast enough. At around 100mph on the autobahn, he started to play silly buggers with Vogts, sitting on his tail. When Vogts accelerated, he chased him down and remained inches from the Porsche's rear bumper.

Sadly for the friend, Vogts's patience was not endless. As I hung back, fearing that 70mph was lethal with black ice around, the BMW closed once more on the Porsche's tail. Vogts snapped.

Slamming on the brakes, he forced the BMW driver to swing the wheel as far as he could to avoid ramming. As he did so, he hit a patch of ice. The big BMW slewed across the carriageway like a drunk, nearly crashing into the central reservation barrier before spinning back across the road and almost down a steep embankment off the autobahn.

I sat back and watched in amazement. It was only pure luck that the guy managed to cling on to the BMW and eventually control it. He could easily have lost it and been killed.

We got to the club around the same time and all three of us got out of our cars. Vogts moved close to his friend and wagged a finger in front of his face. He was not smiling. 'You do not play like zis in zees conditions,' he said. 'It can be very dangerous'.

His pal looked white with shock. Then Vogts and I went inside to do the interview.

⁒ ⁒ ⁒ ⁒ ⁒

NO matter where it was, Munich or Manchester, London or Liege, as a freelance you had to scramble to meet your customers' requirements.

Sometimes legally, occasionally by disingenuous means such as taping up the only public phone box outside a ground and sticking signs saying 'OUT OF ORDER' all over it. At least then that guaranteed you had a phone to use immediately at the end of a game.

So you might have two orders, including one for a live radio job, at West Ham and the guy who was covering the match for you called in sick Saturday morning. Trouble was, by that stage of a busy weekend, all the reporters on your books were busy doing other matches for you. So what to do?

Sometimes you might have a writer free but he had never done live radio reports. So he would call me on a phone I had managed to beg, borrow or steal at a rugby ground where I was working, give me details of the first half and I'd call the radio station and give them a minute's report live at half-time from, er, West Ham. It was all right until the announcer on the rugby ground said something like, 'We welcome back on to the field for the second half, London Welsh and Cardiff.' Doubtless, the guy in the studio at Middlesbrough waiting for my report from West Ham was a bit puzzled by that one.

But improbable circumstances demanded improbable solutions. Like the day I went to report on Tottenham v Sunderland and found myself covering the game for four radio stations. In those days in the north-east, there was a BBC Radio Cleveland station as well as BBC Radio Newcastle.

Then there was the local independent radio station Metro, in Newcastle, and Radio Tees, which was based in Middlesbrough.

But you couldn't use the same name when you worked for a BBC and independent station in the same region. So I had to use four different names at the match. It became impossibly complicated.

If you covered a match for a radio station at that time, you normally gave them a two-minute preview before the start, either live on to air or recorded, then two or three 30-second live updates in the first half. At half-time, they would want a one-minute live report before two or three more 30-second updates during the second half and a one-minute round-up on the final whistle.

In a normal world, one guy would go and cover the game for one radio station. But I didn't often live in a normal world.

What I did have this particular afternoon, doubtless by some illegal means, was two landline telephones in the press box. So I'd be talking live into the programme on one phone, saying something like, 'Sunderland missed a great chance after five minutes, so-and-so shooting wide from only five yards out,' when the other phone would start ringing.

That was my cue to start wrapping up the first report. You would finish your live report with the score line and an out-cue: Peter Bills at White Hart Lane.

Invariably, you had to pick up the other phone while you were still live on air to the first programme which meant that somehow you had to think up a word quickly that would be all right to use in your live report, but convey the fact to the next station that you were ready to go with them. So you might say live to one programme, 'Were Sunderland ready for this counter attack,' and when you used the word 'ready' you'd push the other telephone's mouthpiece right up close to the one you were already speaking into.

Radio station number two took that as its cue. I was ready to broadcast. The producer, unaware I was talking live on the first phone (immediately after saying 'ready', I had put a hand over the mouthpiece of the second phone so they couldn't hear me broadcasting on the other line), would say something like, 'OK Peter, we'll give you the programme,' (which meant you could hear their programme going out live in one ear while you were broadcasting live with the other phone against your other ear).

And as you signed off from the first programme with your out-cue, Peter Bills at White Hart Lane, you could hear the next station's announcer say, 'And now we're going down to London and for news of Tottenham against Sunderland, here is Colin Johnson.'

Then you'd do another live 30-second report. And so it went on.

That afternoon, I was Peter Bills, Colin Johnson, Will Craven and David Peters. And it sure got the heartbeat raised a notch or two to become four different people covering the same game.

It went swimmingly, absolutely wonderfully right up to and through half-time. Not a bother. And then, in the second half, it collapsed into complete disaster. Well, what else did you expect?

BBC Radio Newcastle's man at the game, Will Craven, suddenly metamorphosed into David Peters and Colin Johnson wasn't sure whether he was Peter Bills's blood brother or uncle.

'How come we heard our man Will Craven on Metro radio?' asked one irate BBC studio producer, later. Oh dear.

What was it, Laurel and Hardy's catchphrase? 'Another fine mess you've got me into.'

Part 2

ENGLAND

Diary Notes: early to mid-1970s. Surrey, England.
Around that time, I was doing a series of hour-long interviews for LBC, the London Broadcasting station. Occasionally, they were with sports stars, but I often found others to be more revealing. On this occasion, I am off to interview one of the film world's most infamous characters. But this man also happens to be mad keen on something else. Rugby union. He had played the game and was a keen follower of it.

OLIVER Reed was a quintessentially English eccentric. He could rage, bore, sweet-talk, abuse or charm for England. Whatever the day, however his mood, he was never less than intriguing, absolutely compelling company.

Film stars tend to live within their own self-created bubble. They rarely stray into the real world. But while Reed could move seamlessly into that orbit of faux elegance and make believe, he also had both feet planted very firmly in the real world for long periods of time.

A veritable hell-raiser on legs, Ollie simply loved to prick pomposity. He was like a naughty child with a pin beside a balloon. He told me the story of when he'd invited some Hollywood actress out for dinner in London. 'It's a dress-up do,' he'd warned her. 'My Rolls will collect you from the hotel at seven.'

It probably took the lady that many hours to get ready. And to be fair, even Reed himself looked the part, closely shaven and resplendent in dinner jacket and black tie, when the Rolls cruised up to the hotel entrance in central London.

The luxury car purred smoothly away into the London night – and headed east. To anyone familiar with London, that ought to have been the first warning. They took an hour to thread their way through the evening rush hour traffic but finally arrived at their destination.

It was a transport café somewhere off the Wapping High Street in east London. Regular customers queueing for their burgers or fish and chips were astonished to see the famous actor and his companion, dolled up to the nines, enter the shop and Reed call out for hake and chips twice.

'Coming up, Ollie,' called out the cheerful fryer.

Apparently, he told me with great glee, the Hollywood actress took one look at the place and burst into tears.

So the question for journalists was, how to handle a guy like Reed? He had such a devious, wicked sense of humour that he'd cheerfully lead you up half the garden paths in Surrey. He was a master storyteller and recounted tales with a mischievous glint in his eye that only the extremely naïve could miss. It always spelt danger. The day in question certainly turned out to be one I never forgot.

Reed inhabited a large, rambling stone mansion named Broome Hall which lay on rising ground near the summit of Leith Hill, somewhere between the villages of Ockley and Coldharbour, not far from Dorking in Surrey. With great sweeping views over the hundreds of acres of grounds and out over the fields and hills, it was a vast property of Tudor origins with high ceilings and a rabbit warren of rooms. Grade II-listed, although parts of it were old, much was late Victorian.

Also once owned by a Liberal MP and his suffragette wife, it was said to contain 54 bedrooms and hundreds of radiators. You wouldn't have wanted to have been bleeding those too often.

It was also once inhabited by missionaries who turned it into a monastery. God knows what the missionaries and then monks would have made of Reed's carousing.

'Mine's a pint, Father,' sort of stuff. Ye Gods!

The property had been used by Canadian forces stationed there in the Second World War. They were responsible for building the half-mile-long gravel driveway with concrete base by which you approached the property, so that they could park tanks beside the main house.

Many believed it was used by the film director Ken Lawrence to shoot some scenes in the film 'Women in Love' which starred Reed, Alan Bates and Glenda Jackson. In fact, that was wrong. Reed and Bates wrestled each other naked in front of a log fire at Elvaston Castle in Derbyshire. No matter. That doubtless represented another quiet night in for Ollie.

It was said that when he wasn't drinking late on a Saturday night at his beloved Rosslyn Park Rugby Club at Roehampton in south-west London, he would sometimes invite a group of Park players down to his retreat for a lengthy weekend session. His missus must have looked forward to those events.

Of course, drinking sessions were de rigueur with Oliver Reed. Man, could he drink. It was said that on one occasion, he and 36 friends sank 480 pints of beer, 32 bottles of whisky, 17 bottles of gin and four crates of wine in one session.

Reed later adjusted the story, but alleged on another occasion he had drunk 106 pints of beer in two days just before his second marriage, to Josephine Burge. 'Do you take this woman…' 'Yesh, hic.'

Reed enjoyed his irregular Saturday evenings in the clubhouse at Roehampton. He always exuded a macho image and the game seemed to suit him for that. He'd played the game as a young man and been an avid supporter thereafter.

The great England international Andy Ripley was a Rosslyn Park player in those days and the Roehampton club was one of the most renowned in England, not just London.

Anyway, it was blindingly obvious that a serious drop was likely to be consumed during any visit to Reed's home.

When I got there, at around 10.30am, he was already doing one interview. This was with a pretty young girl from a local paper who had bravely accepted the challenge of an interview with the great man.

Judging by his copious winks to me, as she wrote down various things in her notebook, not to mention her flushed features, that day's alcoholic consumption had already started some time earlier.

In time, she giggled once more and was gone after a long, lecherous kiss from Ollie. Then it was my turn – not for the kiss, you understand, but the drinking session.

It started with Munich beer hall-type steins, filled not with lager but gin. The last quarter at the top, if it was that much, was topped up with tonic water.

We had a couple of those and the taped interview went purringly well. We talked about his passion for rugby, discussed a few great names from the world of cinema and drifted on to a variety of other topics.

The only interruption was when a heron landed in the grounds close by the house. Ollie grabbed a shotgun, opened a window and started blasting away at the bird. 'Bastard things' he swore, as he returned to the interview, suggesting he didn't hit it.

By the time we'd finished, it was about 12.30pm and Reed decided we ought to go and eat something. So we got into his Rolls and cruised down to the local village and his favourite boozer which dated to the 17th century and where his initials were carved into a piece of furniture. There, we started on pints of best bitter.

It's true we had a good lunch, albeit with a couple of bottles of red wine. But as regards driving, neither of us should have gone anywhere near a car for about three weeks.

No matter, these were the days before breathalysers. So with Ollie at the wheel, we headed back up the hill to Broome Hall, where he insisted on one last drink before I left. I'd had so much I can't even remember what it was. Brandy, probably. And it wouldn't have been a small measure. Ollie Reed didn't serve those.

By the time I came to go, the heavens had opened. And would you believe it? My VW Beetle, incongruously parked beside Reed's Rolls-Royce, wouldn't start. It always leaked, that damn car – damp plugs, I suspected.

We opened up the bonnet and plunged our hands inside. After twisting, disconnecting and re-connecting various wires,

Reed professed confidence that it would now start. It didn't. So there was only one thing for it.

'We'll bump start it,' he said, the pelting rain now running off our heads. 'You get in and I'll push.'

It was my last abiding memory of Ollie Reed. As he heaved it forward from the back, I let off the handbrake and the car began to roll slowly down the slope of his gravel driveway. As it gained a bit of real momentum, I plunged my foot down on the clutch, drew it off and the engine spluttered into life. But the action caused it to jerk, and the stuttering momentum fooled Ollie. He first stumbled on the driveway, wrong-footed by the car's checked momentum but then as the vehicle really fired and shot forward, he lost his footing completely.

The last image I had of him was lying face forward on his driveway, completely soaked and waving his arms in farewell as I turned out of the drive and headed home. I couldn't imagine Roger Moore doing the same thing for me.

※ ※ ※ ※ ※

Diary Notes: Heathrow airport, London. A cold, bright, winter's morning. December 1988.

THEY say if you don't ask, you don't get. But even pursuing that truism, this was one hell of an ask. Not even I, the eternal optimist, expected for a moment to get it.

I'm at Heathrow, checking in for a flight to Miami. I've been asked to interview an English footballer in Tampa, a job requested by one of the red-tops, the tabloid papers of Fleet Street.

I spied an opportunity and made a simple request to the paper. Can I go on Concorde?

The precise wording of the brusque reply does not bear repeating in these pages. All I can say is, I've never tried it and definitely won't be doing so in the future, either. The second part of their explanation was more straightforward, 'Not even our staff reporters are allowed on Concorde. You've got no chance.'

Disappointing, yes, but all things considered it could have been worse. I was allowed business-class. It was an offer I accepted. No more discussions, no more prevarication. Or so I thought.

That was until I reached Heathrow on this particular morning when British Airways looked about as organised as a chicken running around the hen house with its head chewed off. My attempt to check in was greeted with an expression of alarm by the lady.

'Oh dear, would you be at all flexible with this flight?' she asked.

'What do you mean?'

'Well Sir, the flight is heavily overbooked and it would assist us enormously if you could travel on our later flight.'

'When is that?'

'In three hours' time.'

Now usually, I am in the mother-of-all rushes, no matter where I am going. The plane/train/boat is usually pulling out when I scramble aboard. Yet today it is different, although that is the last thing I tell her. I have plenty of time because the interview is not scheduled until the next day. I can lose three hours without losing anything. But what might I gain from it?

First rule of journalism: spy an opportunity. Second rule, exploit it. For all it's worth.

There was a deal to be struck here and I knew the one I wanted. The lady's offer of £250 in recompense didn't mean much to me as I was travelling on the newspaper's expenses. So the bargaining came down to mode of transport.

'Sir, as a special concession, I can upgrade you to first-class on the return leg.'

By now, we were following the Marquess of Queensberry's rules; in other words, sparring as if in the boxing ring. So you dance around the point, evading her offer and trying to land the killer blow.

I looked (and sounded) disinterested in the deal. 'Well, first-class only one way and especially on so short a flight probably isn't that special. And I really do need to be in the States as quickly as possible.'

I hoped that the way my voice tailed off might indicate there was still room for her to come up with the knockout offer. I smiled. She smiled.

'Okay Sir, how about first-class return?'

Not a bad offer. But not the one I wanted. I smiled again but sighed.

'Look, I've got a very important business meeting in America. But I don't mind helping you out if I can.'

You have to sound as reasonable as you can. Of course, I was hoping she would realise she had only one more offer to make. But to save her the trouble, I brought it up.

'Look,' I said, ever so nicely. 'How about this arrangement? I stay in business-class on the later flight out. That will help you. But I give you back that £250 you offered me and I come back on Concorde.'

There was a large inhalation of breath, by her initially, and then by myself when she went to check with a colleague. After all, unless you were Sir David Frost, not many freelancers could expect to cross the North Atlantic on Concorde. A fantasy and surely nothing much more than that.

Except that, when she returned to the desk, she was smiling.

'Okay Sir, it's a deal. We transfer you on to the 12noon flight out and you can come back on Concorde.'

There you are. A deal done. So I get to the States a few hours late which is no hassle and eventually do the interview over the next day or two. I then have a day off before returning to London. On that day, 21 December 1988, a very dramatic event occurs.

As I pound out the miles on a running machine in the gym in Florida, I look up at one of the TV screens on the wall above. That infamous phrase BREAKING NEWS is splashed across the screen.

I and the guy next to me reach for our sound controls.

'A Pan American 747 airliner is missing somewhere over the United Kingdom,' said the announcer. A chill ran down my spine. I was due to fly home the next day.

As the time unfolded, the dreaded word 'Lockerbie' was heard. It was the disaster that would reverberate around the world.

The next morning, the American media blazed the news across every outlet. Sitting on an aeroplane awaiting take-off and reading in the newspapers about an air crash the previous day is not exactly guaranteed to calm nerves. But the plane I've boarded at Miami International on this day, 23 December 1988, is enough to divert attention even from that.

You couldn't call the British Airways Concorde waiting at the hangar an impressive aeroplane because of its size. There were, at that time, and of course still are today far bigger aircraft in the skies. But I can't think of a plane I've ever been on that even approached Concorde for style, glamour and performance, even if it was pretty cramped for space.

Flight BA188 is heading up the coast from Miami to Washington but won't go far enough out to sea for the pilot to engage Mach2, twice the speed of sound. That will come over the North Atlantic en route to London Heathrow.

But before then, we pull away from the hangar at Miami and from the tiny windows, I'm struck by the number of airport technicians or ground crew standing gawping at the plane as it rolls back.

Before we reach the end of the runway and our take-off position, the pilot comes on the intercom with a precautionary word. 'Ladies and gentlemen, if this is your first flight on Concorde, welcome on board the world's most advanced aeroplane. It is usual to experience greater G-forces on take-off than on conventional passenger aircraft. This is perfectly normal.'

The roar of the engines and release of the brake bring the captain's words to reality. As the pencil-slim jet streaked down the runway, you could feel the G-forces pushing you hard into the leather seat. There certainly wasn't another passenger jet where you experienced anything of the kind.

The plane seemed to need next to no distance to lift off. As it climbed steeply out over the American eastern seaboard and headed north, you marvelled at this piece of human engineering.

In no time, it seemed, the jet was descending rapidly into Washington DC, the last stop before London. Travelling in a plane that flew so fast compared to most passenger aircraft was exhilarating.

We landed at Dulles airport 75 minutes after take-off from Miami, and headed for the Concorde lounge. You had to say this, too, was the ultimate in luxury. Anyone familiar with the finest first growths from Bordeaux was in their element. Yet in the midst of this opulence, there was, of course, the middle-aged, vastly overweight American shouting for a Coke. God bless 'em.

It might have been the most modern passenger aircraft ever devised but the way Concorde's passengers were looked after was more akin to the days of flying boats and constellations. We were personally guided, in a group, through the airport to the boarding gate.

And with another roar of the engines and the sense of threatening to be buried in the seat by the G-forces, we took off for London.

I have flown in the first-class cabin of several international airlines and there is no doubt, the seats are plusher, deeper and much more comfortable than Concorde's leather-covered, quite hard seats. But no ordinary jet aircraft before or since flew its passengers at such phenomenal speeds.

We climbed out over the sea and set course for London. The champagne they served once we had levelled out became a source of extreme fascination.

Apart from the gentle rise of the bubbles, the liquid inside the cut glass champagne flute just did not move. There was not the slightest tremble. The reason was altitude; we were flying at 60,000 feet, far above any turbulence. It was a strange sensation.

Once beyond the American seaboard range, the cabin digital display soon flicked to Mach2. We were flying at twice the speed of sound. Far below us, the North Atlantic ocean looked no more than a tiny, insignificant blue carpet.

Now I know the tabloid newspaper business can be a shocker, an absolute beast. But I think you have to give credit where credit's due. Eating a plate of the finest beef, washed down with a Chateau Mouton-Rothschild or Chateau Lafitte of outstanding vintage, all on the expenses of a red-top UK newspaper, has to say something about their determination to operate in style. Even if we'd had to tear ourselves away from the Krug to experience it.

Soon, much too soon, lights far below us signalled this exceptional journey was coming to its conclusion. I've never seriously considered hijacking any plane but I'd have loved nothing more than barging into the flight deck and ordering them to turn around and head straight back to Washington.

The sense of the pilot trying to slow this lightning fast craft as we banked and began our approach run into Heathrow, was extraordinary. You got a feeling of being on the wings of a giant bird as it swooped down towards the ground. Except that, at times on the descent, it felt as if someone was kicking the back of the plane as it banked sharply and slowed.

And as Heathrow airport appeared and we touched down, we checked our watches. We'd made it from Washington DC to London, not wind assisted, in three hours 24 minutes. Incredible.

‰ ‰ ‰ ‰ ‰

Diary Notes: Mid-winter, 1989. To Saracens Rugby Club at their old Bramley Road ground in North London to cover an English Cup match.

SARACENS Rugby Club is today one of the best-run professional clubs in England with a multi-million pound budget to match. If you turn up to report a game at the Allianz Park stadium in Greenlands Lane, Hendon, London, NW4, you are assured of facilities commensurate with a stadium and club befitting the 21st century.

Alas, it wasn't always so. Saracens Rugby Club used to play at Bramley Road in Southgate, north London, which they had used since 1945. Until the early 1990s they used a ground owned by the local council. Unfortunately, it was also used by our four-legged friends. Calling cards were a frequent hazard to be avoided as players dashed down the wing or thought about a crucial tackle. Quite often, there was the distinctive smell of something else on a player's kit besides sweat.

But if the pitch was a muddied heap with assorted piles of you-know-what, facilities in the old wooden clubhouse were just as poor. A single electric light bulb of limited energy hung in a gloomy dressing room of concrete floor and rough wooden benches. Very often, the showers were half cold and the mud was everywhere. It must have been a bit like this in the underground hide-outs of the Vietcong.

It was no wonder that, in the early days, they struggled to get first class sides to play them because their facilities were so dire. Those fancy boys from the Harlequins, all city slickers to a man, turned their aristocratic noses up at such a suggestion.

As for media facilities, these were about as obvious as democracy in modern day Russia. Of course, this was in the days before the internet, WiFi and even the second-generation mobile phones which would arrive in the 1990s. There was one telephone, a pay phone, hanging on a wall somewhere under the stand. But it rarely worked, the local yobs saw to that. After that, it was down to the racing pigeons to send score updates.

So anyone intending to report a game at the club in those days had a problem. If the solitary phone on the ground wasn't working, your only possibility was to scramble down the steps out of the stand, nip out of the back and leg it down the approach drive to the road. Opposite, lay a row of suburban houses. People there had landline phones.

You got all sorts of orders for matches in those days. If a Welsh side was in London, BBC Wales might want either a live broadcast previewing the game before the start plus reports at half-time and full time, or just 100 words telephoned through at those stages of the match.

A Saturday evening newspaper, say, in Cardiff, Bristol or Coventry might want 250 words at half-time and another 250 at the end. Whatever it was, without a telephone on the ground, it was exceedingly difficult to communicate and watch the game properly. While you were down the road, using the phone in someone's house, you could miss all manner of scores. Thankfully, you had helpful colleagues back in the stand to bring you up to date when you got back after one of these forays.

The worst day I ever had at Saracens turned out to be one of the best, if that isn't a glorious oxymoron.

A club from the north of England was playing a cup match and the local commercial radio station in the town asked me to cover the game. The order was a nightmare – a two-minute preview before the start, two live reports into the programme during the first half, a full report live at half-time, two more live updates in the second half and a report on the final whistle. Hectic with a phone in the stand, but without one, alarming.

So preparation was key. On a wet, windy winter's afternoon, I banged on the door of a house opposite the Saracens ground and prepared my plea. 'Hi, I work for the media and am covering the game at Saracens this afternoon. Trouble is, the only phone on the ground doesn't work and I have to send live reports to a radio station. Can you help me?

'It won't cost you anything because I can get them to call me if I can use your phone. Is it possible, please?'

The first guy looked blank and closed the door. At the second house, an elderly woman just closed the door. But at the third, a woman perhaps in her late 30s, blonde-haired and smiling, checked my press pass which I proffered and invited me in. This was promising.

She explained there was a telephone upstairs in the bedroom which I could use. She led me up a flight of stairs, we went along a landing and there inside a bedroom on the bedside table, lay the phone. No problem, she said, you can use it as much as you want. Just get the radio station to call the number each time.

I retraced my steps, noticing the white fluffy carpet on the landing and down the stairs. The weather was foul and everywhere was muddy. I grimaced but thanked her profusely and promised I'd be back.

I was. I had pre-recorded the preview earlier. But I'd still need to make six trips out of the stand, behind the pavilion, down the approach path and across the road to the house. Helpfully, she told me she'd leave the door ajar, so that I wouldn't have to bother her every time.

And so I covered most of that match from the upstairs bedroom of a house opposite the ground. To say I saw little of the game would be an understatement. I'd hurry back to the bench that masqueraded as a press facility, catch up on the scores I'd missed and watch about ten minutes of the play before making another mad dash downstairs. It must have been like watching some octogenarian with a weak bladder rushing to and from the loo.

But you do what you can and somehow try to find a way around the problems. When I heard the final whistle sound and hurried down my familiar path, I felt relieved to have negotiated the job somehow, despite the difficulties.

Only trouble was, there was now another difficulty to handle. Firstly, the line of muddy boot marks leading up the stairs and along the landing arrested my focus. But not as much as the next image.

Inside the bedroom, awaited not just the phone but a blond lady now clad only in stockings, suspenders and a bra. Nothing else. She sat there smiling as the phone rang and I began to talk to the sports producer. As I did so, she began to distract my mind far away from rugby balls.

Standing there doing a live broadcast and trying to put over who had scored the tries and what had been the crucial difference between the teams while the lady of the house decided she was wearing far too many clothes on a cold winter's day, wasn't the easiest moment of radio journalism I ever encountered.

And when the broadcast was over, I did what any guy would do in such circumstances. Thanked her profusely for her help, offered her some money to clean up the carpet (which she refused) and left.

After all, I still had 400 words to write for a Sunday paper. By 5.30pm.

‰ ‰ ‰ ‰ ‰

Diary Notes: At home, London, 8 April 1993.
A very unusual letter has just been delivered to my door.

IF a man wearing a hangman's hood and carrying a knotted rope had knocked at my door in the first half of the 1990s, I'd have known in an instant where he'd come from.

Without even needing to think about it, still less actually ask him, I would have deduced he had been sent from Twickenham and was representing the Rugby Football Union.

It would be completely fair and perfectly correct to say that I had been stocking up on missiles, like some Hezbollah devotee, and firing them on a regular basis at the gentlemen who ran English rugby.

The way I saw it, they sat in ivory towers at Twickers, enjoyed damn good lunches and dinners with their increasing number of chums from the commercial world and then signed lucrative sponsorship and advertising contracts worth millions.

Alas, what they seemed unable to grasp, or simply refused to consider, was that they, the so-called guardians of the amateur sport of rugby union, were ushering the game down a one-way street. At the end was an enormous sign and it said professionalism. They were bringing into the sport the great piles of cash which would inevitably turn it fully professional sooner rather than later.

All the rugby unions of the world did it. The RFU snuggled up close to Save & Prosper, the city insurance brokers, the FFR (French Federation de Rugby) got into bed with Credit Mutuel.

In Wales, the Welsh Rugby Union talked turkey with Brains beers, across the Irish Sea the Irish Rugby Football Union (IRFU) did deals with the Irish Permanent Building Society and in Scotland, the Scottish Rugby Union (SRU) supped with the Famous Grouse whisky company.

And a very nice time they had with them, too. Mind you, in the interests of accuracy, I should add that the media, myself included, were not averse to sharing what we might call some of these advantageous contacts.

Save & Prosper staged a splendid dinner each January shortly before the Five Nations Championship got underway. It was always held at one of the old historic livery halls in the City of London.

These were outstanding occasions and the company's hospitality, led by the affable and quietly professional PR executive Simon Curtis, was more than generous. Long, beautifully carved antique tables adorned with candles and the livery company's silver collection which could include anything from tankards and goblets to serving jugs and flower containers, awaited our presence. Such venues represent living history at its most elegant.

The only trouble was, these large sums of money paid by such companies for the privilege of sponsoring England rugby internationals, came at a price. So those charged with keeping the game strictly amateur were dicing with danger by welcoming these great financial benefits.

Yet when any players dared to put their heads above the parapet and say, 'What about us?' they got the equivalent of a ruler whacking a naughty schoolboy over the knuckles. None of the money was for the players, they were told, brusquely.

But who were these tens of thousands of rugby supporters packing into stadia like Twickenham, Cardiff, Lansdowne Road and Murrayfield going to see? Surely they were not there to catch a glimpse of the president of the SRU or the chief executive of Save & Prosper taking his seat at Twickenham?

Increasingly, this disparity became absurd. More and more money was swilling around the international game, like beer in a clubhouse on a Friday night. Yet every country, backed to the hilt by the International Rugby Board (IRB), told its players, you just get on with providing the entertainment on the field. The money is for the game at large, not you.

Was it any wonder the rumblings of discontent among the sport's top players became as loud as a protesting stomach on a senior IRB official overdoing it at another banquet?

By this time, I was editor of *Rugby World* magazine and I used the position to launch a sustained assault on the men at the top of the IRB and the individual unions for its damagingly unrealistic, blinkered approach. I wrote editorials with headlines like 'A Crisis of Leadership', 'J'accuse' and 'A Life of Lie'.

You can accuse me of many things, but I never sat on many fences in life.

Yet amid this fusillade of fire, a most generous letter dropped one morning upon my doormat. A crest of the red rose on the letter revealed its source.

Dated 6 April 1993, a handwritten message said, 'Dear Peter. A brief note. Many, many congratulations on your award as the Magazine Sports Writer of the Year! I am not surprised but it is good to know that excellence is recognised. Well done. Yours sincerely, Ian Beer.' Ian was then the president of the RFU.

I was stunned. How kind of him even to think about writing, especially given my frequent assaults upon his organisation.

Yet this was not the last Twickenham message to reach me around that time.

A subsequent letter, dated 1 November 1994, from the RFU secretary Dudley Wood, said, 'Just a note to say how much I appreciated your editorial in the November issue of *Rugby World*.'

What Wood said at a time when he probably knew it was inevitable the game was going to embrace professionalism in some form or another, contained some highly prescient comments. To say that they have stood the test of time, even 21 years later, would be a gross understatement.

Wood wrote about the future of the game as he then saw it:

'In fact it is not so much the violence aspect which worries me, although I am quite sure we shall see a marked rise in the incidence of cynical fouls, but the inevitable change in the nature of the game. I always list my objections in ascending order of importance. Firstly, clubs simply do not have the income to support payments to players and pressures to retain existing players and buy new ones will drive many clubs into insolvency. The worst-hit will be clubs in Scotland and Ireland!

'Secondly, I hate the thought that talented players following full-time careers will be prevented from playing at the highest level, simply because they cannot afford the time to do so and are unwilling to give up their jobs. We would find ourselves with a very different type of player from those we have today and it is obvious which ones we would lose.

'Thirdly, and above all else, we would all lose our independence of action, unions, clubs and players, as we have to fight in the marketplace and toe the line in order to pay the bills. A fairly dismal prospect!

'Articles like yours help enormously to point out the dangers which we are facing.

'I have no quarrel with top players benefitting from the fame they have achieved and enjoying the comforts of life but if the present campaign is pursued to its logical conclusion, we shall all be the losers, including the vast majority of players.'

If you assume that Wood was one of those welcoming the growing sponsorship sums to Twickenham at that time, then you would have to say his long-term philosophy was flawed. He, surely, helped create the situation where full amateurism was no longer credible.

Yet in many other ways, Wood was absolutely right. Some wonderful clubs, great pillars of the local community, especially in Scotland and Ireland have withered, some dying, in the light of professionalism's arrival.

Likewise, the loss to the game of talented players with full-time careers has been hugely costly. Beyond dispute, it has contributed to the decline of what we might call the cerebral player at the highest level. A game that was once populated by professional men such as lawyers, doctors, teachers, financial experts, City brokers and such like is unquestionably the poorer for their loss.

Of course, generalisations are dangerous. But while it is undeniable that certain skills have been enhanced by professionalism – for example, defending, ball handling and tackling – others such as decision making on the field have declined. This has highlighted a growing void in the field of thinking rugby men. It's true that Jamie Roberts of Wales is a doctor. But most players nowadays are just in the business of making work for doctors.

Wood was also correct in suggesting future financial difficulties for so many clubs once professionalism arrived. Some faded, some died altogether. Others still continue to struggle in increasing anonymity years later.

It is true that a few have prospered. But those good fortunes have been achieved almost entirely by the financial largesse of rich individuals. Without them, even some of the most eminent clubs of the modern game would probably collapse.

※ ※ ※ ※ ※

Diary Notes: To Paris, on a midweek night, in January 1994

Now this is a bright wheeze. We're at Heathrow airport on a Tuesday night, queueing for the British Airways plane to Paris. Sure, it's an odd time to be going there for a rugby writer and photographer. The Five Nations Championship is nigh but has not yet started. So why are we here?

Our other travel companion holds the key. The coach of the England rugby team is in the seat alongside us. And, may he ever more be praised, he's agreed to participate in our madcap idea to produce an outstandingly innovative preview to the Championship.

For in a few weeks, France will play England at the Parc des Princes. As is so often the case, it looks likely to be the decisive match in the tournament or if not THE crucial game, certainly one of the vital ones.

As editor of *Rugby World* magazine, this is no easy job, certainly not when you want to out-smart every rival publication, newspaper or magazine, in the UK media. How do you find a feature that will still be newsworthy by the time of the match a few weeks ahead but also one that your rivals won't snatch in the weeks before your magazine is published? Not easy.

> An interview with a player could easily be overtaken by events, like an injury. In that event, you end up with the nightmare scenario – a front cover story and picture of a player whom everyone knows won't now play in the match you are previewing.
>
> Or another publication could do an interview with the same guy and 'steal' your story line. So it needs careful thought.
>
> In the end, we come up with a fantasy idea. It's far and away the best bet of all the suggestions put forward by the editorial team. But the chances of getting it are slim. So all we can do is make the calls and hope to persuade the relevant parties.

DICK Best was involved as coach of the England rugby team for a total of 17 games in the early 1990s. He was also assistant coach on the 1993 Lions tour to New Zealand. The Lions narrowly lost that series, but with England, Best enjoyed some hugely impressive results.

His record from 17 games, of 13 wins, two draws and only two defeats (both by just a single point), earned him an extraordinary 76 per cent winning ratio as coach alongside Geoff Cooke, the manager. It was also to earn Best something else in August 1994 – the sack.

It came, one Sunday morning, from the lips of RFU official Graham Smith who also happened to be godfather to one of Best's daughters. 'He was pacing up and down in the lounge and couldn't look me in the eye,' Best said later. 'The only reason they gave was that they just needed a change. Clearly Jack Rowell (who had been appointed) wanted to do everything himself.'

That was England for you in those days. About as much style as a Shepherd's Bush horse and cart merchant.

Anyway, as a preview to the 1994 Five Nations Championship, we have inveigled Best to come to Paris with us and participate in a unique conversation with the French national coach Pierre Berbizier.

Now, you have to remember, the English and French do have history when it comes to antagonism. They wind each other up like clocks. So the idea of sitting down the coaches of two such fiercely rival nations, especially when England have won the last six meetings between the countries, might seem a fantasy. But I know both men well and that has helped in setting it up, even though it is just a few weeks before they meet at the Parc des Princes in Paris.

We get to the hotel where the French squad are staying. Actually, it is Chateau Ricard in the tiny hamlet of Clairefontaine, outside Paris. The French players are preparing for their opening Five Nations match of the season this Saturday, which makes our presence here all the more extraordinary.

But remember, these are still, officially at least, the days of an amateur sport. So we first shake hands with the president of the FFR, Monsieur Bernard Lapasset, and then most of the French players who are hanging around. Finally, we dine with Berbizier, a most genial host.

To imagine such a meeting earlier this year between the present French coach Philippe Saint-Andre and England's Stuart Lancaster, would be to warrant a session with a shrink. But this was back then.

Best is intrigued by Lapasset's presence. 'Is he often here?' he asks Berbizier.

'He comes regularly for each game,' explains the coach of France. 'It is important to have the president with the players for a period. He will be president until at least 1995 [actually, he stayed until 2008, serving 17 years in all], an arrangement which offers us a great deal more continuity. If I am going to work with you for only a year, I am not going to get that close to you. However, the president should not stay too long. The last one was here for 25 years!'

There was, to start with, an understandable sense of caution between the two men. But rugby union is, above all, a sport that can demolish barriers, both real and imagined. To talk rugby, to compare attitudes and difficulties induces an animation which quickly illuminates any conversation. So the talk begins to flow.

Berbizier complained that the French national team always came after the clubs in his country. 'We want them to stay fit and fresh and be ready for internationals but it is difficult,' he said.

It was true then and it is even truer today. One week before the 2015 Six Nations Championship began for France with a home game against Scotland in Paris, most of the top French internationals were playing a game in the highly physical Top 14 for their clubs. The situation had got even worse.

This, remember, was little more than a year before the game would turn professional. And they aired and shared views that, in a great many cases, foretold exactly some of the problems that would lie in the path of a professional sport.

Best came up with this highly prophetic statement. 'The status quo will remain until the 1995 Rugby World Cup,' he said. 'But thereafter, there will be more and more pressure from the southern hemisphere.

'I believe the 1995 World Cup will be the signing off of the game as we know it. That should be the stage where we say, "Let's look at another structure for the game." For there must be officially some form of reimbursement for international players.'

Berbizier agreed in principle, saying, 'The players are the ones making the spectacle. But I would not like the context surrounding the game to become more important than the game itself. But today, we take the attitude of the ostrich too much. We are burying our heads in the sand. Everybody knows such difficulties exist but nobody wants to take a decision.'

This debate rolled on for a couple of hours. I took notes and our photographer, Dave Rogers, pictured the duo. When dinner was over, we even managed to set up a front cover photo – the two coaches in front of giant French and English flags we had brought with us.

And at around 11pm the last drop of vintage burgundy enjoyed *plus un petit café*, we shook hands warmly and headed out of the chateau and into the waiting taxi. The evening had confirmed the maturity, vision and respect two great men of rugby football had shared. It had been an intriguing, fascinating experience.

As the taxi crunched its way down the gravel drive of the chateau towards the road, Best shook his head. 'I will never know how the hell you set that up and pulled it off,' he said.

Contacts, that's how. Contacts.

%. %. %. %. %.

Diary Notes: The late 1990s.

To Rye Rugby Club, in East Sussex, to rub shoulders with some
very distinguished company.

IT isn't every day of the week that a journalist finds himself
in an exclusive club like this. But for some reason, I've been
appointed a vice-president of Rye Rugby Club, close by the
historic Romney Marsh region of south-east England.

There are a lot of historic monuments around this part of
the world from old smugglers' inns and watchtowers to forts and
dykes built to ward off possible invasion in Napoleonic times.
And there are a couple more historic monuments here this day;
yours truly plus that renowned humorist Mr Spike Milligan.

In fact, the list of vice-presidents of this club on the Kent/
Sussex borders is revealing. Mr Spike Milligan, Mr Paul
McCartney and Mr Peter Bills are included. God knows what
a humble hack is doing in that sort of esteemed company but
there you are.

Nor is that the end of the celebrity line-up this particular
day. I have managed to persuade an old friend, former Australian
rugby coach Bob Dwyer, plus his wife Ruth, who are staying with
me for a few days, to join us for this fundraising event for the
club.

The Beatle, who owns a house in a village just outside Rye,
isn't actually there. But Milligan is and he's the star of the show.
He's the former Goon who once publicly called Prince Charles,
reputedly his biggest fan, 'a grovelling little bastard'. Twenty-
four hours after that witticism had been splashed across the
world's media Milligan wrote a personal note to the prince,
saying, 'No chance of a knighthood then, I suppose?'

Charles loved irreverent humour of that kind. And Milligan,
who was once voted the funniest person of the last 1,000 years,
did eventually get his knighthood, albeit an honorary one,
because his father was Irish and his son was never willing to
commit to the British crown.

It wasn't a total surprise Milligan became a vice-president of Rye Rugby Club. He had always loved the game and played it during the war during his service years. This day, just four years before his passing, he reminds us of his rugby acumen, taking passes and weaving around imaginary tacklers (albeit in very slow motion) before plonking the ball down over the try line and skipping away in celebration. The years fell off him as he enjoyed himself.

There was only one problem. Spike wasn't amused that would-be tacklers seemed to melt away as he neared the line. 'The buggers think I'm too old to tackle,' he scoffed.

He'd distinguished himself in another rugby arena, one day back in 1973, at Lansdowne Road in Dublin. That day, Milligan had been among the crowd at the famous old ground when Ireland scratched out a 10-10 draw with the famous All Blacks. It was an historic day, too, the first time that Ireland had managed to avoid defeat against New Zealand.

Milligan had marked this unique occasion with a special celebration. Sipping a glass of wine in one corner of a hospitality suite after the game, he spied the New Zealand forward Ian Kirkpatrick entering the room following his post-match shower and clean-up.

Suddenly, a moment of inspiration overcame Milligan, 'I stood there and saw this huge All Black enter the room. I thought to myself, you will never have such an opportunity again. Take this chance.'

Now most sane people would assume Milligan was discussing the possibility of engaging the New Zealand captain in conversation, or perhaps asking for his autograph. But you could never accuse Spike Milligan of being a sane person. Even he would have been affronted at that statement.

So, with a blood-curdling shout aimed at scattering people in his path, Milligan ran across the room and rugby-tackled the New Zealand captain. The All Black's drink went one way, he went another and the pair of them ended up in a tangled heap by the door. Spike always reckoned it was his proudest moment when it came to his association with the game.

In his retirement, he bought a house just outside Rye, down a country lane which ran across the marsh to the old Cinque Ports town of Winchelsea in East Sussex. By chance, my family had a cottage in Winchelsea and we met up on a few occasions.

Not that long after that day at Rye RFC, I was asked to write a book about the history of London Irish Rugby Football Club. Milligan was a valuable source of information because he played a few games for one of their lower sides once the war was over and was then an occasional spectator at the Irish's old Sunbury-on-Thames ground.

Milligan wrote the foreword to that book. In it, he said he'd always loved the Welsh for their passion for the game. 'During the war, the Sergeant-Major at the battery was Welsh and rugby mad,' he wrote. 'If that Hitler and Mussolini had been good players, I'd have used them in my bloody team,' Milligan recalled him saying.

And of nights at Sunbury with the Exiles, he said, 'I remember the drinking was colossal down there before the war. I couldn't keep up with it and once said to the barman, Look, I can't drink all this bloody Guinness – I'll have some wine.

'The bugger shouted down the bar, a glass of white wine for Mrs Milligan.'

Dire deeds used to go on down at the Irish in the 1960s and 70s too. At one time, the likes of Milligan, Richard Burton (once with Elizabeth Taylor), Peter O'Toole and Dave Allen, the comedian, would sometimes turn up for matches. It became the fashionable ticket of the London rugby circuit.

If you ever got out of the place much before 10pm on a Saturday you were doing well. I remember one end-of-season league match the Irish played against Harlequins. Somehow, unbelievably, the Exiles ran up a cricket score against their vaunted foes, one of Quins' worst hidings in years.

That set off all manner of celebrations in the old Exiles clubhouse. I had work to do after the game for at least an hour but when I joined the throng in the bar well after 6pm, they were still about ten deep trying to order a pint of the ubiquitous

Guinness. Cut an Irishman open and his body won't run red with blood. Black with Guinness, more like.

A few pints later, nearing the hour of 8pm, I suddenly remembered with horror I was expected at a dinner that night. When I left, there were literally hundreds of cars still in the car park and the bars were doing a roaring trade. Those were the great nights down at the Irish.

That story had a strange ending. The following Monday morning, the club began to receive a great many calls mostly from the City of London. Companies eager to sponsor the club perhaps? There was a simpler explanation.

Most of the calls went like this, 'I wonder if you can help. Our chairman/managing director/chief executive was at your ground on Saturday and he seems to have mislaid his car. He is wondering if he left it at your ground when he went home on Saturday night.'

Milligan firmly approved of nights like that. So when we arranged to meet at his home in the Sussex countryside, I took him a very special bottle of red wine. It was from the Clare Valley, one of Australia's finest regions, and was a great vintage. He cradled it in his arms with the loving care of a mother with her newborn.

I often thought one of the main reasons Milligan bought that house was its address. Okay, there was a glorious view across the marsh to the English Channel from the large picture windows in the sitting room. But the actual address was Dumb Woman's Lane. Spike had a good few jokes ready in association with that.

He hated two things above all else; smoking and noise, especially unnecessary noise. So on the front door was a large sign that said, 'This door can be closed without slamming it. Try it and see how clever you are.'

Every August, Rye Rugby Club holds a 15-a-side Spike Milligan Memorial Tournament. Buried in nearby Winchelsea churchyard, his gravestone bears the inscription 'I told you I was ill'.

Special man, Spike, and the devotee of a special game.

AUSTRALIA

Diary Notes: London, autumn 1984.

The arrival of the 1984 Australian rugby touring team, the Wallabies, in England. To central London to attend the tour arrival press conference.

Australia. The brave new world. A country filled with perennial hope.

'Have a go yer mug' is a national catchphrase. Call it arrogance if you like, and plenty do. But it's more to do with a deep-seated belief in self.

How often has this revealed itself within Australian sports teams? A bunch of ragtag operators can turn up at the training ground, but give them a garish blazer or put a silly cap on their heads and they're suddenly transformed into world-beaters.

Not that the class of 1984 fitted a category of ragtag operators. There had been plenty of imposters in the previous ranks of Australian rugby union players and teams pitching up in the UK down the years and failing lamentably. But not this lot. They absolutely exuded class.

THE year of 1984 was an important one for Australian rugby. The Wallabies arrived in London that autumn determined to make history by becoming the first Australian touring team to do the grand slam on a northern hemisphere tour. In other words, beat England, Wales, Scotland and Ireland on the same trip.

Some very good coaches, the likes of Bob Templeton and Bob Dwyer, and a decent number of very fair players had failed to achieve the feat. By now, those years of failure had started to resemble a possum bite on an Aussie backside. It was a festering sore.

This time, the man chosen to mastermind the attempt was unusual. Alan Jones was about as far removed from a Dame Edna Everage image as present Aussie Prime Minister Tony Abbott from an Asian boatyard owner.

An erudite former Oxford University student and schoolmaster, Jones had become a political scriptwriter for the former Australian PM Malcolm Fraser and had mixed in circles rather more elevated than those to be found in a muddy, sweat-stinking rugby dressing room.

In 1982, Jones had been appointed manager of the New South Wales rugby union team and a year later, he became coach of the Manly club, guiding them to the NSW domestic title for the first time in 32 years. That achievement propelled him into the ranks of international rugby union.

He was officially listed as coach of the 1984 Wallabies but in truth, at times he was more like the CEO on that tour. Jones shaped the philosophy, tactics, everything. In terms of on-field matters, he had the astute coaching brain of Alec Evans, his assistant, and the quiet yet influential words of captain Andrew Slack to assist. That was no slur on Jones and his capabilities. After all, each to his own. Jones excelled both in the world of oratory and motivation. His vocabulary was vast and he used it with considerable wisdom and judgement. Then there was motivation. The former England fly half Rob Andrew once summed that up perfectly.

Andrew spent a winter season playing club rugby in Sydney, and he talked often with Alan Jones. Afterwards, he would explain how half an hour's conversation about rugby with Jones would make him want to get his boots on and go out on to any rugby ground. Even if it was 2am.

That was Jones, a hugely inspirational human being.

Some rival coaches and media men of the time had to have Jones's philosophy of the game explained to them.

A journalist turned up at the Australian team hotel one afternoon during that 1984 trip and asked to see a player.

'He's training,' replied Jones.

'Oh, I was told you trained this morning and the players were just having a rest this afternoon,' said the hack.

'We did,' responded Jones. 'They're sleeping right now. That's part of their training.'

The hack departed, bemused.

But it's fair to say no other country in the rugby-playing world, with the exception of New Zealand, would have understood such a philosophy at that time.

Once, analysing a player's fall from grace, in terms of a poor personal performance just days after a supreme display, Jones scoffed, 'One day King Rooster; the next, feather duster.' Not bad.

But even the loquacious Jones was left speechless at the first press conference he gave, at the Australians' St Ermin's Hotel in central London. They had flown in that morning and rather than dragging the media out to Heathrow airport, decided the arrival press conference would be held at their London base. Nice touch.

We'd heard a lot about Australia's latest coach and the guy in front of us didn't disappoint. There he sat, at the top table, resplendent in his crisply cut green Wallaby tour blazer with smartly pressed white shirt and green, impeccably knotted Wallaby tie, fielding questions like a full-back under the high ball who never remotely suggested he might drop one. But then he did.

All seemed to be going smoothly until a soft voice from the back of the room that told of the Welsh valleys, enquired of the great man, 'Are you worried about going to Wales? It's just that, six years ago see, when you played them in Australia, Pricey [tight head prop Graham Price] had his jaw broken by a punch.'

Jones bridled and swatted the question aside as if it were some irritating fly that had dared to land on his nose. 'Oh that was all a long time ago. I'm sure they'll have forgotten all about that by now in Wales.'

To which a disingenuous English voice at the back of the room was heard to mutter, 'Forgotten? The Welsh are still arguing about a try that was disallowed in 1905.'

Three years later, I was to get to know Alan Jones better when I lived in Sydney for seven months after the first Rugby World Cup had been held in Australia and New Zealand. We collaborated on a book which for various reasons was fated never to see the light of day. But working with this intellectual colossus was never less than an eye-opener, an invigorating experience. You couldn't get bored in the company of this man.

He'd ask me to go to his home, the top floor of a converted warehouse in Newtown, one of Sydney's inner suburbs, on Sunday late mornings. The top-floor, open-plan single room which went from front to back of the building, was vast. An enormous dining table and chairs stood at one end, an elegant sofa at the other. You'd have had to hail someone standing at the other end of the room, like a watchman trying to make human contact on a foggy night. One section was partitioned off for his bed.

From the back end of the top floor, you stepped past floor-to-ceiling glass doors out on to a terrace from which Sydney's western suburbs were laid out beneath you. Up in the sky, Qantas jets cruised past on their final approach run into Kingsford Smith International Airport at Botany Bay. It was all a bit surreal (and very minimalist), not least when the master of the house turned up.

He'd come in carrying an enormous bag of those fresh prawns which they sell by the truckload, not to mention assorted other fish which he'd bought that morning at Sydney's superb fish market at Pyremont, not far away. A huge bowl would be procured and the prawns tipped in, ready for us to devour over lunch. He'd pick at the food and pour me a glass of very good Australian chardonnay – Jones was neither a heavy eater nor drinker. It was as though he became bored by such mundane activities. We would discuss the world, life, events, cultures, politics, trends, pretty much anything in vogue at that time.

You only had to mention something, whether it was the work of a Titian, a Sibelius suite or the qualities of a great world politician (pretty rare, that species, nowadays, it has to be said) and it would be like a scene from a Frankenstein movie. The body would suddenly move, its eyes would open wide and instantly the brain, by now activated, would engage and pour forth with intellectual comments.

The vocabulary sparkled like a new dollar coin lying on a sunny Sydney street. Oxymorons would be condemned outright, phrases of exquisite beauty judiciously constructed without the slightest hesitation. His grasp of the English language could hardly have been bettered in all Australia, and most of England for that matter, too.

We rarely discussed rugby until the time came, lunch over, when he would close his eyes, yawn profusely and exclaim, 'God, I am tired.' It was no wonder. Each morning, he was up by 3.30am or 4am to get into the radio station 2GB for which he worked in the city. There, he was steadily building a reputation as one of the sharpest, cruellest and yet wittiest observers of the scene anywhere in Australia.

Most callers to his early morning programme entered these waters with the trepidation of a bather in a crocodile-infested creek up in Australia's Northern Territory. But not all.

Like the lady who phoned up one morning to complain that she wasn't getting enough social assistance off the Government. 'I think it's dreadful, Alan,' she moaned in that familiar, high-pitched Australian nasal whine. 'I've got three kids, ma 'usband's gone off and I have to manage on this amount. Well Alan, I can't do it, I need more. It's so expensive out there and the kiddies eat like grown-ups.'

Jones let this tide of verbal diarrhoea wash up perilously close to his own doorstep.

'How much d'you get off the state?' he asked briskly. Still, the caller didn't pick up the warning signs of an impending storm.

'Oh Alan, they only give me a few hundred bucks a week. I mean, that's not enough for anyone on their own, is it? Never mind someone with three kiddies to find for.'

Jones all but spat out the next question. 'And how long have you been drawing that?'

'Oh, for about three years, Alan. But it's not gone up enough, you see. The food and the kiddies' clothes and everything – that's all gone up. But my money hasn't been enough to keep up with it, Alan.'

By this stage, those of us who knew Alan Jones well were donning tin helmets and preparing to dive under the nearest table. We knew what was coming. I pictured in my mind a kettle boiling its head off with no-one around to turn off the electric supply. Even so, the steam coming out of it probably wouldn't have been as much as the amount blasting out of Alan Jones's ears at that particular moment.

'You're just a bludger,' was his opening salvo, or words to that effect. His message was brutally clear. 'Who owes you a living? Why should everyone else have to keep you and your family? There are jobs out there; go and get one. Get some money into your purse and some pride into your life. Stop thinking the world owes you a living and will do for ever more. Get off the state's back.'

The radio station controllers, or more likely Jones himself, didn't give the woman the chance to reply. But then maybe she couldn't. Perhaps she was flat out on the floor in shock.

After five days of this sort of high-octane, knockabout stuff, it was no wonder the man was exhausted. So when he finished lunch with me on a Sunday, he'd close his eyes and I'd groan to myself, 'Here comes a wasted afternoon.'

He might need as much as two minutes to recharge those astonishing human batteries. But maybe not as long. Talk about the Duracell bunny. Quite suddenly, as if subjected to electrical stimulus, he'd open his eyes and say, 'Right, where do you want to start?'

I'd fire a question or a topic at him and off he'd go. Two or three hours later, I'd stumble out of the place mentally shattered, as if I'd been the guy getting up in the middle of the night every day of the week. That was Alan Jones. An incredible guy and the most stimulating company you would ever find. He was like a breath of fresh air in the sometimes fetid world of rugby football in those times.

It really wasn't a great surprise his 1984 Wallabies did the grand slam and made history. Led by the quiet yet authoritative Andrew Slack, to this day one of the most impressive men I have ever met in top class sport anywhere in the world, those Australians were a class apart. Mark Ella (who scored a try in each of the four Test matches) was the brilliant visionary cog by which the whole team worked, Simon Poidevin never knew the meaning of doubt or easing off, Roger Gould was a rock of a full-back, David Campese, a threat at every unpredictable turn.

Then there were the youngsters, livewire scrum half Nick Farr-Jones, a hugely intelligent young man (typically, Jones had noticed that long before the tour and earmarked him as the Test half-back) and the young but fast-learning Michael Lynagh outside Ella. What a talent he would become.

Then there were others like giant lock forward Simon Cutler, a guaranteed source of line-out possession, the elegant Michael Hawker, Bill Calcraft, Matthew Burke, Topo Rodriguez, Tim Lane; the whole lot of them just oozed class, whether you were talking about a match situation or off-the-field moment.

Why on earth Slackie never went into the Diplomatic Corps I will never know; through his quiet authority, he helped ensure a group of highly divergent individuals were welded together with marvellous aplomb.

When it was all over, when they'd beaten the best that England, Wales, Scotland and Ireland could throw at them, not to mention the Barbarians in the traditional end-of-tour fixture where dear old Bill McLaren ran out of eulogies to describe them, especially Campo, they rounded it all off with a late-night boat trip down the River Thames. They insisted the media was banned, except for yours truly. Why I got an invite, a Pom at that, I'll never know but what a night. Wild horses wouldn't drag the secrets out of me. But friendships made on that tour and on that boat have lasted a lifetime. Not too bad for a simple game.

※ ※ ※ ※ ※

Diary Notes: Dunedin, 23 August 1986.
New Zealand 13 Australia 12.

By glorious irony, the year 1986 when Alan Jones was still Australian coach, was the last time the Wallabies won a Test match at Eden Park, Auckland. And that meant that as 2015 kicked off, their 29-year wait continued. As for Jones, it's fair to say he settled in most New Zealand stomachs about as uneasily as a piece of bad cheese.

Oxford-educated, suave, elegant, composed, brilliant and supremely confident plus a superb orator – Jones wasn't lacking in too many qualities and his levels of intelligence were elevated, to say the very least.

JONES could be an extremely generous man to his friends, a vivid supporter and a wise counsel. But he could be as tough as a bag of nails, too, and he didn't suffer fools gladly.

In Dunedin in 1986 on the Wallabies tour (again led by Andrew Slack), they faced the so-called Baby Blacks in the First Test because so many of the senior All Blacks had undertaken a jaunt to apartheid South Africa. Shame on the lot of them too, they put themselves and, allegedly, their own financial well-being, ahead of the plight of millions of downtrodden black people in that troubled land.

A rugby tour by an overseas team, any tour, was positively the last bloody thing those poor people needed at a time when the vicious South African apartheid police were still shooting and torturing innocent black citizens. As the slaughter of seven black men in a confrontation with police in Gugulethu, just outside Cape Town in 1986, showed.

So when Australia won the first of that three-Test tour, the only surprise was that their margin of victory in Wellington was just a single point, 13-12. But as for the expected Wallaby win in the next Test in Dunedin, that appeared an inevitability. Or at least, it probably should have been but for a couple of expensive errors by the mercurial David Campese.

Now it has always been denied by Jones that he laid into Campo after that game at the old Carisbrook ground. Yet the word was, he tore the wing apart, metaphorically speaking, in the dressing room afterwards, allegedly saying, 'I told people you were the Bradman of rugby – now you have let me down.'

Well, maybe he did and maybe he didn't. But what happened later that night was pretty revealing.

It had been a soaking wet night at Carisbrook. And as Campo was the first to admit, defence was not the greatest part of his game. The All Blacks (I personally never subscribed to the Baby Blacks idea – in 50 years of watching them, I've never seen a rank bad New Zealand team) had chosen a very different side to the first Test team, forgetting about the bans on those who had gone to South Africa and recalling ten of the previously suspended players for the Dunedin Test.

They exploited a couple of errors by Campese and squeezed out a 13-12 win to level the series at 1-1. Even so, it needed a ludicrous decision by Welsh referee Derek Bevan to refuse a try by Aussie number eight Steve Tuynman, who had ploughed over the line, admittedly with a couple of would-be tacklers on his back like a koala with its joey, with just four minutes left.

It was obvious to everyone, even the New Zealanders, that Tuynman had scored. Bevan disagreed so the All Blacks escaped with the win which guaranteed a series decider in Auckland. Remember, the Australians had yet to win a Test series in New Zealand.

Campo wasn't to know it that wet, grim night in Dunedin but his try would clinch victory for the Wallabies in a 22-9 win in the final Test the following week. But before that, there was a long night ahead.

By the time I'd finished work at Carisbrook, it was dark and deserted. No taxis outside; there seemed nothing for it but to trudge back into town through the rain and cold of a New Zealand south island winter. Until, that is, I spotted the Australian team bus still waiting outside the ground.

There in the front row, sitting on his own, was Campo. He leaned outside and shouted, 'Mate, in here. Come and sit here.'

It wasn't exactly usual for a journalist to get a ride on the team bus back to their hotel. But we chewed the cud a short while en route to the team base where I was also staying. Once there, the players went off for dinner and I went to my room to finish some work. An hour or so later, I wandered downstairs. Sitting at a table all on his own, just eating and staring into the beyond, was Campese. He beckoned me over and we started chatting.

He talked freely and openly, confiding in me about his feelings and what his coach and mates had said in the dressing room. He didn't request confidentiality but I made the decision myself that it should be. We talked and talked, about any and everything. It might have been a foul night outside but the growing conviviality inside was a welcome distraction.

Eventually, all the players drifted into the lounge and began some fun and games. I think it was a lesson called 'How to get a Test loss out of your hair'. After a while, with livewire half-back Nick Farr-Jones as the master of ceremonies, running a fictitious horse race across the floor with huge shouts of excitement and encouragement from the whole Wallaby squad as the dice rolled, projecting certain 'horses' owned by different players or conglomerates into the lead, I left them to it and went to bed.

But I never forgot David Campese's kindness and willingness to be as frank and open as he was that night. Thereafter, we became good mates and a few years later he would ask me to write his autobiography.

Most of the rugby world of that time had one word to describe Campo. That word was arrogant. It was shouted in scorn (and maybe perhaps a touch of fear?) when he stalked the rugby fields of the world. And it was chortled out, like some hoary old cliché, whenever his name had appeared in print, quoting him on some topic concerning the game.

It was also about a million miles wide of the truth. To call David Campese arrogant was about as accurate as dubbing Richie McCaw thick. You couldn't be more wrong.

What appeared to be arrogant was the way Campese played the game. His brash interventions, astonishing acts of high-class skill and searing pace (before he began to bulk up after the 1991 Rugby World Cup and he lost that exceptional speed he had always possessed) might have looked arrogant.

But Don Bradman was said to be arrogant and if you watch the tapes of him smacking bowlers through the covers for four all day long, you might conclude that was the case. But we in society too readily confuse genius with arrogance.

If you are a genius, it is 99 per cent certain that your game will be so good, whatever your sport, there will be a touch of arrogance about it. That is the natural way. The plodding partisans who labour in the slipstream of the greats, all panting, sweaty, hot and bothered, invariably look anything but arrogant.

It is the difference between artisans and labourers. Those who play with an easy elegance are too often dubbed arrogant. It is a casual insult, a glib but usually uninformed comment.

Away from the rugby field, Campese offered the outside world an image of a bloke shouting his mouth off. But in my view, there were two reasons for that. The first was that, by his own admission, David Campese had hardly enjoyed what you might term a first class education. Some of his reading and writing skills were deficient to say the least. He was a boy who came from a humble, basic background in the country of the Australian Capital Territory (ACT) and there were no fancy words or phrases in his vocabulary as he grew up.

This is only a personal opinion but I have always felt that Campo deliberately tried to mask this weakness with loud talk. He used the traditional Australian image of loudmouth, brash characters for his own purposes. If he was saying things – (albeit some of his comments were naïve in the extreme, almost guaranteed to get him into trouble) – then perhaps, I suspect he reasoned, people would focus on the content rather than the way they were delivered.

The second reason, I think, was that deep down, David Campese was always a touch uncomfortable when the off-field spotlight was on him. Those who don't really know him might ridicule such an assertion. But I reckon I got to know Campo better than most people. When we worked on his book, I went to

Australia and spent time with him there. Then I went to Milan where he was playing for an Italian club for a while (together with Mark Ella) and we lived together in his apartment. Finally, he came to stay at my home in Kent.

It was an old oast house, where they used to dry the hops which were grown in the local fields. We would go for training runs down the valley, through the fields and along the lanes. We spent quite a bit of time together and neither I nor my family ever detected this so-called arrogance.

He mucked in at the house, helped with the dishes and did other odd jobs. This was no King turning up his arrogant nose at humble surroundings, no big-headed, bolshy guy moaning at having to stay at someone's house rather than in a five-star hotel.

Campese was happiest out of the limelight, not in it. He was a different bloke away from the media pack and the TV lights. What he produced on the field was a God-given gift not even he could comprehend at times. He once told his Randwick club and national coach Bob Dwyer, 'Mate, I don't know where I'm going or what I'm going to do on the field. I just go where my legs take me.'

Dwyer, asked to explain how as a coach he handled such individual brilliance, backed up that philosophy with a gem of his own, 'I make it a personal habit never to interfere with bloody genius.'

But off the field, Campese lacked many of the social skills a player of his eminence requires in the modern world of intense scrutiny of our leading sportsmen and women.

Consequently, he found it hard to, as they say in political circles, work a room. By that they mean, walk in with a broad smile firmly in place, go up to complete strangers, introduce himself, ask for that person's name and chat in an easy manner so that the stranger meeting the celebrity is somehow made to feel as though he is one of the most important people in that person's life. It is a real skill and not an easy one to acquire. Bill Clinton was apparently a master at it and someone else who was superb was Dickie Davies, the former ITV Sport presenter.

Campo could never do that sort of thing. Sure, he might try to bluster his way through and be more successful at it on some days compared to others. But I have seen him cringe on many occasions when total strangers have cornered him. Not because he was arrogant and just not interested or because he thought he was superior to them. But making small talk with people he had never met was simply not his forte.

I flew back to London's Heathrow airport together with the Australians after that astonishing, incredible performance of Campese's in the 1991 Rugby World Cup semi-final when his genius was the principal cause of New Zealand's demise in Dublin. As we entered the arrivals hall at Heathrow, TV arc lights were switched on, an army of people engulfed him, microphones were thrust under his nose all to the cry of unknown numbers of media folk and supporters, 'There he is.'

The real arrogant sportsman would have revelled in it; this, after all, was his moment, his theatre. The fame and the adulation came at him like curtains of rain on an English winter's afternoon.

So what did David Campese do, who did he go straight to? A two-year-old girl in a dress, clutching her mother's hand and looking bewildered by the throng of media and people, but awaiting the arrival home of her Daddy after a few weeks away working. Campo picked up the little girl, cuddled her and tousled the hair of her elder sister who was just four. My two daughters.

It was a hilarious scene. TV and radio men fighting deadlines to get Campo's reaction to a semi-final that had stunned the world because of his genius, simply stood around waiting while he chatted to my family. And then eventually, when he had finished, he was hauled off for the interviews.

It was a side of David Campese that didn't surprise me because I had seen it often enough. But it surely would have astonished those still tempted to use the word arrogant.

℀ ℀ ℀ ℀ ℀

Diary Notes: To Australia & New Zealand for the first Rugby World Cup, 1987

A new innovation this, in the world of rugby union.

They've managed to bury (probably alive) or at least gag and tie to a chair, the diehards among rugby's administrators who swore they'd take up arms before agreeing to such a thing as a World Cup in rugby.

If you are reading this in the year 2015, then yes, pinch yourself and say it is true. Because it is.

To a man, rugby's administrators in the northern hemisphere retorted 'over my dead body' when the heretical suggestion of such a tournament was mooted, chiefly by the southern hemisphere nations. In their world, in which a fog of cigar smoke and warming brandies seemed to linger endlessly, there was no room for reality or the wishes of spectators or even players. Perish the thought. What would they know about 'our' game?

But somehow, in the final years of the 20th century, rugby managed to drag itself, albeit kicking and screaming, into something approaching the modern world. Of course, it was easier once the gentlemen on the International Board had been assured that they'd be required to spend six or seven weeks in Australia and New Zealand observing this new tournament.

What was that I heard from one committee room? 'We ARE flying first-class, aren't we?' Surely not. My ears must have deceived me.

And so we all decamped down to the southern hemisphere (most of us NOT in first-class) to witness the birth of this strange new infant the game had never imagined conceivable. Perhaps the old farts wished they'd followed Spike Milligan's maxim – contraceptives should be used on every conceivable occasion.

But whatever, it was alive and here among us. In truth, like most newborns, it wasn't a lot to look at, to start with anyway. But studying the television upon arrival in New Zealand provided the first shock.

In this so-called amateur sport, as it allegedly still was at that time, there was one famous All Black advertising a tractor he used on his farm. Others had their names attached to car makers, hire car companies and such like. Eyes were opened. It was like open season down here in the southern hemisphere. The old world had been left behind, in more ways than one.

Of course, what all this meant was that a country like New Zealand was far better prepared for the tournament than any other. Presumably, players who were advertising tractors and such things had more spare time. And also presumably, it was a safe bet that much of that extra spare time would have been used in training and preparing for the World Cup.

While players from the old countries back in the northern hemisphere played an international match on a Saturday and still caught the train to work on a Monday morning, those in New Zealand were driving tractors around farms in front of film cameras.

Two different worlds existed and the old game was living a lie. It had to change.

IN an era before mobile phones arrived to chain employees to their masters, staff journalists on japes like this one could still lose themselves, should they so wish. I was reminded of that at 3am in a Sydney hotel room on my first night of the trip.

A distinctly smooth English voice was on the end of the line when the telephone rudely interrupted my slumbers.

'Sorry to bother you, old boy, but I'm afraid we've lost our rugby man. He's gone missing. Have you seen him?'

It was *The Guardian* in pursuit of David Frost, then its esteemed rugby correspondent. Frostie, the most laid-back man I ever saw outside a boxing ring, had decided to break the long journey to Sydney by stopping off somewhere en route and staying with friends for a few days. Who and where was a mystery. But the fact that a UK national newspaper was desperate for some copy, a story or two from their man, was of no concern whatsoever to Frost.

Of course, I wouldn't have shopped him even if I'd just spent the evening with him. You don't. Besides, he was a lovely guy, a special man loved and respected by all. But needs must.

'Would you be able to give us 700 words on one angle, another 500 on another?' enquired the voice from London, ever so politely.

'It's three in the morning here,' I replied.

'Yes, awfully sorry but you know how it is.'

Oh, the joys of being a freelance.

'How long have I got?'

'Oh, about an hour.'

So at quarter past three on a Sydney morning, I put on a few clothes, got the lift down 24 floors to hotel reception and crossed the street into Kings Cross – to find, among the drunks and good-time girls, an all-night dairy selling the first editions of the *Sydney Morning Herald* and *The Australian* newspapers.

Both were stuffed with World Cup stories none of which, in this pre-internet age, had yet made their way back across the air waves to London. *The Guardian* desk readily agreed to my two suggested angles, both heavily influenced by what I had just read in the Australian papers.

By 4.30am, both stories were in London and I was back in bed.

David Frost did arrive and covered that first World Cup. But I don't think anyone ever found out where he'd vanished to for two or three days before it all started.

%, %, %, %, %

Diary Notes: A Sydney bus stop, winter 1987

There's no doubt about it. You get a better class of wisecracker in Australia than almost any other place in the world, with the possible exception of Ireland.

ON a freezing cold but bright and sunny winter's morning, while I was living in Sydney, my partner and I decided to take ourselves and our six-month-old daughter Hannah off to the world-renowned Doyle's restaurant for lunch.

Now those boys who sailed the *First Fleet* to Botany Bay way back in 1788 sure knew what they were doing when they chose a location to land. Presumably, Doyle's was already there, a favourite watering hole of the local Aborigines who were presumably chewing fresh calamari and downing mouthfuls of Chardonnay even as the strangers sailed in.

Doyle's is a seafood restaurant that occupies one of the most dazzling settings anywhere in the world. In summer, you sit outside this quite small abode (they have expanded in more recent times) looking from Watson's Bay right up Sydney Harbour, almost from the entrance out into the Tasman Sea.

We had no car while we lived there, partly because we found public transport so convenient and reliable. To get to the city, we'd take the bus up the hill from Balmoral Beach, past Mosman and through the suburbs to Taronga Zoo. There, a ferry would meet the bus and chug its way across Sydney Harbour to Circular Quay, right at the heart of the downtown area.

I suppose there are better commutes into a city in the world but right now, I can't think of any, with the possible exception of Cape Town. But this particular day, we're going the other way, from the city out to Watson's Bay. And we're standing waiting for the bus, together with a few other hardy souls on this crisp mid-morning, when my attention is drawn to a young lady dressed, as you might say, somewhat scantily and standing on the balcony of a building overlooking the road.

The area was King's Cross, which also happens to be the number one red light district of Sydney. It was clearly this particular young lady's place of work.

The cold morning certainly wasn't inhibiting her. The brief glance I gave her revealed a flimsy garment apparently over very little indeed. Her eyesight and humour were equally transparent.

As the cold bit into me, I rubbed my hands together vigorously. It evoked a message and an invitation.

'I could show you something a bloody sight better to do with yer hands than that,' came the call from on high.

Most of us at the bus stop cracked up at the offer.

> **Diary Notes: To London, for the start of another Australian tour. It's not only the players you look forward to getting to know on these tours. Then there are the real characters, the journos.**

ONE of the Australian writers on this particular tour was extremely partial to a drop. Now that's astonished you, I know. So much so that he would periodically go off on a bender lasting a few days. Whether there was a Test match being played at that particular time and his paper back home might actually expect quite a chunk of written text, was of no relevance whatsoever.

But 'mate' is a sacred word in the Australian vocabulary. In their world, you do what you have to do to get your mate out of trouble. That's the first law of the land. Always has been.

So with our pal cosying up to another bottle of Scotch or whatever tipple he'd selected that particular day to send him crashing into oblivion, arrangements are hastily made among his mates working for the other Australian papers. Besides doing their own work, they would file a separate report to their mate's paper, under his name, of course. After all, someone had made sure his computer had been brought to the ground even if its owner had gone AWOL.

You had to say it was extremely well organised and it worked wonderfully. True, his mates went to bed each night a tad weary. But the most important thing was, his desk back in Australia apparently never twigged.

Nor, you could say, did our friend until he eventually came out of the bender. That process began when he awoke in a blind panic in his curtained hotel bedroom at 11pm, after three days of being out of it.

Throwing his clothes on and chucking what he thought he needed into his bag, he rushed downstairs in the hotel, all unshaven, bleary-eyed and with hair as criss-crossed as a railway junction outside Sydney Central.

Hiring a taxi, he leapt in. 'Twickenham, and make it quick please mate – I'm late for the game,' was the order.

The driver studied him suspiciously. 'What do you want to go there for?' he asked.

'I'm covering the match and I'm late. Hurry up mate,' replied our friend.

The reply was simplicity itself. 'Well, there's no hurry because they won't be playing until tomorrow afternoon.'

By now, it was 11.30pm, a salient point completely overlooked by our grossly hungover scribe.

%% %% %% %% %%

Diary Notes: Hong Kong airport, the second half of the 1980s, en route to Sydney, Australia.

So YOU get your Christmas office party as a perk, correct? Well, I get this trip, the annual jaunt to Asia for the renowned Hong Kong Sevens, as my perk for the year.

Cathay Pacific, the airline of Asia, fly a group of UK journalists out to the old colony each March for what has become one of the great fun events on the global rugby calendar.

The first thrill is landing at Kai Tak airport. If you never did that (and you won't now because a new, bog-standard airport was constructed a few years ago out in the New Territories which took away all the fun and drama of Kai Tak) then you missed out.

Pilots had almost to stand the aircraft on its wingtip when they came over the mountain overlooking the former colony. When they twisted the craft around, steering a path between giant skyscraper apartment blocks in the process and all the while negotiating the capricious crosswinds, there were thrills aplenty. To see the cabin crew blowing their cheeks after a particular landing is to know it has been hairy.

At one point, shortly before you reached the start of the runway, you went over the top of shopping streets and could clearly see stalls selling fruit and vegetables below. You don't get that sort of eyeful coming into Heathrow.

So we'd get transported to some luxury hotel and be expected to write something and stay just on the right side of moderately sober for three days, to justify our stay. The tournament took two days and the climax, on a Sunday evening when the final was staged, was followed by a big celebratory dinner at a top hotel.

Not much sleeping was done in the entire weekend. So by Monday evening when you'd made your way back to Kai Tak, you were ready for a good long sleep on the flight home. But this particular year, I'm not returning to London. Instead, I team up with the Aussies because I'm going down to Sydney to work with David Campese on his autobiography.

But if that sounds a simple enough journey, you could not be further from the truth.

WE are greeted at the airport by a scene of Asian chaos. There must be the best part of 3,000 people either inside or trying to get into the airport terminal. Some are thronging check-in desks, others standing around talking, still more already stretched out on the floor.

It turns out that all the computers are down and none of the waiting aircraft can produce a boarding plan. The delay stretches to beyond two hours.

That doesn't matter so much. After all, you have to get these things in context. No-one has died so far so it can't be that important.

The problem is that when the computer system is finally restored and the planes begin to be filled, the clock is ticking towards curfew time. And because of noise restrictions over the residential areas of the city, they close Kai Tak at 11pm.

So we board the Qantas flight for Sydney and leave the gate, slowly edging our way out through the darkness towards the end of the runway.

The pilot reveals disconcerting news. 'Good evening ladies and gentlemen,' says the familiar Australian twang. 'There is good news and bad news. You're all on board, which is good. But the bad news is, we're tenth in line for take-off and the curfew falls at Kai Tak at 11pm. That's not much more than 20 minutes away so it's going to be tight. If we don't make it, I'm afraid we'll have to return to the gate and you'll have to spend the night in the terminal. Our first scheduled departure will be at eight in the morning.'

Audible groans greet this news. And suddenly, everyone takes on the intensive demeanour of a Formula 1 motor racing timekeeper. Watches are scrutinised every 30 seconds or so, pulses are racing.

We get down to the last five, but there are barely ten minutes remaining. A roaring sound twice over, signals that planes five and four ahead of us have blasted away into the night. Then a third. Two to go and we're down to less than five minutes from curfew.

As the exhaust fumes from the plane directly in front us dissipate over Kai Tak airport, our pilot manoeuvres the 747 into place at the end of the runway. We're ready to roll.

And then, wouldn't you believe it, Kai Tak control tower comes on to the pilot.

'Sorry Qantas, it is 11pm, curfew starts. Please return to gate.' Or words to that effect. And the lights down the runway are switched off.

To which the Aussie pilot, God bless him, responds, 'Kai Tak, we are going. If this thing ends up in the sea, you are responsible.' Or words to that effect.

We were never told what Kai Tak control tower said in response. But the 747 jet thrust forward, forcing the issue. The runway lights went on again. We climbed away into the night, en route for Sydney.

Directly behind us, the British Airways 747 bound for London Heathrow, on which sat one of my journalist pals, turned tail and tamely trundled back to the gate for the night. They left at 8am the next day.

Aussie pilots, eh? You gotta love 'em. And do you know what? Only one major airline has, to date, NEVER had a major crash.

Qantas.

⁄⁄ ⁄⁄ ⁄⁄ ⁄⁄ ⁄⁄

Diary Notes: June 1990.
To Sydney, for the three-Test French tour of Australia.

Now the Aussies have a few guys in these Tests who can really play. Nick Farr-Jones, David Campese, Jason Little, to mention but a few. You'd go a long way to see that lot.

As for the French, try Serge Blanco, prince of full-backs before he became Le Michelin Man, Philippe Sella, Patrice Lagisquet, Pierre Berbizier, and more.

In other words, it was worth crossing the world for this contest. Only trouble was, once the series started, it was hard to see anyone actually play.

NOW to call this just another tour would be substantially wide of the mark.

It wasn't so much a rugby Test series as a right royal rumbustious affair with boxing sometimes the chief sport on view.

The French travelled with their usual accoutrements – some good music on their personal systems, copious packets of Gauloises, a few decent novels, packets of condoms and such like. There was probably the odd rugby ball somewhere in the kit bag but that never featured very prominently on these French tours of the southern hemisphere.

Trouble was, by the time they even got on the plane at Charles de Gaulle airport in Paris, they were exhausted. The French domestic season had run from late August to the start of June. Now they were being asked to undertake a rigorous seven-match tour of Australia containing three Tests.

So interest was not exactly intense. At the airport in Paris, there were long, wistful sighs when the flight to Nice was called. A few weeks on the Mediterranean would always be infinitely preferable to the weary French rugby men than some slog around faraway Australia.

So they dragged the squad, moaning and complaining, up the steps on to the flight. And when they disgorged in Sydney, about 20 hours later, the classic Gallic shrugs and sighs were omnipresent.

However, from a journalistic point of view, at least there was to be something to write about on this tour. Oh yes. You always sensed there might have been a bit of rugby trying to break out occasionally. But alas, most of the time it failed.

The trouble started early in the first Test at Sydney. French forward Abdel Benazzi lasted only 13 minutes before being sent off for an act of gratuitous violence, a cowardly and vicious stamp on the head of Australian lock Peter FitzSimons.

Fitzie, who was later to become a brilliant and most prolific writer of, among other things, military history, would enjoy his own moment of madness later in the series, when he launched a vivid impression of a one-man wrecking machine.

But before that, there was another furious fight in the second Test in Brisbane. Benazzi, obviously not someone able to learn his lesson, again stamped on FitzSimons's head as he lay on the ground. Perhaps he just didn't like the Aussie's hairstyle. Or more likely, it was a settling of old scores from the time when Fitzie played in French rugby for the Brive club.

This time, FitzSimons's team-mate, number eight Tim Gavin, came to his defence and shoved Benazzi, raising his arms. At which stage, French tight head prop Philippe Gallas hit Gavin with a short, sharp right-hander which flattened the Australian. The blow would have been more at home in Madison Square Garden than a rugby ground in Australia. The Frenchman was promptly sent off by Welsh referee Clive Norling.

Two Tests gone, two sendings off. I was covering the tour for *The Times* in London and wondering what on earth would come next.

We thought all it needed for the High Noon showdown back in Sydney was to have Clint Eastwood riding into town on his horse, over the Sydney Harbour Bridge. In the end, we weren't to be disappointed because he wasn't needed. There were still some gunslingers intent on plying their trade even as late as the third Test. We certainly didn't have to wait long for the explosion. And when it came it was mayhem.

FitzSimons was big but he wouldn't have been the biggest guy who ever played Test rugby, not by a long chalk. But what

Fitzie had was ticker, real heart and commitment. He was scared of no-one.

So when some dark deed was enacted by a French foe, the historian in FitzSimons clearly mistook Sydney for Gallipoli. It was time for slaughter. The first couple of French forwards who squared up to him were laid out as if they'd been hit by a shell from a battleship lying just off the coast. Then, someone else was reduced to pulp.

This was impressive stuff, in pugilistic terms. I was never quite sure what it had to do with rugby but still, I'm certain he had his reasons. However, not even Fitzie could have anticipated the assailant who finally put an end to the fighting.

According to the French media covering the tour, no-one could ever remember centre three-quarter Philippe Sella even raising a fist in anger before in his illustrious career. Sella was a lovely bloke; modest and thoroughly self-effacing.

But now, seemingly incensed by the puny efforts of his forwards in the dark arts, Sella launched so immense a haymaker at FitzSimons that the Aussie was knocked flat.

When he finally got up, English referee Tony Spreadbury sent him off, the third dismissal in three Tests of the series. God, it was fun covering the French on tours like that.

But in those times, something else happened. Once everyone had put down their weapons and buried their dead from the battle, sorry, match, they all got dressed up and went to an after-match banquet. That's what it was like in those days.

People who had been hurling punches and kicking the heads of opponents were to be seen engaged in quiet, philosophical conversation while sipping a beer or a glass of chardonnay.

Welcome to the human species: a fascinating, disturbed element of the animal kingdom.

The media were invited to that end-of-tour dinner and I remember it well. We enjoyed a good meal and even better rugby conversations. All the players were there, rugby men and boxers combined. And you could chat with anyone you wished.

Eventually, the interminable official speeches came to an end and we made our plans for the night. The players headed off to a club and I headed back to the hotel to pack for a flight back across the other side of the world.

But in the wee small hours, what started as fun became sadness which was about to turn into tragedy.

French forward Dominique Bouet from the Dax club had played in the Test earlier in the day. It was his fifth cap. Bouet was a typically strong, squat French front row forward – 1.83m tall and weighing 103kg. Not the best in the world but a worthy adversary and a decent, reliable practitioner of his trade.

So as the night developed, the French decided it was party time. They went through the night in Sydney and virtually straight to the airport the next day. But they weren't going directly home. Instead, they had planned a few days' rest and recreation in New Caledonia, one of the Pacific islands, on the journey home.

So they flew up to Noumea from Sydney, allegedly continuing the drinking.

It didn't stop when they got there. So by evening time, the proverbial skinful had been sunk. At which point, it is further alleged, Dominique Bouet was all but out of it. His mates took him back to his room to sleep it off. Alas, it turned out to be his final sleep.

With a young wife waiting for him back in France, Dominique Bouet lay on the bed of his hotel room, threw up and, rendered helpless by drink, choked to death on his vomit. At the age of 26 years and 93 days.

When the French finally flew home, they did so with a coffin in the hold. Back in Dax, there was an explosion of grief at the loss of the young man's life.

It is said over 30,000 attended his funeral, bringing the centre of the town in the Landes department to a complete standstill. Wallaby flanker Simon Poidevin flew from Australia to represent the Australians.

Should Bouet's captain, Serge Blanco, have done more to avoid such a tragedy? Should a captain be responsible for his players on AND off the field? Should the captain of any group of young men offer guidance concerning their behaviour?

These questions were pertinent at the time and remain so to this day with regard to the leadership of young people. No-one is saying Serge Blanco was to blame for Dominique Bouet's death. But is it not conceivable that young men, especially in a group a long way from home, need some directions, some sage advice from time to time?

Whatever the answer to those questions, the truth is that Bouet's death was a tragic, crass and stupid waste of a young life.

※ ※ ※ ※ ※

Diary Notes: to Sydney, 1994. To do assorted interviews.

YOU never had a hope of doing any work once you got to Sydney unless you took the lunchtime Qantas flight out of Heathrow. It became, at one time, the business fraternity's best kept secret.

You'd board the 12.15pm departure and settle down to work or read. There was only one stop, Singapore's Changi airport, and you'd arrive there after one night in the air.

After an hour and a half refuelling, you would set off on the rapid seven-and-a-half-hour leg on to Sydney. All of which meant you landed at Sydney airport at around 7pm. You had time to get into the city, check into a hotel, go out for dinner and then crash out for the night. Most times, you'd get a good night's sleep and be ready for work the next morning.

By awful contrast, if you left London or anywhere else in Europe late at night bound for Australia you would have two nights in the air. The consequences were appalling. When you arrived on the other side of the world, heavily jet-lagged, at around 6am, you were no use to anyone that day or for about three days after it.

I did it once with a photographer pal and we soon discovered the reality. We flew in early on a Saturday morning and were due to work at a Sydney club match that afternoon.

Trouble was, we had been warned about not going to sleep during the day we landed. Otherwise, said the experts, you'll feel like death and be awake all the following night. 'Best to stick it out, somehow get through the day and then you can sleep,' was the advice.

So we tried it.

Feeling dreadful, we got into the downtown hotel, dumped the bags and went for a big cooked breakfast. We felt even worse after that. So I insisted we get a large intake of caffeine to wake us up. We did that and felt marginally better for an hour or two.

But when your body is racked with tiredness, you just don't seem able to think clearly or function properly. Quite obviously, the messaging service between brain and body had been seriously impaired, like electrical wires shorting.

Anyway, we managed to find the right bus to take us to where the club match was being staged out in the Sydney suburbs. It was one of those shocking Australian winter days, just the type you get in Sydney. A warm, blindingly strong sun beat down and its rays induced more longing for sleep in the bodies of two of the weary travellers on this particular bus.

By some manner of miracle, we made it and I caught up with one of the guys I wanted to interview for *Rugby World* magazine back in the UK. Even more astonishingly, I managed to talk enough sense for long enough to get a decent interview with him.

When it was finished, and the afternoon Australian sun was casting a beguiling light across the ground, I asked my interviewee if he'd do a few pictures.

'No worries mate,' came the reply. 'But if that's your mate down the touchline, he won't be much use.'

We walked a few yards down the side of the pitch to see a most extraordinary sight. Curled up in a heap that half resembled a foetal position and surrounded by large camera lenses and other paraphernalia lay my photographer pal. Completely dead to the world with a rugby match being played just a few feet away.

We always made sure we got the lunchtime flight after that.

%. %. %. %. %.

Diary Notes: To Sydney, July 1994 to empathise with a player who'd just had a lousy 24th birthday.

No, I didn't go all the way to Australia for someone's birthday party. It just so happened that the Australian rugby player Tim Horan had celebrated his birthday on the day his team, Queensland, played the final of the 1994 Super 10 competition.

The Aussies had flown to Durban to play Natal in the early days of Super Rugby finals. But what was to occur that day almost wrecked Horan's entire rugby career. Even today, only he truly knows the agonies he went through after his shocking injury.

I HAVE seen rugby players suffer some grievous injuries in my time associating with the game.

Many years ago, on the morning of one England v Ireland international match, I went to New Beckenham, one of the London suburbs, to see a game between rival banks. One of the London banks was playing the Northern Bank and Willie John McBride, the great Irish and Lions forward who was a bank manager in Ballymena, Northern Ireland, was playing for the Northern Bank.

Very often, an international player would appear alongside quite ordinary players in those bank teams. McBride himself remembered the time when his Northern Bank played Midland Bank one year. Barry John, the legendary Welsh fly half, worked for a subsidiary of the Midland and had been drafted in to play.

With a minute or two left, Midland won a line-out close to the Northern line. If they scored, they would win the game. John got the ball, chipped up into the air and dashed over the line to catch it. McBride, sensing what was about to happen, ran across and as Barry John caught the ball, the big Irishman caught John and carried him over the dead ball line before he had a chance to touch the ball down. Northern Bank won the match and Barry John was livid.

The newspaper I was working for that day in London, the *Belfast Telegraph*, wasn't much interested in the actual game but wanted a report on how McBride got on.

But before I could focus on him, there was an appalling injury that stopped the game for 20 minutes or more. As I stood on a touchline, a player ran across the field in my direction with the ball. He was tackled, perfectly fairly, but somehow fell badly. What ensued made for grim viewing.

When he finally came to a stop amid a scream of pain, it was perfectly obvious to anyone that his leg was badly broken. It was leaning in two different directions where he had taken the impact. With the bone protruding through the skin, the poor guy was screaming his head off in agony.

A medic on duty rushed over, trying to do what he could to ease the pain. But in those circumstances there isn't very much you can do. He didn't have an oxygen cylinder, which could have helped the victim. So they gave him a chunk of wood to bite on to try and manage the pain.

Eventually, an ambulance drove straight across the fields from the entrance to the sports ground, parking right next to the injured man. His face was contorted by pain as they gently lifted him on to a stretcher and got him into the back of the vehicle. I noticed that even strong, tough-looking rugby players looked distinctly queasy at all this.

It was just as sad a sight in November 2014 at Cardiff's Millennium Stadium when the South African captain Jean de Villiers wrecked his knee in a second-half tackle against Wales. The timing could not have been crueller. De Villiers, who had been forced to fly home early in South Africa's winning 2007 World Cup campaign in France due to injury, was just 20 minutes from the end of his long 2014 season.

He had captained the Springboks with great quality, as much an impressive man off the field as on it. Now, in South Africa's last match of their autumn tour, he was looking forward to getting home and a good rest over Christmas/New Year with his family.

But then it happened. His leg was trapped in a pile-up and the damage to his knee was horrendous. He ruptured the anterior cruciate ligament (ACL), ruptured the medial ligament, dislocated his knee cap and tore the hamstring.

De Villiers was carried off in agony. Suddenly, his future looked very different to the one he had been contemplating – having a holiday, preparing for the 2015 Super Rugby tournament and then, in all likelihood, leading the Springboks into the World Cup in England, in September 2015.

The initial injury prognosis confirmed his, and our, worst fears. Jean needed a total knee reconstruction, a major operation and lengthy rehab. He came through the operation okay but 2015 developed into a race against the clock, not knowing whether he would be fit in time for what was certain to be his last Rugby World Cup.

And yet, players do get through the most horrendous injuries and play again at the highest level. Take Tim Horan.

Horan was a tremendous player, good enough to win 80 Test caps for Australia between 1989 and 2000. In 1993, Wigan Rugby League Club made him what was then a massive financial offer of £250,000 a season to turn professional. Happily for union, he rejected it.

But in the Super 10 final of 1994 in which Queensland beat Natal 21-10 at Kings Park, Durban, he suffered a terrible knee injury which looked certain to end his career prematurely. The surgeon who was to operate on him told him later it was a good thing he had skin on his leg. 'Nothing much else was holding together the top and bottom half of your leg,' he remarked laconically.

Like Jean de Villiers, Horan had to undergo a major operation to reconstruct his knee. He had shattered both cartilages and completely torn both the medial collateral and cruciate ligaments. He too had also dislocated his knee cap.

But if the shock and initial pain from the injury was severe, then Horan was destined to plumb an even greater hole of pain and despair when his rehabilitation programme got under way.

When I went to see him at his temporary home at Palm Beach, an hour up the coast from Sydney, he told me about the agonies he had been through and how they continued every day of his life. One look at his withered leg hanging limp told you all you needed to know about the extent of the injury.

Photographer Dave Rogers and I took him down by the water at Palm Beach to do some pictures. But what happened next shocked me.

Just as we were about to take a final picture, a rogue wave came higher up the beach than we had anticipated. Tim was caught by it, utterly helpless and unable to move out of its way. His clothes got soaked but you could tell that wasn't the chief wound inflicted.

Here was a strong, superbly fit young sportsman, one of the best rugby players anywhere in the world, reduced to helplessness and almost complete immobility. He didn't stand a chance of getting out of the way of a simple wave. How would he ever play top-class rugby again?

Tim was brutally frank about his aspirations at that time. 'I am not even thinking about playing rugby again,' he told me. 'I just want my leg to recover sufficiently for me to play with my children in the park someday, to run enough to kick a ball around with them. Right now, that is the extent of my ambitions.'

Tim had to go through hell to achieve it. Only he would truly know the pain and physical torment he endured.

'I could hardly bend the knee at all even weeks after the operation. I think Greg Craig, the Wallabies physio, got a big shock. But it was nothing compared to what I had when he started to bend and move the knee. I wasn't ready for the pain it was going to cause. It was painful when I did it but the pain under physio treatment was much worse. It was excruciating.

'You know something of what is coming but you have got to go through it. The only way to explain it is that they are trying to bend the knee to break down the scar tissue.

'It's like bending your finger back until you can't handle any more pain, and then bending it a lot more. You get to the pain barrier and you are screaming into the pillow. Then you go past that barrier but you are still feeling it.

'You are close to fainting at times. One day, I thought, "How long will this go on, how much more can I take?" The pain kept happening and happening.'

Big tough rugby players able to grin and bear it? Get a life.

He had physio work on the knee every day for his first three weeks at Palm Beach. Each session lasted from 7am to 1pm. Then he'd try and sleep, before another horror session from 4pm to 6.30pm. The continuous pain so wrecked his appetite that he lost 12kg in three weeks.

In seven weeks, he had only two weekends off from this torturous programme. Always, he kept focused on the chief goal in front of him. 'I am going through all this so that I might be able at least to walk properly in the future,' he constantly told himself.

Yet astonishingly, Tim Horan returned to Test rugby the following year. It was a triumph of willpower over physical agony. Few players have ever been braver than Horan.

※ ※ ※ ※ ※

Diary Notes: May 1997. To Twickenham for the Pilkington Cup Final. Leicester are involved and Australian Bob Dwyer is currently coach of the Midlands club.

I've talked a few times in this book about how rugby union is a sport that creates such special friendships they can last a lifetime. None fits that category better than mine with Bob Dwyer and his fantastic wife, Ruth. This particular day, a dramatic one for me, would demonstrate what deep friendships are about.

IT wasn't a telephone call I could have anticipated. A phone ringing just before the start of the English cup final should have been the radio station I was working for that day. Instead, it was from a friend and the note of anxiety in the voice betrayed alarm.

My father, on holiday in North Wales, had just had a major heart attack. He'd been rushed to the nearby Bangor Hospital but they didn't know if he would live or die.

And then the whistle went at kick-off. So what to do? Abandon my work, jump into the car and drive north? Or somehow try to stay focused, do the job and then see whether the journey would be made in hope or sorrow?

I did what my dad would have insisted I do. Stay and do the job, even if it was devilishly hard to concentrate 100 per cent.

At the end, there was one more job to do. Cover the press conference. In particular, get some quotes from the Leicester coach.

As the media took their seats, I hung around the door from the dressing room area where the coaches would arrive. Thankfully, Dwyer was first. But I needed a favour as I didn't have time to sit through the press conference.

So what did he say when I explained my dilemma? 'Fire away, we'll do it now before the press conference.' And I went through the questions I had while the media at large waited patiently, doubtless bemused at the sight of myself furiously scribbling notes as they sat around, many with deadlines to negotiate.

We finished and shook hands. 'Get there as fast as you can but safely,' counselled Dwyer. He knew what I was capable of doing in a motor car. Killing myself, to put it succinctly.

I made it rapidly, but most importantly, my dad made it, too. As befitted the keen cricketer he was, his innings wouldn't end until he was 102.

I couldn't tell you how many times Bob Dwyer's hospitality, friendship and help have left me speechless. But put it like this: if Ruth Dwyer had a dollar for every meal she's ever cooked me, she'd have a very large bucket full of coins on her kitchen bench.

If I ever doubt the ongoing values of this game, one that has given the opportunity to unknown numbers of people around the world to establish and cherish friendships like this, I think of people like Bob and Ruth Dwyer. You can't repay them for their kindness and they wouldn't want you to. But you can keep at the forefront of your mind the merits of a wonderful sport that allows such relationships to flourish among human beings.

% % % % %

> **Diary Notes: April 2002. To the Auvergne region of central France and the atmospheric Stade Marcel Michelin for a French club match, A.S. Clermont-Ferrand v Stade Toulouse, a repeat of the previous year's final.**
>
> I am here partly to interview someone for an article. But I have been asked to fulfil another task this particular day. It could help an Aussie mate of mine, the former international hooker Michael Foley, who is coaching at Bath, where I live at this moment in time.

IN terms of physical attributes, Alessio Galasso was no shrinking violet. A tight head prop who stood 1.8m (5ft 11in) and weighed in at a handy 103kg, Galasso was good enough to represent Montferrand in the 2001 final of the French Rugby Championship.

True, neither Galasso nor his mates got a hand on the coveted Bouclier de Brennus, the French Championship log, that night. Stade Toulouse won that final 34-22 and the Auvergne club's search for a first French title went on. But I have come to the Auvergne for another reason. Bath, whom I have helped advise about player recruitment for a year or so, have asked me to run the rule over a tight head prop they have had their eyes on. Born in Dakar, Senegal, his name is Alessio Galasso.

One year earlier, in 2001, Galasso won two senior caps for France, as a replacement against Romania and England. He has also played for Toulon so is clearly a man who knows the scene. Bath are interested in him because decent, reliable and solid tight head props are like hen's teeth in these times. Even some of the ordinary ones seem able to command vast salaries.

So can Galasso play? That is my brief from Bath. Can he scrummage strongly enough, can he hold up a set scrum and dominate an opponent? Bath want some clear indications as to whether they would be spending their money wisely or foolishly if they recruited him.

Well, the last question, the bit about whether he contributes around the park, takes no time at all to answer. Fact is, Galasso never has the chance to prove himself one way or the other in that respect.

At just about the first scrum of the game, Galasso packs down opposite a man mountain wearing a Stade Toulouse jersey. His name is Cedric Soulette, he is their loose head and he has the kind of facial expression Al Capone used to adopt when he was lined up for a mug shot upon entering Alcatraz.

Unshaven and unsmiling, Soulette is of the old school of French props. Look like a villain, act like a villain and waste no time in finding out the worth (or otherwise) of your direct opponent.

Now the great tight head props of the world are mean men. Their philosophy is not to give an inch, especially to some Fancy Dan loose head prop. Tight head is the guy who is the real man of the scrummage. If he does his job, his team's scrum should enjoy at the very least parity and maybe superiority, assuming others play their part.

But when loose head prop Cedric Soulette packed down alongside his Toulouse team-mates and readied for the impending collision with the Montferrand front row and tight head prop Galasso, it was very obvious that achieving parity, in other words, just holding his opponent, was far from Soulette's mind. Instead, he was hell bent on inflicting damage, the more serious the better.

Far be it for me to cast wild, unfounded allegations. Let's just say that when the two clashed, Galasso quickly resembled an item of clothing in the washing machine. He was sent spinning around helplessly. Worse still, a fist – surely it wasn't a Toulouse hand inflicting it? – then smacked him one flush on the chops. Alessio Galasso went down like a corpse.

Now the odd punch from a member of the opposing pack at scrum time was not exactly unknown in those days. It was more like a rite of passage, an early tester just to see if the intended recipient was worth anything. Alas, in this case, he wasn't.

Even when they got him up, Galasso looked like he'd been hit by a passing bus, not a simple fist. He staggered off, was replaced and never came back.

Alas, this presented his assessor in the stands with something of a problem. How do you judge a guy who has fallen flat at the first whiff of cordite? By going and talking to his team-mates at the end of the game, of course.

An hour or two after the match finished, I had managed to work my way into the official reception where all the players had by then gathered. I found a group of the home team and sidled up.

'How is your prop, Galasso?' I enquired, matter-of-factly.

A strange, collective expression seemed to invade all their faces. A couple of them dispensed with words and just rolled their eyes. I got the message.

Next morning, in the car heading south through the rolling hills of the Auvergne, the phone rang in the car. It was the finance director of Bath, Ed Goodall.

'Peter, did you see Galasso?'

'Briefly, yes. But he didn't last long in the game. Only as long as the first scrum,' I reported.

There was a brief silence at the other end of the line. 'Oh dear, so do you think we'd be wise to buy him or not?'

'In the eyes of his own team-mates, he's a pussycat,' I told him. 'Save your money on him and buy the Toulouse loose head. He can play both sides of the front row, he's an animal and he'll be a huge success for you,' I advised [they did later invite Soulette to Bath for talks but owner Andrew Brownsword wouldn't pay the money he wanted, which also went for other players I got to the club for talks such as South African flanker Corne Krige and the French internationals Serge Betsen and Sylvain Marconnet].

The denouement to the story, unknown to me at the time, came later that day when Goodall called Michael Foley to relay the news.

'Michael, we have a problem. Peter Bills saw Galasso play yesterday and has told us not to touch him.'

Foley's reply was succinct. 'Who is the coach of this club, Peter Bills or me? I think he'll do a good job for us, I want to get him.'

Of course, it was the fatal flaw made by coaches of sports teams the world over. 'I can make him a great player,' the coach tells himself, whatever the evidence to the contrary. So Bath signed Alessio Galasso, at a reported £180,000 a year on a two-year contract.

And what happened? Galasso played just a handful of games for Bath in the 2002/03 season, only eight as a member of the starting line-up, the rest as a replacement. He never remotely looked like being the answer to their needs and was moved on after a single season.

Not even Michael Foley, one of the great men of world rugby and a World Cup winner in 1999 with the Wallabies, could make Galasso a great player. Foles and I still laugh about it even now, years later.

SOUTH AFRICA

Diary Notes: Johannesburg 1972

The world was a very different place when I first went to Johannesburg. The year was 1972; some year that turned out to be.

The last American troops were withdrawn from Vietnam, terrorists of the Black September group launched their murderous assault on the Israeli athletes at the Munich Olympics, a break-in at the American Democratic party offices, Watergate, ultimately led to the resignation of Richard Nixon, President of the United States and 16 survivors, including members of a rugby team, from a plane crash in the South American Andes were rescued after being forced to practise cannibalism.

YOU might think that was enough to be going on with. But even more astonishing than all that lot put together, England sent a rugby team on tour to South Africa and actually beat the feared Springboks, 18-9, in their own Johannesburg lair, Ellis Park. Why so remarkable? Quite simply, because England were usually complete rubbish in those days.

Rugby was amateur and even players likely to be chosen for the national team would do daft things like go skiing over Christmas and sometimes break a leg which ended their rugby activities for the season. Trial matches were held at Twickenham, usually on the first weekend of January, between an England XV and The Rest.

Anyone who could be bothered to lift themselves above the usual torpor of those grim, often fog-bound occasions, was just about guaranteed an England cap in the first international of the season. Otherwise, the selectors had to rely on the form of players in club matches such as Rosslyn Park v Richmond and Harrogate v Broughton Park. It was all so haphazard as to be bizarre.

Quite how England managed to go to Johannesburg and beat the mighty South Africans after another modest season back home in the Five Nations Championship of that year, has remained a mystery ever since. But they did and even completed the seven-match tour unbeaten.

Those of us who were there rubbed our eyes in disbelief and then hung around afterwards to talk to a few of the players to hear their views. Mostly, they didn't have a clue how or why they'd won, either.

Years later, England second row forward Peter Larter remembered, 'We were labelled no-hopers which I suppose was understandable since England had just lost seven consecutive internationals. One incentive was that we were the last of the four home countries to tour South Africa and none of the others had managed to win a Test there.

'It was a marvellous team effort and the emotion in the changing room after the game was quite amazing – something I will always remember. It was also incredible to realise that we had become the first international touring team not to lose a game in South Africa since the 1891 Lions.'

So then we headed to the Glasshouse, bastion of white South African rugby men in their renowned rugby backyard.

The Glasshouse was where the so-called 'elite' were invited to after-match receptions. No-one got in there unless they had been born with a certain skin colour. Let me put it like this: if you'd got deeply tanned on holiday beside the Mediterranean earlier that year, they'd have looked at you very dubiously.

But other entry qualifications were required, too. You couldn't go in unless you were wearing a shirt, tie and jacket and looked respectable. One former Transvaal player of that era recalled years later, 'All I can remember is a room full of Dutchmen, Dutchmen and more Dutchmen.'

The England wing that day, Keith Savage of Northampton, had showered and changed and stuffed his tie into his kit bag, which he'd left on the team bus. All the protests in the world to the white Afrikaner on the door that actually, this guy was one of the England players, met a non-bending wall of resistance. If Cecil John Rhodes himself had strolled by and offered to vouch for the England rugby man, it wouldn't have made a fig of difference. In that familiar South African guttural voice, the man explained that this Englishman wasn't being allowed in because he didn't have a tie. Full stop.

Those of us who did were grudgingly admitted to a world of privilege. The reception was crammed full of white men and their ladies, dressed as if for church on a Sunday. They sipped their drinks and delicately consumed nibbles of food and you thought for a moment you were probably at Henley-on-Thames or an Oxford college, not in Africa. But then, apartheid was always about window dressing, creating a mirage. Below the surface, another world existed.

Just a week earlier on that trip, I had been down a goldmine outside Johannesburg and seen the inherent hatred among the white bosses for their black workers. It made me feel physically sick.

We'd donned overalls in the miners' changing room and then squeezed into the cage of the lift shaft. But banish from your mind images of commercial lifts gently descending. These things drop like a stone into the depths. And they keep going endlessly.

About a mile and a half underground, with your stomach left halfway back up the shaft and making a vain attempt to catch up with the rest of your body, the lift begins to slow. You step out of the cage into a dimly lit, claustrophobic underground cavern where the dust, dirt and noise assail your senses.

The boss man waiting at the bottom looked down his rather large nose at the visitor and snarled, 'Where's your helmet, man?'

'Wasn't given one,' I snarled back.

At which point, the black worker charged with bringing me underground was seized by the Afrikaner. I thought he was going to tear him apart limb by limb.

'You kaffir bastard, why didn't you give this man a helmet,' he roared. The poor black worker looked terrified. He had every reason to – a verbal assault that would have reduced most human beings to pulp was then launched at him, like a missile. I was sure if I hadn't been standing there, he'd have cheerfully killed him. I had never seen such deep, intrinsic hatred by one human being for another.

They found a helmet in the end and we set off along dark corridors where the rock had been blasted out. Soon, we arrived at the face to find a scene of grim, primitive endeavour. Two miners, stripped to the waist amid the sweltering heat and humidity and in goggles to protect their eyes, lay on their backs each holding up a long, lethal-looking mechanical drill which blasted into the rock face. Lumps and splinters flew off in every direction and were shovelled into waiting trucks on a rail line, ready to be hauled to the bottom of another lift shaft ahead of delivery to the surface and sorting to unearth the nuggets of precious gold.

If the working conditions were dire, the people in charge were even worse. I spent an hour or so underground before being catapulted back up towards the sky, the sense of relief as we stepped out of the rickety cage, simply overwhelming. I had every reason to be fearful – soon after, several workers at another mine nearby were killed when the lift cage plummeted into the bowels of the earth, suffered a mechanical failure and failed to brake.

Still, the good news was that I'd seen for myself the sadistic torture chamber for unknown numbers of black workers underground. And that helped me to arrive at a key decision. I'd get out of this aesthetically beautiful country which had sadly been irrevocably stained by the white fanatics and never return until apartheid had been lifted. I was true to my word – I left in 1972 and never went back until 1995, when the new South Africa hosted the Rugby World Cup of that year. Even though I had some dear friends there who were nothing like fanatics.

But you had to wonder, why on earth couldn't other sportspeople see the reality? It was a scandal and disgrace that, long years after sports such as cricket had put in place rigid isolation of South African teams, dear old rugby was still playing with the evil apartheid regime in South Africa.

As late as 1980, almost 17 years after Nelson Mandela and his colleagues had been incarcerated on Robben Island following the Rivonia trial, the British & Irish Lions, led by the avuncular Bill Beaumont, were still touring the white-dominated Republic and enjoying the apartheid regime's lavish hospitality at the expense of the great majority.

Shame on them, they should have known better. At least another Englishman, the late, much lamented Andy Ripley who toured South Africa with the Lions in 1974, admitted years later he had been 'a shit' to go. And it is important to state that the Welsh flanker John Taylor, who had toured New Zealand with the 1971 Lions, flatly refused to have anything to do with the 1974 tour. By doing so, he revealed himself a man of considerable principle.

I don't recall any such gesture or confession from most of the 1980 Lions. They sipped the wines, lived the life and closed their eyes and ears to the grim reality all around them. All they could do was trot out the banal mantra of that time, that sport does not have anything to do with politics.

I can't think for one minute anyone actually believed that claptrap, but if they did they must have been the most naïve human beings on the planet. Nor could they have heard of the youth uprisings of 1976 in Soweto when 13-year-old schoolchild Hector Pietersen was shot dead by police. Maybe they knew but just didn't care.

Yet there were just a handful of players from that 1980 tour who understood the reality. Even today, the Irish fly half Tony Ward recalls the Lions place kickers practising at the University of Cape Town's fields under the shadow of Table Mountain.

When they finished their practice and began to leave the ground, they were stoned by white students from the university. There was a reason for that.

Ward himself had not understood why the black supporters at rugby grounds had supported the Lions, not the Springboks. He quickly came to see the truth.

With the European Cup at the Bayern Munich training ground in 1975

The analysis. Coach Jacques Fouroux discusses a game deep in the bowels of the Parc des Princes with, from left, Jean-Luc Joinel, Jean-Pierre Rives and, on right, Pierre Lacans who was tragically killed in a car crash in 1985

The French rugby squad, elegantly attired for their 1990 tour of Australia. It was an unusual tour. The Test matches degenerated into a series of punch-ups and hooker Dominique Bouet (second row from back, second from left) came home in a coffin after a night of wild excess. It was a tragedy that stained French rugby

With former Australian coach Bob Dwyer before the 2003 Rugby World Cup Final in Sydney. It must have been before the start: Bob wasn't grinning after Jonny Wilkinson's drop goal had won the cup for England

One of the most genuine men I ever met in world sport: on the terrace of Jack Nicklaus's private office at his West Palm Beach, Florida, base after a three-hour interview. Typically generous and completely unprompted, he signed a golf shirt for me as a parting gift

With my family and the great Nelson Mandela at his home in Johannesburg after an exclusive interview in June 2002

Another man of towering modesty whom I was privileged to meet and interview: Jose Carreras, in his room in a Sydney hotel, June 2004

Two of the giants of British & Irish Lions rugby in their heyday discuss old times at a reunion in the Hotel Plaza Athenee in Paris. Former Ireland and Lions wing and record holding try scorer, Tony O'Reilly, chats with ex-England and Lions scrum half Dickie Jeeps. Photo Hannah Bills

This giant, ungainly trophy of a square lump of heavy wood is what French rugby players smash the hell out of each other for throughout the long winter season. Here, Paris club Stade Francais has won the trophy and among the guests at the night's reception is a young fan, my son James

Another incredible night with former French coach Jacques Fouroux at Claude Lafitte's great restaurant in Auch. Here Jacques is clearly protesting at another glass being poured by the owner. Some problem, some night

At the Groot Constantia wine estate outside Cape Town. Moments after this photo was taken, my mobile rang, the caller demanding to know where I was because the President of South Africa, Thabo Mbeki, was waiting for me to interview him

Emmerson's World Cup view: Warning - the global economy is going pear-shaped - Thursday Sep 22, 2011

A cartoon which appeared in the New Zealand Herald *on 22 September 2011 during the Rugby World Cup. New Zealand Prime Minister John Key, clad in All Black training gear, is telling his finance minister: "The new French Head of the IMF reckons the global economy isn't playing like a winning team. I'd be keen for a second opinion. Ask that rugby writer Peter Bills: he seems to have his finger on the French pulse."* Cartoon by Rod Emerson

New Zealand fly half Dan Carter amidst the hurly burly of an autograph signing session. Photo Hannah Bills

A stunning close-up portrait taken in New Zealand of the Maori links to rugby football. The two are inseparable. Photo Hannah Bills

A pensive moment on the Mediterranean coast and a beautifully poignant image of giant South African forward Victor Matfield, playing for Toulon at the time, with his young daughter Jaime. Photo Hannah Bills

One of the most famous men of rugby union in silhouette. If you know the game, you should pick the face. They key is the background, the rooftops of Rome. The figure is South Africa's Nick Mallett, taken while he was coach of Italy. Photo Hannah Bills

On reflection: Wales coach Warren Gatland after an interview with him at Cardiff Bay Hotel. Photo Hannah Bills

The calm before the storm. A revealing close-up portrait of the Racing Metro front row: the sweat, grime and intense focus paramount in the photo. Photo Hannah Bills

The moment of impact: Racing Metro scrum half Jerome Fillol looks on as the two packs hammer into each other in a brilliant blur of speed, colour and aggression. Photo Hannah Bills

The former South African captain, Corne Krige, photographed in Cape Town with the book we wrote together after his retirement. We had a great working relationship

With the great Willie John McBride at his home in Northern Ireland in 2015. I came to know his home well after working with him on his autobiography: a revealing, fascinating book that told of the many hard times in his life as well as the rugby triumphs

Winner of the Magazine Sportswriter of the Year award in London 1992, presented by former Wasps and England rugby man Peter Yarrington (left) and a sponsoring official

A faithful old friend. Before computers came to dominate our lives, I carried this old Olivetti all around the world

A collection of some of the mementoes, press passes and programmes from so many years of watching international rugby. Photos Katie Bills

'I refused to travel back out there with Ireland in 1981 on grounds of conscience i.e. what I had seen and experienced on that Lions tour in 80 when, much like Rippers [Ripley] in 1974, I went without even thinking. I just wanted to be a Lion. I too listened to the building bridges case but ultimately decided that through isolation alone, given the distorted importance of rugby to the Afrikaners, could change of any description come from within. I sure wasn't going to change the world but it was the right and only thing to do. I wasn't back until about 1997, I think.'

Sadly, the fact was that very few of the Lions party took the trouble to get out on their own and try to see the reality. Some, like Tony Ward and his fellow Irish half-back Colin Patterson, tried to make secret visits to certain townships. Lions captain Bill Beaumont was another who tried to join them on one occasion, attempting to visit the oldest existing township outside Port Elizabeth, New Brighton. But the authorities, aware of the potential cost of allowing these visitors to see the truth, quickly moved in and prevented them getting to their destination.

However, on another occasion, Ward did manage to reach a township and what he saw appalled him. But too often, his were a lone pair of eyes.

As for the rest, shame on the lot of them for their selfishness. And of course that includes the 1986 so-called New Zealand Cavaliers who were still happy to play with the apartheid monsters only eight years before they finally fell to their doom. Rugby has a shameful record in such fields.

When at last I went back to South Africa, apartheid leaders like the dreaded John Vorster was, thank God, by now pushing up the daisies, although the equally odious P.W. Botha, Prime Minister from 1978 to 1984 and then State President from 1984 to 1989, was to linger on until 2006. Botha, perhaps appropriately, was known as Die Groot Krokodil (Afrikaans for The Big Crocodile). He was vicious and slimy, that's for sure.

Equally happily, I now found a country where most people had a respect for their fellow human beings. You could go and have a beer with a black pal and a white man could make love to a black woman without risking landing them both in a criminal court. Human beings from all backgrounds were meeting one another and talking, like victims surviving a nuclear attack and emerging, blinking, into a new world. What a step forward for mankind.

Maybe the best comment ever made on the evils of the apartheid regime was by the revered English cricket writer John Arlott, at the end of MCC's 1964/65 tour of the Republic. When you departed the country in those days, you had to fill out a lengthy form at customs and immigration. One of the questions was race.

John Arlott dutifully filled in the form and wrote in reply, 'Human'.

The Afrikaans official at customs took one look and growled, 'You get on that aeroplane Mr Arlott and never come back to our country.'

'I have not the slightest intention of ever setting foot in this place again,' he is said to have replied. But then Arlott, like Tony Ward and Andy Ripley, had principles. Too many others didn't.

※ ※ ※ ※ ※

Diary Notes: London, late April 1995 with all eyes looking to the Rugby World Cup in South Africa this year.

HONESTLY, I really think some people do this deliberately.

You're sat there in the offices of *Rugby World* magazine at Waterloo on London's South Bank. The offices perched up on the 16th floor overlook the River Thames and you can see right out across the city and down the sweep of the river in either direction.

Unfortunately, the one thing you can't see is any movement from the fax machine in a corner of the office. And this particular day, at this particular hour, that silent, inactive machine has become the focus of our entire lives.

We've slaved, every single one of us, to put together a rip-roaring, bumper issue of the magazine that is a special souvenir edition previewing the Rugby World Cup.

It will start in South Africa on 25 May and finish on 24 June. It promises to be an absolutely fascinating, riveting World Cup, the best yet. For a start, South Africa will compete for the first time.

So we've pushed the boat out for this edition. There is a brilliant series of photographs by Dave Rogers of David Campese around Sydney Harbour. We've got great pictures of the Springbok full-back Andre Joubert with his wife on the beach at Durban, super interviews with the 1991 World Cup Final captains, England's Will Carling and Nick Farr-Jones of Australia. Then there are further exclusive features from Tony O'Reilly, Dean Richards, Andrew Mehrtens and many others.

We have slaved to get this far. And now we are sweating, big time.

Unfortunately, the ONE piece we really want, everyone covets, has not arrived. And we can't keep pestering him for it. You don't phone up the President of the Republic of South Africa and tell him to pull his finger out.

Of course, it was always a long shot. You try and get an exclusive, personalised message from President Nelson Mandela about an event as huge as the Rugby World Cup in his country. I imagine he and his staff have a few other things to think about.

Nevertheless, they said he would do it. But when? In time for the 2023 World Cup, perhaps? Clearly, the President's office has forgotten the deadline we set. Or perhaps there was never an intention to do it. After all, no-one else in the UK is going to get a personal message from Mandela, not even *GQ*, *Esquire* or any of the UK's national newspapers. And with the minutes ticking away before our deadline for closing the magazine, it doesn't look as though we are, either.

People mope about the office, waiting, wondering. Everything else in the magazine is done. These are the last two pages that will be sent off to print the issue, a colossal 196-page effort that, time will prove, will sell in excess of 55,000 copies.

The whole team has busted the proverbial gut to make this the best edition I've edited since I came on board. But now the crème de la crème, the one item that would make us really stand out, looks as though it's not going to arrive.

I beg an extra hour and then half-hour from the printers, just in case. And lo and behold, suddenly the machine fires into life. The first thing I see, on the top of the first sheet, is the seal stating OFFICE OF THE PRESIDENT. The hairs stand up on the back of my neck.

Below it, the title says President Nelson Mandela's exclusive greeting to *Rugby World* readers.

It says the following:

'The opportunity for South Africa to host the 1995 Rugby World Cup Tournament is a great honour bestowed on our country. To the organisers of Rugby World Cup 1995, I would like to extend my heartiest congratulations for undertaking this gigantic task. I am convinced that the 1995 Rugby World Cup Tournament will provide keen competition and that we will see rugby of an exceptional standard. It is also my sincere wish that this event will be played in a spirit of goodwill and true sportsmanship, which characterise the game of rugby.

'I would also like to extend a hearty welcome to all visitors and participants. I trust that they will not only enjoy the tournament, but also the scenic beauty of the country and the warmth of our South African friendship.

'It is above all my sincere wish that the 1995 Rugby World Cup Tournament to be hosted in South Africa, will make a vital contribution to the global endeavour to promote peace and unity among the people of the world through the medium of sport.

'Finally, I wish to say that we as South Africans are committed to organising the event successfully – thus demonstrating to the world that we have the capability in human and physical resources to host major global sports events. I believe that this momentous event will, among other things, not only showcase our attributes and world class facilities, but it will also stimulate the grassroots development of rugby in South Africa.'

We ran it as a double page spread, a great photo of Mandela on the left hand page with his message beneath the President's seal opposite. It was a proud moment for *Rugby World* and everyone involved in that edition.

%% %% %% %% %%

Diary Notes: Johannesburg 1997, the Lions tour of South Africa.

Unless you have pressing business in the city centre you would hardly head for downtown Johannesburg these days. I don't know, maybe it's me being silly and over-sensitive. But you tend to get put off by the sight of guys shooting up in broad daylight as they wait at traffic lights.

However, there are a few isolated, splendid places to see or visit in the city centre. The Rand Club with its wood-lined dining room walls and old fashioned gentlemen's lounge is one. To dine within its hallowed rooms, where the likes of Cecil John Rhodes ate, is to experience a taste of Empire and how it must have been all those years ago.

But once darkness falls the city becomes a crime playground. Just up the hill from the centre is the notorious Hillbrow region where Nigerian gangsters and drug dealers of all nationalities hold sway.

Unwanted strangers, outsiders are not so much discouraged as despatched, a fact that was high on my mind as I headed unwittingly into Hillbrow on the night of Saturday 5 July 1997.

By 1997, Hillbrow was a very different place from 1972 when you could walk around it late at night in total safety.

So you do your homework, think you've done your planning and then this happens.

I'D planned this and arrived hours early for the last Test on the 1997 Lions tour of South Africa. The series was already decided, the Lions winning in Cape Town (courtesy of Matt Dawson's outrageous dummy, the biggest outside Mothercare) and in Durban thanks to Jerry Guscott's low, Exocet-type drop goal which skimmed over the bar to win the match and seal the series.

But at Ellis Park, the world famous rugby ground in the suburbs of Johannesburg, we knew the wounded Springboks would hit back. National pride was on the line; a nation demanded a response. South Africans bettered in sporting contests generally react like slumbering lions who have had a stick jabbed up their backsides.

The denouement to the Test series required careful planning because I was booked on the 9pm British Airways flight out of Johannesburg for London that Saturday night. That had seemed in loads of time when I booked it long before, assuming a 3pm kick-off. But the reality was different; television demanded a 5.15pm start, which cast a shadow over my schedule.

But as long as I knew the quickest route to the airport, seven miles east of downtown Johannesburg, I figured it might work out. Doubtless, it'd be the usual rush for the gate, dragging assorted bags and collapsing into the seat as last on board. But that was nothing new.

So getting clear instructions was the key and who better to ask than a senior police officer outside the stadium. I'd parked in a propitious spot, close by the stadium within a two- or three-minute run from the main gate. And Sergeant van der Merwe, or whatever his name was, could not have been more helpful.

'Go up this road, turn left, take the next robot and you arrive on the main street. Go through three robots, then turn left and you will see the sign for the motorway. Ja.' Easy.

I rehearsed it all in my mind in the couple of hours I had before kick-off. It became as clear as one of those lovely sunlit, golden afternoons for which South Africa's high veldt is renowned in mid-winter.

So the match was played, South Africa won (35-16) and at 7.20pm, with 40 minutes to make the airport, drop off the hire car and negotiate check-in and security, I was on schedule. Alas, 15 minutes later I began to realise my life was in serious danger.

Darkness had fallen by the time the game kicked off. In winter, it creeps up on you in the southern hemisphere like an assailant. Which wasn't the worst analogy given I was heading out of Johannesburg, one of the most dangerous crime hot spots in the world back in 1997.

I put the car into gear and my brain into auto-pilot at the same time. My hire car didn't have a sat-nav and I wouldn't have had the damn thing on anyway. If your idea of a fun drive is to have some frustrated human being constantly nagging you to turn left, turn right, don't go down the next street but go through the lights, don't sniff, don't wipe your nose on your sleeve and don't take your right hand off the wheel, then I wish you well. It isn't mine. I had a mental sat-nav. What could go wrong?

Well, probably nothing if I'd been given the correct directions. As it turned out, I might as well have asked Sergeant Plod for the quickest route not to the airport but the Botswana border. He sent me totally the wrong way.

With meticulous care (quite unlike me on the road), I followed his directions – and ended up down an unlit cul-de-sac. What was worse, it was in an area you clearly wouldn't have wanted to be in even during daytime, never mind at night.

Someone long ago coined a phrase about pubs in such locations – the kind of place you wipe your feet when you come out.

Reversing at speed the wrong way up the street and back on to a road, while trying to avoid scraping parked cars, was decidedly difficult.

By then, I was hopelessly lost. But when you see lights you think you'll find life and I found some, all right. Unfortunately, it was the worst sort. As I passed a street sign saying Hillbrow, my heart sank. What was equally disconcerting was the sudden thinning out of the traffic.

Hillbrow is not a place you want to be at any time. But in the darkness it looked especially threatening. Gangs of youths loitered at the traffic lights perhaps waiting for some misguided fool actually to stop on the red light. As I slowed to a crawl to approach one set down a poorly-lit street, a car drew up alongside. I looked across at my fellow traveller and saw a look of clear unease etched deep into his face.

Winding down the window, I shouted across, 'Which way to the airport from here mate?'

His reply was less than comforting. 'I don't know but I'd get out of this area as fast as possible. And don't stop at any lights.' There wasn't any hint of a joke in his voice.

He turned next left and disappeared in a cloud of exhaust smoke. There was no-one else on this lonely road.

With a growing sense of alarm deep in the pit of my stomach, I took a right turn, mainly out of interest rather than any sense that it might be the way out of the area. And as another set of red lights loomed and I caught sight of a rough bonfire burning on the side of the street with a few characters around it, it began to look a forlorn hope.

Five or six minutes later, I'd driven straight through two sets of red lights, narrowly missing a car without any lights at the first set coming in the cross direction at high speed, reversed the wrong way up a one-way street and then found a fairly major road. Mind you, you'd probably see more comforting sights on a city street than guys shooting up without a care in the world and then flicking the needle into the gutter as you drove past. You don't get that in Casino Square at Monte Carlo on a Saturday night.

At the next lights I turned left and suddenly spied a small sign for the M2 motorway. Whether it was the right or wrong way to the airport didn't concern me; just escaping Hillbrow was the chief priority.

By pure chance, I joined the motorway heading in the right direction for the airport. Eventually, I drove into the car rental shed, grabbed my luggage and reached check-in. It was 8.20pm, 40 minutes before take-off. And there was still a live radio report to send overseas from the lounge before boarding.

The sense of elation as the 747 picked up speed down the runway and lifted off into the clear, cold South African night bound for London, was hard to define. And to think, some people actually say they dread airline flights.

‰ ‰ ‰ ‰ ‰

Diary Notes: June 2002 and a very special exclusive interview.

The phrase 'exclusive interview' became a bit devalued some time ago in the world of journalism. There was a time when it genuinely meant something – a paper had secured a real scoop. But circulation wars among the UK tabloids undermined the whole meaning of it. When some sub-editor or writer on your paper pinches a story off the internet, re-writes it and blasts 'WORLD EXCLUSIVE' across the top, then you know the process has become seriously flawed.

But just occasionally, you did get a genuine world exclusive. And when it happened, it tickled the taste buds like fine wine.

YOU didn't get world exclusives with this man. Quite simply, he was beyond all that, too elevated in the world's consciousness even for a journalist to dream of a one-on-one interview with him.

So we've flown into the country scarcely believing this is all going to work out. It has been arranged by my boss Sir Anthony O'Reilly, head of the Independent News & Media group, and for sure, I've been promised the interview. But promises can be amended, broken even.

We've flown in? Sure. I've dragged my whole family right across the world for this occasion. The person is that special.

Mind you, kids being kids, we've had some lively debates about the value of it all. Katie, my younger daughter, was due to go on a school trip when I told her about this journey. It clashed with hers and she reckoned she wouldn't bother; she'd go with her school pals to Devon, she decided.

That decision was revoked pretty well the moment she got to school next day and told her friends about the contrary offer.

'Are you crazy?' they chorused. 'You've got to go there, you'll never get that chance again,' they said in unison. Ah, the wisdom of youth.

So we all make the long flight, collect a hire car and two mornings later, find ourselves wending our way through the leafy suburbs of the city. Presently, we find the house and park up.

Guards with pockets bulging with weapons and others clutching AK47s, beckon us inside the compound. We are led into a comfortable, large family home of a property with well matured trees shielding the garden from the warm midday sun.

The security may be obvious but the rest is the personification of simplicity. I am shown into a room with a few bookshelves, a large desk and comfortable chairs. An old man's crinkly, withered hand is outstretched to meet me.

Mr Nelson Mandela.

So we talk about rugby. He recounted his days, talked of his emotions as a young man, standing on the terraces of one international ground in the only small area allocated for black people, watching the 1955 British Lions touring team, in which Irish wing Tony O'Reilly was one of the star performers at just 19 years of age.

He talked too of the 1995 Rugby World Cup and the effect it had on him, watching that tense final between South Africa and New Zealand. He expressed his belief that rugby football, with its many great qualities, could help unite his country.

I asked him for his memories of that famous 1955 Lions tour and this is what he said:

'The 1955 events included the rugby tour by the Lions. Many thought that it was the strongest side that ever visited South Africa. It was the first team that came to South Africa by aircraft.

'They won two Tests on the fast fields of the high veldt [in Johannesburg, 23-22, and Pretoria, 9-6] but they lost two Tests at the coast [25-9 in Cape Town and 22-8 in Port Elizabeth]. That is what I remember of the 1955 Lions.

'As for Tony O'Reilly, the Lions' wing, his reputation preceded him because as a 19-year-old he came here and he was a sensation due to his height, strength and ability to run at full speed. He was very difficult to stop. During that tour he scored 16 tries but he was at times weak on defence as the South African player Tom van Vollenhoven would testify. He passed Tony and scored three tries in one match.

'But nevertheless, that did not reduce Tony O'Reilly's ability as a sensation in rugby. But of course, later, we have known him as one of the most amazing businessmen in the world.

'We admire him for his readiness to support worthy causes inside and outside our country. He is a man I admire very much.'

What did rugby mean to Mandela? 'I wouldn't say rugby played a significant part in my life and I also would not like any particular sport to be isolated because although I have always understood that rugby is a very important game in South Africa to both whites and blacks, nevertheless it is sport as a whole that has played a significant part in our lives because sport can unite a nation. It also speaks a language which is understood by everybody no matter from what country that person comes and what their backgrounds are.

'Sport is extremely important and in that context rugby has had a tremendous influence in regard to the uniting of our people.

'Without doubt, my most cherished rugby memory was firstly the 1995 World Cup which South Africa won. I was very much involved of course as an outsider because the first match was played in Cape Town. I went to see our boys [before the game] and I told them that the team that won that particular match would go right through to the end because South Africa was playing Australia who were the world champions.

'In encouraging our boys this is what I said and that proved true. When our boys beat Australia they were able to go on and beat every opposition until they met the All Blacks in the final.

'I was lucky to be alive after that match. I had never been so tense when there was not a single try in the match. It was penalty goals and drop kicks only. But we won and that created tremendous excitement among both blacks and whites in this country. It was a great day.'

I asked Mandela about earlier times in South Africa under the Colonial influence.

'The history of Colonialism is very long. And a process like that which exercises a tremendous influence on the thinking on the part of many people cannot be destroyed just overnight. The process to destroy Colonialism takes a long time. It has left its scars on…our…society and those scars are still visible today.

'Although there is no doubt that the Empire is now a thing of the past, it is now the respect for the ability of a leader to hold the various parts of the Commonwealth together and Her Majesty, Queen Elizabeth, has achieved this. But the Empire itself we have destroyed.'

The thorny issue of whether the 1974 Lions were right to tour apartheid South Africa at a time when Mandela and his fellow freedom fighters had been imprisoned for life and repression remained rife, reverberates to this day. What did Mandela think of this contentious issue? Should those Lions have toured or not and did the Springboks' defeat in that series help change minds generally in society?

'In the sense that the Lions destroyed South Africa in that series and created a tremendous excitement among the oppressed people in this country, we always favoured a foreign team that came to play in South Africa. The fact that the Lions crushed South Africa helped our struggle.

'You must also remember that that tour was only two years before the 1976 youth rebellion. South Africa was going through turbulent times and that rugby tour had a contribution.'

What of the 1995 Rugby World Cup and its legacy? How significant was that and has its legacy been entirely successful or not?

'The 1995 Rugby World Cup was absolutely significant. It united our people as never before and the fact that our team was now supported by all segments of the population was a very important factor indeed.'

Yet at the end of the day, is rugby not just a game and therefore an irrelevance or did he see it as a major factor in the future of his country?

'If you take rugby in isolation, although it was important it cannot be said that it had an overriding effect. All sports in this country, whether rugby, soccer, cricket, basketball, golf or others have united the people of South Africa and put this country on the map. Because if you forget for the time being the reverses that any country has in sport from time to time, nevertheless South Africa has been shining in sport. Therefore, sport has put our country in the limelight.

'It is not only one sport that will hasten integration. As I have said, sport as a whole has had that role of hastening development in the country...and bringing about...the rejection of all forms of race discrimination. That is how I would like to put it without isolating a single sport.'

Did he think the sporting world should have enforced a blanket sporting ban on all contacts with South Africa from the 1960s onwards? Would that have brought faster change to the country?

He shrugged. 'It is no use crying over spilt milk. But the important point is that the sport boycott had a great effect on the apartheid rulers in this country. And the fact that they were regarded as the polecat of the world and boycotted by the entire world did help to hasten reparation.

'But we must not forget that it was not just the boycott. It was the unprecedented fight and resilience of the people of South Africa. If they had not stood up on their feet and fought back, the world would have done very little to help us.

'The reason why the world rallied around us was because human beings admire heroes and heroines, brave people who can stand up and fight back. That is what we did and that is why we were able to rally the entire world to support us.

'But we must always understand that it was the common masses of the people of South Africa, black and white...African, coloured, Indians and some whites who stood up and fought and therefore impressed and mobilised the entire world. That is how I would like us to think of the whole role of sport.'

It was an unusual interview. Well in advance, I had to supply a list of questions I wanted to ask him. I was warned that any deviation from those questions and the interview would be terminated immediately. So supplementaries were impossible.

Throughout the half-hour long interview, a pair of cold eyes watched me like a hawk. Their owner, a lady from Mandela's private office, brooked no nonsense. The minute he had answered my last question, she stood up.

'Madiba,' she said, 'you agreed to meet Mr Bills's family.'

'Oh yes, bring them in,' he replied.

In terms of eliciting world-shattering quotes, you couldn't say the interview itself had been the greatest triumph of my career. But maybe actually getting the interview and being there, was. But then came the revealing stuff, an insight into the real Mandela.

He shook hands with my wife and cracked a well-rehearsed joke. 'How did you catch this man?' he asked.

With a bottle of good red wine hanging on the end of a rope, she might have replied. But she smiled warmly and introduced our three children. He talked to each of them in turn, first Hannah, the eldest, then Katie and lastly turning to James, who was still quite small for a 12-year-old.

Sitting him on his knee, Madiba asked him what he wanted to do when he grew up. Anything but be a journalist, he probably thought.

But Madiba probed more. 'When you are older, would you do something for me?' he asked James, in all seriousness.

'What is that?' was the small boy's reply.

'When you are old enough, will you come back to my country and help my people in some way?' he asked.

Five years later, with Mandela by now an increasingly ailing old man, that promise was fulfilled. A friend in Cape Town, schoolteacher and rugby coach Louis Mzomba, agreed to let James work for two weeks at his school, helping out in the classrooms whatever way he could. He was writing a project on the differences between two schools in the Cape – Bishops, probably the outstanding school of the Cape Province with its fabulous setting beneath Table Mountain, and Nomlinganiselo Primary School, Mzomba's school in Langa township.

At one stage during his two weeks with Mzomba, James came upon a group of teachers puzzling about an interactive whiteboard connected to a computer so it can reflect what the teacher is doing on the computer, and all students can see it.

They didn't have a clue how it worked but James did. His own school back in Bath in the UK had used it, too.

With his expertise, he set it up so the township school would benefit from it. You might say it was a small act but his promise to Mandela all those years earlier was redeemed.

It was a day and interview never to be forgotten. And I gave thanks that when the great man finally passed away, on 5 December 2013, I was in South Africa, on the Cape coast overlooking Robben Island where Mandela had spent so many years locked up. Somehow, I felt closer to him and his memory than I could ever have done back in the northern hemisphere.

%% %% %% %% %%

Diary Notes: July 2004. Second Test, South Africa 26 Ireland 17 at Newlands, Cape Town.

Sunday lunchtime. At the beautiful Groot Constantia wine estate, outside Cape Town.

It wasn't that I was on personal speaking terms with every South African President. But a funny thing happened at lunch one day, 24 hours after a rugby Test match at Newlands.

IT had been the usual intensive rugby Test match weekend. Cover the match, talk to players afterwards, write reports and comment pieces into the small hours. As was about usual, I'd finally finished work around 3am on the Sunday.

Next morning, there were the normal follow-ups to be done, reports for Monday morning papers (in South Africa, Ireland and London) to be written or pored over to change, amend or partially re-write. Tell me a writer who is ever 100 per cent satisfied with a piece he or she has written and I'll find you a serial liar.

But when the whole process is at last completed, it's around midday. Where to go for lunch in or around Cape Town? Of course, a wine estate.

Sitting in one of these places on Sunday lunchtime, with fine food and spectacular views to enjoy, is one of life's great pleasures. The countryside is fabulous, the company (of local people) always fascinating and the food, almost always outstanding.

We've had the meal and are lingering over a coffee when, my mobile (or 'cell', as the South Africans call these things) rings. A strange conversation ensues.

'Is that Mr Peter Bills?'

I react with extreme caution. No newspaper person would address me in such a manner, still less a personal friend. And I'm not expecting any other calls at this time. So caution drips from my every word.

'Who wants him?' I ask, with, I must admit, obvious suspicion and perhaps a hint of sarcasm. The somewhat indignant reply jolts me out of my lethargy.

'I am *********, and I am the personal secretary of the President of South Africa, Thabo Mbeki.'

I start listening seriously at this point.

'Mr Mbeki is sitting here waiting for you to come and interview him,' was the response. 'Where are you?'

I told him and they reckoned it was 20 minutes away. I said simply, 'We are leaving this minute.'

The President had been at a meeting at the luxurious Steenberg Golf Estate outside Cape Town. He'd allowed an hour to see me and do an interview which I knew nothing about. Except that, then I remembered.

Some time ago, I'd had a meeting with my boss, Tony O'Reilly, when he'd come to Cape Town. Among other things we'd discussed, we'd talked about potential exclusive interviews and, in an ideal world, which ones we'd like to do.

He knew Robert Mugabe from a long while back and I wanted him to set up an interview for me with the Zimbabwean tyrant. After all, it takes a special skill to turn your country from a beautiful land known as the bread basket of Africa to a financially ruined, starving, ramshackle place where those still interested in the theory of democracy were either tortured or killed. Or both. Mugabe had long since managed that with considerable aplomb. So I wanted to talk with him about his life's work.

Alas, O'Reilly didn't fancy the idea. He probably judged (rightly so, I guess), that I'd say something inappropriate and end up in some Harare jail. Then he'd have to come and get me out.

Sean Connery was a potentially easier target. He was on an advisory board of the then Independent News & Media group. So my wife settled that – I had to go to the Bahamas to interview 007. Guess who wanted to come with me.

Actually, he came to where I was. The board held one of its annual meetings in Cape Town and we all got invited to a dinner-dance at the historic Cape Town Castle. But to see an ageing, slightly stooping 007, long, straggly, greasy hair (there wasn't any on the top of his head) hanging down over his collar, rather shattered the Bond image. He looked what he was – an old man past his time. I didn't pursue the interview idea.

But an exclusive with the President of South Africa was worthwhile. Only trouble was, Tony or his office had forgotten to tell me about the interview he had arranged. So the hire car got the mother of all workouts on the road from Groot Constantia to Steenberg.

The 20-minute journey took just under eight. I might have shaved a few millimetres of rubber off the tyres, especially on a few tight bends, but what the heck? When the President of a country is sitting twiddling his thumbs waiting for you, you've got the perfect excuse if a cop car pulls you over.

So we raced through the gates of the golf estate and headed towards the main building. Raced? Well, we were going fast enough, I noticed, for the President's security personnel, standing around waiting for him outside the entrance, to clutch their automatic weapons to greet this lunatic flying up the driveway towards them.

The car slewed to a halt right outside and I jumped out. 'Where's the President?' I asked. The closest security guard looked dumbfounded. He probably couldn't quite decide whether to shoot me there and then or get me carted away by the men in white coats.

Luckily, the President's personal secretary was close by.

'Mr Bills?' he asked.

It wasn't quite that 'Dr Livingstone, I presume, moment of African history, but it would do. I confirmed it wasn't Jody Scheckter (the former South African F1 world champion) on a return visit to his homeland.

I was led inside and a familiar face appeared.

'Mr President, I must apologise profusely,' I began. But my apologies were waved aside. We had most of the hour allotted, then chatted, as you do with the South African President, about his times as a student at Brighton University back in the UK, the aesthetic delights of the South Downs and English pubs and, strangely, how he liked the Scottish tradition of first-footing at New Year when you go around to people's houses clutching a piece of coal.

He couldn't have been nicer – especially about the mess I'd made of the golf estate's driveway.

※ ※ ※ ※ ※

Diary Notes: Port Elizabeth, June 2005, South Africa v France

A new stop, for me at least, on this merry-go-round circuit of Test rugby. I've been fortunate enough to cover rugby Tests at almost all the great South African grounds; Newlands, Cape Town, Kings Park, Durban, Loftus Versfeld, Pretoria and Ellis Park, Johannesburg. On the Lions tour of 2009, I would see some of the new stadia, too, which had been built for the soccer World Cup South Africa was hosting in 2010.

Now you have to be careful about stadia. It's too easy to state blandly that the new concrete edifices are a vast improvement on the old grounds. Take Paris. The Stade de France out in the northern suburb of Saint Denis is a vast, 80,000-seat stadium but it has about as much soul as a dead parrot. And not one that's 'just resting', either.

But take the Parc des Princes on the south-west side of Paris, where France used to play all their international rugby matches until 1997. It is still a concrete edifice and it only holds just over 48,000. But atmosphere? I doubt it was better in the Coliseum when the 60AD Lions were touring Rome and performing to crowds led by that rugby fanatic Emperor Nero.

The place was an absolute bear pit of sound, raw emotion and atmosphere, the best in Europe. That brass band belting out La Marseillaise on a raw cold February afternoon, sent a shiver down your spine. So you see, each ground has its own individual characteristics.

Take the Boet Erasmus stadium, just up the road from the seafront at Port Elizabeth on South Africa's vast, rugged southern coast. Behind one side of the old ground was parked up on the top of the embankment, an old steam train, complete with a few coaches. Some bright spark even took over the rights for use on Test match days so that punters could dine in the old carriages and look out over the ground. I'm not sure anyone ever parked a steam train behind Twickenham or Cardiff Arms Park. This was different.

PREPARATION. Ah, the oxygen cylinder inside the journalist's briefcase. Fail to prepare as the old saying goes, and prepare to fail. True in most cases. But not today.

It's one of those gorgeous South African winter days when a sky of deep blue contains a sun emitting extraordinary light.

I'd flown in the previous Sunday and been in town all week. When you cover a Test match overseas, you need to be in town where the team is for daily press conferences and interviews. I'm not sure that Port Elizabeth (or plain and simple PE as it is known throughout the Republic) would be in my top five list of worldwide locations where I would wish to spend the rest of my days. Paris? Maís oui. The Cote d'Azur? Bien sur. Cape Town? Yes please.

Nevertheless, the sun shone that winter week at PE, my hotel looked out directly on to the beach and ocean and once work was done I could train and train: as much beach running and street running as I wanted. It was idyllic and there wasn't a lot of slack time given all the work to do, as well.

Arriving early in Test match week allows you plenty of time to do your preparation. Like going to the ground and checking whether there are any telephones, whether WiFi has been heard of in these parts and whether you are actually on the list of accredited media. For the fact is, you never know.

It transpired that relying on the WiFi working in the rickety old press box at the Boet Erasmus would be an act of faith. And I was never a true believer.

No worries, an alternative plan was available: leave the computer all wired up and ready to go in the hotel bedroom, and the minute the game was over I could make the five-minute run down the hill to the seafront where the hotel stood. By doing that I was guaranteed an internet system that worked. At the ground, it was a gamble. So what do you do – take the 50 per cent chance in the press box or go for the 100 per cent certainty back at the hotel?

No decision to make. I would leg it back to the hotel. I reckoned I'd even be back there before the after-match interviews were done so I could make shorthand notes from them off the television.

Nothing went wrong; well, initially. South Africa trimmed the French 27-13 and I was out of the ground in a flash at the end. No heavy computer to carry, just a notebook, binoculars and a few other bits so I was flying down the road. As a beautifully sunny winter's afternoon declined into a sunset of rich colours and darkness approached, I saw the ocean ahead of me down the hill. I wouldn't have wanted to be anywhere else at that particular moment.

Alas, I had about three more minutes to enjoy this Valhalla. Unbeknown to me, Armageddon loomed in my path.

I got into the lift, stepped out on my floor and hurried to my door. I opened it and honestly, I doubt if Nelson Mandela had been sitting at the desk welcoming me, I'd have had a bigger shock. My computer wasn't there.

The wires still trailed out of the wall socket but no computer. And time was tight for the first edition story back in London on the Sunday paper.

There was a shout that encompassed anguish, anger, alarm and panic in a single outburst. What the hell had happened?

A brief search of the room told me it certainly wasn't there. Conclusion? It had to have been stolen. But with reports to write for papers in Ireland, London and South Africa, I couldn't dwell on the theft itself. I had to find an alternative.

The first escape route was to call my office back home. Through the panic and anger, I managed to ad-lib the better part of 800 words for one of the Sunday papers in Ireland. That done, I went downstairs to reception and launched a furious tirade against the nearest recipient. Poor creature, but then when the adrenaline is flowing like a fast flood it is better not to be anywhere near.

'What sort of a hotel is this? My computer's been stolen from my room, what the hell am I going to do to send reports to newspapers?' probably contained some of it. You couldn't say it was a hot early evening on a PE winter's night but boy, was I starting to sweat as my voice and anger rose.

In fairness, the hotel did their best. Like plunging a sizzling hot coal into a bucket of water to cool it down, they thrust me into one of their offices, set up a Word document on their computer and I started pounding out a 1,000-word analysis of the game for the South African Sunday papers. It is amazing how fast fingers can work when they're being controlled by someone fighting an inner rage.

I sent that report around South Africa and then started work on another one for London. Somehow, I also managed to pick up some quotes off the TV from the two captains to incorporate into the report.

By 6.30pm, as I was winding down my work for the Sunday newspapers, the hotel manager had been busy investigating the theft. What he uncovered was maddening. Sure, you could say I shouldn't have left the computer out on the desk. But hell, I had kept the key with me so who else would go into the room?

It quickly transpired what had happened. No sooner had I left the room, locking the door behind me, the maid had arrived to clean it and make the bed. Ah, the thief uncovered? Not so fast.

The local African maid had started work in the room. And, as a standard procedure of hotel regulations, she had left the door wide open. Here was the rub. She had been cleaning when someone walked down the corridor, looked through the open door and saw my computer.

Brazen as a brass monkey, he walked in, explained himself to the girl as a friend of mine and said I had asked him to take my computer downstairs to me as I waited in reception. Now you probably wouldn't have made her Employee of the Month for her actions. But even though the poor, duped, bewildered girl had handed him the machine and he disappeared, I couldn't bring myself to criticise her. I did wonder, however, at a hotel policy that insists guests' rooms should be left wide open and visible to everyone, even when the maid was out of sight cleaning in the bathroom.

I had little time to go into the details on that torrid Saturday evening. I needed to see the South African coach and some of his players to get some quotes for part of my Monday morning newspaper comment pieces. It isn't that you want to reproduce vast columns of quotes from players in what you write – I hate that trend and besides, nowadays it is pointless because they're just like puppets.

Even when they open their mouths, they have been trained to say nothing.

But back then, it made sense to chat with some of the players, Springboks of immense intellectual and rugby capacity like centre Jean de Villiers, captain John Smit and that fine, knowledgeable lock forward, Victor Matfield, to ascertain their overall views. They may have formed a very different impression of the game than you did up in the press box.

So I trudged across Port Elizabeth to where the after-match reception was being held. By the time I arrived it was in full swing.

As I wound down mentally from the rush of deadlines and panic combined with dismay at losing my computer, my spirits sagged. I walked into the reception with a hangdog expression writ large upon my face.

The Springbok coach Jake White, with whom I had forged a very business like and amenable working relationship since his appointment to the job in 2004, saw me and came over.

'What on earth happened, Peter?' he asked. 'You look awful.'

I explained the sorry saga. So much was lost; a nearly new computer, so many columns and files, by no means all on sport but including travel and political stories which I was also writing at that time for the South African media. And then there was the gross inconvenience.

Now one of the many attributes Jake White brought to the Springbok coaching job was being positive. He was usually bright, breezy and cheerful. And what he said next stunned me.

'Peter, I am telling you, you will have your computer back by lunchtime tomorrow.'

'How so Jake? Did YOU pinch it?' I responded with a wry grin.

He smiled one of his confident smiles that even half-convinced me, in the depths of my despair, that something good was going to come out of this saga after all.

'I know all the senior guys in the township around here. I'll pass the word. I'm telling you, it'll be back by tomorrow.'

You couldn't doubt Jake's willingness to help or his deep-seated belief. Alas, he had made one major miscalculation.

The unspoken assumption was that it was someone from a local township who had got into the hotel and stolen my computer. How wrong could we have been?

When the hotel management interviewed the maid, she confessed she had handed the computer to the WHITE gentleman. So it was a bastard white honkey who had thieved my computer.

I wrote a not terribly flattering story about it for the *Star*, the Monday morning newspaper in Johannesburg. The hotel had not put any soap or loo paper in my bathroom and now they'd left my door wide open for some opportunist to steal my computer. And this was a leading hotel in a city destined to host some games at the 2010 soccer World Cup.

Beneath a banner headline that blared 'No soap, no loo paper and no computer' I asked, in the Monday morning editorial opinion article, 'What is going on in this country?'

The answer didn't take long to arrive. Before 9am on the Monday, as I packed my remaining gear before heading to the airport, the bedroom phone rang.

'Good morning Mr Bills. My name is ***** and I am the general manager of the so-and-so hotel group in South Africa. I have read your story in this morning's newspaper here in Johannesburg and I am deeply concerned.

'I want you to know. Your computer will be fully replaced whatever the cost.'

He was as good as his word. It was. And very quickly, too. Nevertheless, the whole manic affair had probably taken a few years off my life. But that's the job, I guess.

※ ※ ※ ※ ※

Diary Notes: Rustenburg, 2006

International rugby has been played at some pretty weird places down the years.

Aberdeen, Florence, Wollongong, Nantes, Huddersfield, Auch, Milan – these are far removed from the usual suspects like Cardiff, Dublin, Auckland and Cape Town.

But one place surely qualifies for the daftest location of all. It was as daft as a brush. Or should that be bush?

Three hours' drive north-west from Johannesburg through the South African scrub and not far from the border with Botswana lies the town of Rustenburg. Within its geographical boundaries stands the grandly named Royal Bafokeng Sports Palace.

Owned by the Royal Bafokeng nation, the ground, which was opened in 1999 and renovated and expanded to a 42,000 capacity ten years later, is located at Phokeng, on the R565 road from Sun City to the Botswana border.

It hosted five first-round matches and one second-round match at the 2010 FIFA World Cup in South Africa. A lot of people always thought the Italian manager Fabio Capello was away with the fairies given some of his actions and comments while in charge of the England national team.

That may or may not have been true but what marked out Capello as a nailed down certainty for the nearest loony bin was his decision to base the England soccer team at Rustenburg for part of that World Cup. Worse still, a fact which proved him completely delusional, he then spent thousands of pounds of the Football Association's money on stocking a library in one of the team rooms filled with classics by the likes of Shakespeare, Wordsworth and Wilde.

The closest most of the cerebrally challenged who inhabit England football teams ever get to a proper book reminds me of that old joke: I read a book once; green it was.

Thus, you will deduce from this that there were probably not quite raucous celebrations within the corridors of the New Zealand Rugby Union back in Wellington when news trickled across the world that the All Blacks' Tri-Nations fixture of 2006 in South Africa would be played in Rustenburg, rather than Johannesburg. Or Pretoria. Or Durban. Or, heaven forbid, somewhere the New Zealanders might really like, such as Cape Town.

What would have occupied their minds once they had actually tracked it down on a world map was how the hell to get there.

International rugby teams are not exactly keen on three-hour coach journeys these days. They want to fly in, take a coach for the short ride to a city centre hotel and then seal themselves off hermetically from the rest of the world. In the zone, is the team speak, whatever that may mean. Or, in the soup in the case of England.

The trouble with Rustenburg was that even getting to Sun City, that extraordinary gambling fantasy created by the pint-sized South African entrepreneur Sol Kerzner, took a bit of doing. Course, the high rollers destined for the gambling tables flew by helicopter from Johannesburg. But NZRU funds hardly stretched to a convoy of Chinooks.

As for mere mortals like your correspondent, the solution was to stay in Johannesburg and put up with a six- or seven-hour round trip by road on the day of the game. And God help you if you wrecked a tyre or the suspension disappeared down a pothole, at some stage of the journey. For hour after hour out there in the dark, there is literally nothing and no-one. Plenty of animals, for sure, but few people.

I was willing to hire a car and drive myself until dark tales began to filter through regarding such an enterprise. Wouldn't do that if I were you, warned various locals.

'Why not? Lions and tigers loose on the road at night?' I jokingly enquired.

'No, it's the donkeys that end up killing you because you never see them and at 75mph [120kph], they make rather a mess of a car,' someone replied, matter-of-factly. Funny, but I'd never regarded Eeyore in that light.

So it was decided that hiring a car complete with local driver was the answer.

HE arrived bearing one of those trademark African smiles, white teeth shining out of a dark mouth, and a shy, proffered hand to shake. True, the teeth looked as if most had been re-arranged, like Lego pieces in the wrong location, at some point in time. But there was no doubting Moses's determination to see the job through and provide a first class service.

Now it's important to be realistic when you travel in Africa. Unless you happen to be the President or Chief of Police, travelling in a high powered Mercedes is not the normal mode of transport. Nevertheless, the locals do their best and genuinely want to help and give you a journey to remember. Well on that score, Moses certainly led us to the Promised Land.

We set off out of the drab Johannesburg suburbs on a bright, chill winter's Saturday morning. James, my 15-year-old son, was on a treat trip – a visit to the Kruger National Park and then a Test match.

The Kruger hadn't disappointed. 'Take a right down the next track,' he had advised me as I steered our hire car around the tracks and byways of the Kruger Park. 'What for, it says it's a dead end,' I argued.

'Well you never know,' he persisted. Driving in the Kruger is like that; you pay your money and takes your chance. You might see everything or nothing. So we plough slowly down this muddy track, ease around a bend and standing barring our way, just five yards ahead, is an enormous white rhino.

The following day, we'd driven slowly past a copse of trees. 'What's that up the tree?' said my sharp-eyed son. We reversed to witness a leopard halfway up a tree, resting on a bough with a barely dead buck in its mouth.

At nightfall, the Kruger is equally alive. You make camp, staying in one of the rondavels and light a barbecue (or braai as the locals call it in South Africa) to cook your meat. If you do it in a London suburb like Sidcup or Islington, or maybe Tallaght on the outskirts of Dublin, the meat may sizzle but not against a soundtrack of lions roaring across a nearby river.

Even when we'd finally eaten half a shelf of the nearby supermarket's meat, sunk some beers by the fire and bonded as fathers and teenage sons should, the evening's entertainment was not over. As we lay in our beds listening to the sounds of the African night, a great commotion was heard inside the camp.

A hyena, which had doubtless fancied dining beneath the stars on some discarded lamb chops or sausages, had slyly dug a hole under the perimeter fence and got into the compound. In the morning, we found teeth marks on the fridge on our terrace. Surely he couldn't have expected a beer to wash down the fragments of bones and meat?

In one sense, Moses's car this winter's morning for the journey to Rustenburg reminded me of the one in the Kruger. Both rattled disconcertingly. But they seemed to keep going which was the important thing.

We passed through small villages and crossroads where locals tried to sell you anything from oranges, to grapes, to figs, to table decorations. Those grapes: well, a box big enough to last you a week cost about Rand 20 – in those days, less than £2.

Africa, wherever you travel in it, is beguiling. There is always something or someone to watch, to study. It might be the little children playing beside the road, the women carrying gross weights around a village or, in an aesthetic sense, just the sunlight on the rich soil.

Eventually, as Johannesburg receded far behind, the sealed road came to an end. Soon, that trademark vista that somehow denotes Africa – a vehicle with a plume of dust pouring out from the back like a vapour trail from an aircraft – could be seen behind us.

It was a good thing it wasn't summer and baking hot. Had it been, we'd have probably arrived covered in dust looking like extras from a Crocodile Dundee film.

With Moses sitting back and content to make steady rather than spectacular progress, the time ticked on. Three hours became three and a half which then edged towards four.

Eventually, a growing number of dwellings suggested we had reached the outskirts of Rustenburg. And there we stopped. Two or three miles from the stadium, the queue of cars inched forward. At such a rate of progress, I estimated we would at least see the second half or perhaps just the last 20 minutes of the match.

Europeans unfamiliar with the ways and workings of Africa might have despaired. But we had Moses to lead us and all would be well with the world. Turning around to the back seat, a wide smile lit up his face as he suggested, 'Ah noo a good route to this ground. Not thees way.'

'Moses,' we chorused, 'show us your skills.' The grin widened still further.

'Yes, baas,' came the reply.

The car was thrust violently into reverse and the steering wheel yanked fiercely to the right. We jumped forward across the road, mounted a kerb and found ourselves on rough ground. It soon got a whole lot rougher.

At one point, we seemed to be trying to thread the car down a narrow passageway between a row of houses on either side. Back gardens ran into the passageway and children scattered as we powered on.

If this all seemed a bit unlikely, an extraordinary sight then greeted us. Turning around as we bumped along the rough track, we spied a convoy of about 20 cars following in our wake.

'Moses, you got company,' we said. 'Either that or the local police want you.'

The smile again lit up his face. 'No baas, no police,' he said, a couple of teeth seeming to sway out of the way as the words came out. 'Thees men want Moses's route map.'

Great guffaws of laughter followed this statement and for a moment, to demonstrate the point, both hands were removed from the wheel. James, a young man about as laid-back as a buck having its innards eaten by a leopard, merely shrugged. I was too intrigued at our cross-country approach to this stadium to be concerned.

We drove over fields, round the back of shacks and over building sites. Occasionally, we spotted the gigantic queue of traffic stacked up on the nearby road, a sight Moses was naturally keen to point out.

At last, after the long journey, we suddenly spied the Royal Bafokeng Sports Palace stadium right ahead of us, its tall, angular concrete columns rising out of the African soil seemingly in the midst of nowhere. We ground to a halt in a cloud of choking dust, got out, shook ourselves down, gathered our gear and made our way into this concrete bowl. Nothing is ever what you expect on this continent and one thing was for sure: I'd never arrived at Twickenham in such fashion.

Moses, of course, was under strict instructions. 'Meet us at 7pm, beside the main gate near the car park, and we will be there. And no drinking this afternoon.' Moses beamed his agreement.

No-one was ever quite sure just how much this sports fantasy hidden away in the African hinterland had actually cost. But whatever the cost, the boasts of the locals must have exceeded any price imaginable.

'Baas, we got everything for you,' they said. And I was led to a press box with spacious, comfortable seats, a regal view of the pitch and a wide bench which was said to have WiFi available to all.

In this business, your needs are very simple. Most of us frankly don't care whether the hotel room is offering only a bed of nails and the toilet is a hole in the ground. As long as the telephone works. Likewise at the rugby grounds of the world.

You can put up with uncomfortable wooden benches for seats or even part-restricted views of the field as long as the internet works and you can file in time for your deadline. Nothing else matters to the working scribe, not even the match or its outcome. For the fact is, if you can't file, as we say in the trade, in other words get your report through to the newspaper desk, then everything else becomes an irrelevance.

On this particular day, the match swung backwards and forwards like the pendulum of a clock. New Zealand were ahead at one point, then South Africa came back, then the All Blacks got ahead again only for the Springboks to score again. In the end, it came down to a single kick by the South African outside half Andre Pretorius. He landed it and the Springboks won 21-20.

Now given the nature of the Test match and the Springboks' victory, back pages were being cleared ready for the story in newspapers across South Africa. Durban's *Sunday Tribune*, for example, picked the best of the wired photographs and ran it big on the back page. The team worked in the headline pretty quickly. All they needed now was my story. And I'd written all 1,000 words of it within 20 minutes of the final whistle, which was pushing hard.

You get down your analytical thoughts, detail of the game, trends you have perceived as crucial and descriptions of the key moments. What you do NOT do, or at least shouldn't, is write a report which says, 'A passed to B, he took the ball on, gave it to C and D scored.'

Why? Chances are, anyone interested enough to read this on a Sunday morning would have seen the game anyway. To produce lengthy accounts of moves they have seen already is to insult their intelligence. They want a dissection of the match and crucial moves, some opinions, what were the key factors, such as a mis-pass that cleverly created space, a missed tackle, an erroneous sideways drift by the defence; who dominated the set pieces or was prevalent at the breakdown and why. You will offer brief descriptions of the relevant scores but cannot write stuff that will have been blindingly obvious to everyone.

Once your fingers have flicked and flittered across the keyboard, like the pianist at his craft, you take a hard, cold, viciously critical eye to the text. Anything that looks inferior is jettisoned, anything that risks stating the obvious or is technically wrong, deleted. The depths of concentration required for this rapid review under pressure of deadline are immense. The process, even if it only lasts ten minutes, can exhaust you.

Only then, after facts and everything else has been checked, you press the SEND button. Which I now did. The sense of relief is huge. You're too tired to feel celebratory, too mentally shot to contemplate much, apart from a cold beer perhaps which begins the gradual winding-down process.

One last task awaits. You check with the newspaper desk 'Has it dropped?' The answer here was alarming. 'No.'

Nor did it when I re-sent it. At which point, I went scurrying off to find the local electronics expert to see if he could help. He arrived with an assured, confident type of expression that immediately put a rogue feeling into my bones and promptly went through the process, loaded the file again and pressed the SEND button. Once more, it disappeared, presumably into the ether somewhere above those backyards and passageways Moses had been driving down hours earlier.

But this wasn't funny anymore. Voices were being raised on sports desks in Durban and Johannesburg.

'Where is it, we can't see it,' they said.

'Hell, I'm sending it and it says "message sent",' I retorted, a growing sense of desperation in my voice.

As ever, the clock, enemy of all journalists, continued to tick. Deadline was 6.30pm and we had passed 6pm. But I was not alone. Four or five seats further along the press box, fellow English journalist Barry Newcombe was trying to file for the London edition of the *Sunday Times*. Newcombe had flown to

Johannesburg and from there had journeyed to Rustenburg solely for this Test match.

He, too, had written about 1,000 words but was also having his day ruined by the technical problems. In the end, he picked up a telephone and spoke to a sub-editor on the desk back in London who had seen the game. Newcombe gave him short comments on key issues and the inventive sub put together the 1,000-word report. That's where good sub-editors are worth their weight in gold.

Given that it was now no more than eight minutes to deadline, I did not have that option. Hence, the increasingly frantic behaviour of the computer operator.

Basil Fawlty's wild assault on his car with the branch of a tree after it had refused to start came to mind. There was much shouting and screaming, Fawlty-esque lines such as, 'You bastard, I've warned you, you've tried it on just once too often.'

At 6.25pm, Durban suggested one last thing. 'What system have you been sending it on?' I was asked.

'Hotmail.'

'Do you have another system?'

'Yes, AOL but that never works in South Africa. It wouldn't even work in the hotel in Jo'burg this week so it isn't likely to work out here,' I replied.

'Just try it; for Christ's sake, do something,' was the response.

At 6.27pm, three minutes before deadline with a blank back page still awaiting my story, I pressed the SEND button on AOL. There was a wait of perhaps ten seconds which seemed closer to ten hours as I held my breath. Then came a voice down the phone line, 'It's dropped.'

My 15-year-old, who had watched the game in the stands but by now had joined me in the press box, surveyed the dishevelled, wrecked-looking human being slumped across the desk in front of him and said laconically, 'This job will kill you one day.'

Actually, he was wrong. It wasn't the work that nearly killed me that particular day but the drive home.

As the smoke and smell from myriad braais drifted around the back of the stadium, an enticing prospect given my fatigue, a familiar face appeared beside the main gate. There was the trademark smile and a car door opened. I slumped inside Moses's car and prepared for the three-and-a-half-hour journey back to the hotel in Johannesburg.

Alas, I slowly began to realise nothing could have prepared us for this journey. It became obvious as we made our way down the road towards and then past Sun City. We were driving in the middle of the sealed road.

With no traffic in sight, indeed no lights anywhere to be seen, this didn't seem to matter. But things then got more disconcerting. At the top of a long hill which we were approaching, I spied a pair of headlights. Slowly, inexorably, they came closer towards us.

First 500 yards, 400, 300, 200, and Moses didn't move a muscle. We were lined up right in the middle of the road and he wasn't going anywhere. Nor, it seemed, was the other driver coming straight at us. What was this? A renegade suicide driver from Dagestan? Or a game of chicken with a local mate?

At 80mph, 200 yards disappears rapidly into nothing. No matter, cool hand Moses left it until the other car could barely have been 100 yards away when he swung the wheel to the left. No sooner had the other car shot past than Moses swung the wheel back to the right and settled once more in the middle of the road.

We became intrigued by this behaviour because it happened time and again. Was he seeing the wild donkeys I had been warned about? Or was he just seeing things? Had he been on the moonshine all afternoon? What became clear was that we were going all the way to Jo'burg straddling the middle of the road.

By some manner of means or a passing miracle, we eventually tumbled out by the hotel in Sandton. We'd become so accustomed to Moses's party trick that we'd even fallen asleep for some of the journey. God knows how close he left it to turn the wheel on those occasions.

So out we stepped and a thought suddenly struck me. I walked around to the front of the car and took a look. For sure,

Moses had lights: two sidelights. The glass and bulbs on both his headlights were smashed to smithereens.

Our intrepid driver had managed to negotiate his way through the darkness for three and a half hours not that far from the Botswana border back to Johannesburg on sidelights.

South African taxi drivers? Like the French police at Calais, I'll never have a word said against them.

‰ ‰ ‰ ‰ ‰

Diary Notes: Johannesburg, 2007

The point was, never rely on technology. And just to underline the point, I then had something similar occur even at a five-star hotel in Johannesburg.

THE Southern Sun hotel at Sandton is an extremely comfortable, upmarket hotel which does a very healthy trade offering elevated levels of hospitality and accommodation for people from all over the world.

I'd flown in that morning and got a cab from the airport. Check-in was smooth and professional. But oh dear, if only connecting up the internet in my room had been anything like as easy. The room had everything: a sweeping panoramic view over the Sandton suburbs towards the pyramid-type dump of residue from an old gold mine which scars the Gauteng landscape, a deep Jacuzzi bath with faux gold taps, a luxury sofa, bed big enough for an entire family and thick pile carpet. It also had a working desk and a most promising looking internet cable with which to connect to your computer.

What could go wrong? Well, let's start with what could go right. The answer was, nothing. I spent the best part of the next 90 minutes vainly attempting to get online. I put wires in here, wires in there, crossed wires, changed plugs, turned the computer on and off half a dozen times, re-booted the thing, just booted the damn thing, and nothing worked. It didn't want to know. Wires ran across the desk like cables alongside the track of the London Underground. But whatever they were carrying, it wasn't power.

I hate admitting defeat in anything but this devious little piece of electronic technology had me done. There was only one thing for it – call the hotel's telecommunication expert. Yes, he really existed: he featured prominently in the hotel's big information pack, offering all kinds of advice on things like what to do, where to go in the hotel, where to go in Gauteng, what to eat, what to drink, how to relax.

How to relax. That's a joke, I thought. How can you relax when you have two stories written and edited but you can't send the damn things? But maybe Jeff, the hotel expert, could solve the problem.

He knocked at the door and my word, you had to say he looked an impressively reassuring figure. A tall African, he was neatly shaved, wore an immaculately pressed white shirt with a tie knotted smartly at the throat and a well-cut dark suit. What is more, Jeff had an assured manner. You had the immediate sense that he was on top of his game, knew all about these computers and could solve your problem in a trice.

'How can I help?' he smiled. If you'd been looking for the cavalry to come over the hill and save you, you couldn't have found a more convincing guy.

He came into the room, sat down at the desk, made himself comfortable in the manner of a concert pianist and familiarised himself with the surroundings. Then he began. He put the internet wire into the proper socket in the computer, and went through the entire connection process.

You know full well what is going to happen – the guy will get it working first time and you'll look like a complete fool after 90 minutes of mucking around and failing to discern any sign of life whatever in the machine. How often does that happen?

Except that, in this case it didn't. Gradually, after more fiddling around with the connections, wires and computer the assured smile was steadily fading, to be replaced by the first furrowed brows of concern.

Jeff's patience seemed to know no limits. But after a further hour he was no nearer finding a solution than I had been. It was then that he made the fateful decision.

'I think we must call the help centre and ask them to find the answer,' he said.

Now I have nothing personal against the people who work in help centres. For all I know, the whole lot of them may be good, clean-living souls who read their children a bedtime story every night before lights out and go to church regularly every Sunday to pray for the good of the world.

It's just that, I think the whole lot of them are useless. I wouldn't call a help centre if I'd fallen through the Arctic ice pack, had a couple of enraged polar bears about to attack me and broken both legs in the process. They just aren't going to solve your problem. Fact. And the sooner the world's population comes to grasp this salient point the quicker companies around the globe will save billions of pounds, rupees, dollars, euros or whatever employing these well-meaning but basically hopeless people.

The help centre for this particular machine was in Bangalore, India. My heart sank deep into the Indian Ocean.

But Jeff was a marvel. He retained every ounce of his composure, patience and manners as the help centre worker asked for all the facts.

'What is the problem, Sir?'

'Well, we connect all the wires in the right places but cannot get a final connection.'

'Have you tried disconnecting the machine and then turning it back on?'

'Yes, five times.'

'Perhaps you should try again.'

'Well we can but it has not done anything before.'

'Well, maybe try it.'

So we did, and it didn't. The conversation resumed.

'What is your name?'

'Jeff.'

'Is this your computer?'

'No.'

'Oh, I need to speak to the owner of the computer. Is he there?'

'Yes. I will put him on the line.'

'Good morning, Sir. Is it a nice day where you are?'

'Well, not awfully. My computer won't work, you see.'

'Oh dear, but don't worry Sir, we will have it working soon.'

'Do you promise?'

'Oh Sir, I will do my best.'

'Good man.'

'Sir, what is your name?'

'Peter Bills.'

'Thank you Sir. My name is Sanjay. Where are you from?'

'England. But I am in Johannesburg.'

'Oh I see. How can I help you?'

'Well, I thought you were.'

'Oh, I was speaking to another gentleman in Africa.'

'Yes that's right, he is in the room beside me.'

'But Sir, I thought you said you were from England.'

'Well yes, I come from England but I am in Johannesburg.'

'Oh, I see.'

'Are you sure?'

'Yes, Sir, I am sure.'

So we swapped ideas on where the wires should go, whether the sockets were loose and, for all I can remember, what time of the night it was in Bangalore at that particular moment. And then there came this conversation-ending, completely ridiculous help centre defining comment that summed up beautifully the whole insane process with which I was engaged.

'Mr Peter. There is just one thing I cannot understand,' he said. I expected some hi-tec explanation that might solve the entire nightmare. Instead of which I got the following:

'Mr Peter. You say you are from England and you are in Johannesburg.'

'Yes, that's right.'

'But tell me, which part of England is Johannesburg in?'

Unless he reads this book, and the publishers have warned me that sales are not expected to be mega-big in Bangalore, Sanjay will never know whether my computer lived or died. I killed the call. It was better to quit before someone died.

‰ ‰ ‰ ‰ ‰

Diary Notes: Johannesburg, 2009

Number 54 Sauer Street, in central Johannesburg, is a typically late 1960s/early 70s office block architectural creation. Nowadays, it looks as visually enchanting as a large red spot with a white head on the end of a teenager's nose.

However, Number 54 is a very famous building, for all its design shortcomings. In an earlier incarnation it was named Shell House after its owners, Royal Dutch Shell, who cheerfully continued to do very profitable business with South Africa's apartheid regime through that grim era of repression which lasted from 1948 to 1994.

The African National Congress party (ANC) paid Royal Dutch Shell 20m Rand in 1993 to acquire the 22-storey building. And it quickly acquired notoriety.

Twelve months later, as South Africa prepared for its first truly free elections since the disbanding of apartheid, around 20,000 supporters from the Inkatha Freedom Party marched on Shell House to protest against the election, which Inkatha was planning to boycott.

Nelson Mandela said later that it had always been the ANC's intention to defend themselves and the building. That defence became brutal as 19 Inkatha supporters were gunned down by ANC security guards.

In 1998, Shell House was renamed Luthuli House after the former ANC chief Albert Luthuli. It remains on the same site today. Quite by chance, right across the street from Luthuli House stands the Johannesburg offices of the Independent News & Media company, owners of South African newspapers such as *The Star, Johannesburg*, *The Mercury, Durban*, *Pretoria News* and the Cape Times group. *The Star* is printed in the bowels of the old building.

You could hardly envisage a more convenient spot for a newspaper office, given the frequent demonstrations, marches and protests that are regularly held outside the ANC headquarters.

> The only problem with this location is that it is frequently the victim of city centre traffic gridlock. Marches quickly block the streets of downtown Johannesburg, laid out on an old-style grid system with wide boulevards where ox wagons once turned around in olden times.

MOST visitors to Johannesburg nowadays stay at Sandton, the smart, upmarket suburb which is a 20-minute drive away from the city centre. It's what you'd call a sanitised suburb, designed and built very much with the international tourist in mind.

Within the whole vast, sprawling Sandton complex you can find luxury hotels, outdoor and indoor restaurants, banks, luxury shops and such like. Apart from a giant (and not very good – the proportions seem all wrong) sculpture of Nelson Mandela in the aptly named Nelson Mandela Square which is at the heart of the complex, you could be in any city centre anywhere in the southern hemisphere.

So I'm at a meeting at the Independent News & Media offices in the city centre and it's a familiar story. I'm late leaving.

I need to be back at Sandton by 1pm for an interview and lunch appointment but have forgotten the mobile number of my dining companion, whom I am due to see. And then, when I leave the newspaper offices, oh no! There must be thousands of people blocking the main road. They can't all be looking for a taxi.

It turns out there is some protest march going on. 'Don't go out on to the street looking for a cab; we'll call one from here,' they'd told me in the newspaper offices. Trouble was, I didn't have time to wait 20 minutes for a car to turn up. I was sure I'd pick one up on the street.

I might have done, but for the demonstration. Actually seeing a car was rare and when you did it was hemmed in by hundreds of people. Life is basic in some of the streets of this city. Just down the road where they sell fruit, technical gadgets and such like on an array of orange boxes on the pavement, I asked a shopkeeper for a taxi.

'Down to the bus station, best place,' he advised.

It wasn't far but for sure it didn't look like the best place. It didn't look like the safest, either.

This underground bus station was in fact a vast pull-up for hundreds of the famous African minibus taxis, the 12 to 16-seater vans that ferry a whole people to and from the townships into work in all the big cities of South Africa. You risk life and limb in them; few have not had major crashes which is no surprise given the speed at which they are driven and the general state of repair of most.

One other thing was a touch disconcerting. Amid all these taxis and hundreds of locals, there wasn't a single white face to be seen. Clearly, no tourists ever came down into this particular parking area. I noticed that a lot of eyes followed my movements.

A couple of the drivers looked menacingly at me when I suggested they might be able to help with a lift. They weren't going anywhere, especially not for the white stranger.

Someone waved a disinterested arm towards a piece of rough ground just outside the underground parking lot. If the standard of vehicle looked even worse out there at least there were more four-seater cars masquerading as taxis, whose owners might be interested in doing the job.

'Where you wanna go, man?' asked one.

'Sandton.'

'Four hundred Rand, man,' he replied. I smiled and moved on. Two hundred and fifty was enough.

Out on the far corner of the rough ground, a strange, somewhat acrid smoke drifted across the parking lot and teased your nostrils. It came from the cigarette of a guy of about 40 who had one eye half-closed and the other dipping down, rather like the late afternoon sun into the sea.

The car was about as dishevelled as its owner. Vintage? Almost certainly pre-war, I mused. Boer War, that is.

I assumed he was still of this world because at least he replied when I asked him how much to Sandton. 'Two hundred Rand, baas,' was the reply, as he drew heavily on the smoking weed.

'Listen man,' I said. 'You get me there in 15 minutes and I'll give you 250.'

It was as though a wire with an electric current had suddenly been attached to his backside. His eyes bulged and lit up, the weed was flung aside and he ordered, 'Jump in, baas.'

When I look back on it now, I figure it was money well spent, an absolute snip. The ride of your life for 250 Rand? It had to be a good deal. But at the time, other thoughts came to mind.

We'd revved up and bumped across the rough ground, swinging out of the car parking lot in seconds. We joined the main road and nearly killed three pedestrians before he'd found second gear. Up the hill we accelerated out of the city centre towards a set of red lights which seemed set firmly on, well, red. But my man was in no mood for compromise.

With me in the rickety old front seat, the plastic cover peeling off and chunks of the foam missing, he drove straight at the red lights without considering the brake. Amazingly, as we were within about ten feet of them and doing around 50mph they changed to amber and we went through in the spare lane. Timing, pure timing.

That seemed to invigorate him in terms of the challenge. But it was about to get even more appealing. The quality of street surface on Johannesburg's roads can be decidedly variable. Some are as smooth as billiard tables, others like a beach full of rocks. Alas, it was our great misfortune to hammer straight into a pothole at about 50mph.

The car shook violently as my man struggled to keep it on the road. And suddenly, there was a cracking, creaking noise and the front passenger door began to fall off its hinges. I made a lunge for it and, luckily as the window was down on a warm day, grabbed hold of it. Air conditioning? Please, be sensible.

My man smiled. 'Good thing you here, man,' he grinned. 'No good car with no door.'

And so we continued: he swinging the ageing, half-wrecked car all around the road and me, hanging on desperately to the front nearside door which was now only attached by a slim piece of metal at the bottom. But no-one should ever underestimate the determination and inventiveness of Johannesburg taxi drivers. With a final roar of acceleration, we hammered up the hill into Sandton as the clock ticked up to 14 minutes and Arnold had won his prize.

His smile was worth the prize money alone. 'Did well baas, yes?' he said.

'Arnold, you're a champion,' I replied as I thrust the notes at him. Maybe, just maybe they'd have paid to have his front door welded back on, too.

It just showed how you can find helpful locals wherever you are, if you look hard enough. But there was a sequel to the tale. A week later, I was in another taxi in Johannesburg and regaling the black driver with the story.

A growing expression of anguish and fear infused his face as the tale unfolded. With a touch of disbelief in his voice, he said, 'Man, you went down into that taxi station? Man, you're crazy. Even we don't go there.'

%. %. %. %. %.

Diary Notes: Covering Test matches in South Africa

I've tried to illustrate already that working in Africa isn't like anywhere else. They say only surgeons operate – wrong. Journalists sent to work in Africa have to operate, too, albeit in a different way.

Nothing is as it seems on the African continent. South Africa might seem a whole lot different, developed in many more ways compared to the likes of some other African countries. That's partly true. But you still need your wits about you whenever you are there.

Working in the great rugby Test grounds of South Africa is a huge privilege. The 1995 Rugby World Cup highlighted that but also the intrinsic challenges of operating in the place.

WE had found our way to Durban, and soon came the storm and floods on the day when South Africa met France in the semi-final. I watched the storm come rolling in from the Indian Ocean that afternoon, in my hotel room which looked out to sea. It was formidable; huge dark clouds, lightning and thunder followed by a downpour which went on for hours.

When it rains in these places it rains. The city was awash; Kings Park, too.

The iconic image of that day was a line of African women with brushes trying to sweep some of the water off the pitch. This was like using a couple of cans of fly spray to kill off the Tetse fly in central Africa. Understandably, they weren't very successful given the amount of water that had fallen.

It meant the game was delayed which guaranteed complete travel chaos at Durban airport later that night. Most of us in the media box had booked on a flight back to Cape Town afterwards, together with thousands of supporters.

So when the kick-off was delayed at Kings Park, a decision was taken to hold all the planes at Durban to wait for everyone at the match. This was some decision.

When the game finally ended, thousands and thousands of people somehow had to make their way to the local airport. They did so by commandeering cars, taxis or just persuading some locals to give them a lift. It was like a great migration across the African savannah.

When we got there, all was utter chaos. Perhaps as many as 20 planes were waiting to ferry this human army down to the Cape, but with airline desks and computers swamped by the numbers, a shambles ensued.

As more and more people arrived at the airport, many barely able to get inside the terminal building such was the crush of people, what it came down to was whether the airlines would forego the usual meticulous arrangements and just start stuffing people on to planes. If they didn't, there seemed a very strong chance of a riot breaking out.

Just about every type of plane was lined up on the tarmac: a couple of 747 jumbo jets, McDonnell-Douglas MD 80s, 737s, old 727s, the odd DC10, even. And some brave soul somewhere then took the courageous decision – fill the planes whatever ticket people were holding and let them go.

For those with some flying experience, this was like a sort of aerial happy hour. For what it meant was that those who could leg it fast enough to arrive first at the steps up to the plane were guaranteed the best seats. They'd abandoned the notion of individual seating; it was every man or woman for him or herself.

You've never seen such a bun fight. People carrying large African drums barged past women carrying cuddly toys for their children back home; there was the occasional Zulu spear to be seen (remember, this was pre-9/11) employed to secure its owner an improved position going up the aircraft steps.

Of course, you needed to be fairly clued up on your aircraft. There wasn't much point rushing towards an old, creaking Boeing 727 and expecting anything special. Most set their sights on a huge 747 which stood on the tarmac like the first prize.

You had to be quick and you had to have strong hips to barge aside some latecomers trying to squeeze past you as you mounted the steps. I'm not altogether sure you could call this Fleet Street's finest hour but within moments, the fittest and wiliest among us had reached the top of those steps, turned left rather than right and flopped down in the sanctity of the first class cabin. Strange how that filled up faster than a watering can with a hose at full blast inside it.

When the mob following on behind had filled the economy seats, we rolled out to the end of the runway, splashed down it on take-off and bumped our way through the Kwa-Zulu Natal storm clouds to level out at 36,000 feet. Then we could enjoy first class service on the two-hour flight down to the Cape. It was about midnight when we finally took off which meant a 2am arrival in Cape Town. The weather wasn't much better there.

Arriving at airports anywhere in the world at two in the morning isn't a whole lot of fun. It's even less amusing if you are not sure where you are going. The car hire place was about to shut when I reached it and then there was a problem with the security device on the vehicle I'd been given. Out in the dark, isolated car park, I reloaded all my gear back on to a trolley, trudged back to the terminal, only to find everyone had gone home from the car hire company.

That meant wandering around the airport to try and find someone who might help. It took an hour before I eased out of

Cape Town airport. At three in the morning, in lashing rain, it is not the best time to be driving into the city past the sprawling townships of Gugulethu and Langa.

Under every bridge on the road huddled groups of Africans. This was their home on such a night and it put first class on the 747 into sharp perspective. I thought too; if this car breaks down out here, I could have a problem.

Eventually, I made the city, went over the Kloof Nek road out towards Camps Bay and found the apartment I had booked.

Shortly before 4am, a very lively night finally ended, to be followed the next day by the drama of the second semi-final, New Zealand's comprehensive 45-29 demolition of Will Carling's England team.

It was an extraordinary semi-final epitomised by the man mountain New Zealand wing Jonah Lomu running through and over the top of the England full-back Mike Catt for one of his tries.

A French journalist nearby stood up and exclaimed, 'Zis is the first time I see a man run over a cat.'

And the last, thank goodness.

%. %. %. %. %.

Diary Notes: February 2015.

To Cape Town, to work on various projects and escape the snow, ice and rain of a northern hemisphere winter.

Hands up those who have a better excuse to head to the southern hemisphere at this time of year.

I open a Sunday newspaper one weekend and am confronted by an odd-looking story.

In the South African *Sunday Times* the headline reads 'Nobody wants me', says blocked former Springbok coach Peter de Villiers. In the story, de Villiers made the assertion, 'I'm not allowed to be part of rugby in this country any more.'

At the time, de Villiers was coaching the University of the Western Cape, although his contract coaching in club rugby was due to expire in a few weeks' time.

Whatever the rights or wrongs of such a claim, it was not made clear in the article as to who was preventing him being part of rugby in South Africa any more. Indeed, he was quoted as saying he was being blocked 'everywhere I go' in South African rugby. But why and by whom? Few answers emerged in the article. It was like a great Whodunit. Who blocked de Villiers?

Now all this set me thinking. It reminded me of the time when Peter de Villiers was bidding to become the first non-white coach of the Springboks. Despite Jake White leading South Africa to the 2007 Rugby World Cup crown, the powers that be in SA Rugby made it clear they wanted a new coach. That's the way it works in SA Rugby – you win a World Cup and you're on your bike. Nope, I don't understand it either.

By the start of 2008, it was clear that either de Villiers or the Blue Bulls coach Heyneke Meyer would likely get the job.

In the end, de Villiers got it but he was not helped by a curious public statement from the SA Rugby president Oregan Hoskins, suggesting that his rugby credentials were not the only reason for the appointment.

'We have made the appointment and taken into account the issue of transformation when we made it. I don't think that tarnishes Peter; I'm just being honest with our country,' said Hoskins.

To me, this statement was about as filled with wisdom as former South Africa President F.W. de Klerk greeting the outcome of the 1995 democratic election with words like, 'We have given this opportunity [to the country] and taken into account transformation. I don't think that tarnishes Nelson; I'm just being honest with our country.'

You could almost hear the welcoming mat or carpet being pulled out from underneath de Villiers's feet. It would surely have been much better left unsaid by the president of SA Rugby.

Of course, what such words did was undermine de Villiers from the start. When the president of a country's rugby board indicates to the world that they have chosen a national coach on reasons other than his rugby knowledge, the man's whole status is opened up to question by too many people. Not least some of the players in his charge.

It was also alleged around that time that the South African Rugby Board had initially offered de Villiers a contract worth anything between Rand 200,000–400,000 less than the deal Jake White had been on. And another allegation circulated that a clause in de Villiers's contract stipulated that if he were to lose a Test series, his position could be open to review. If Peter de Villiers thought he heard the sound of a gun being loaded he was probably correct.

These allegations were never proven. But they swirled in the air, leaving an unpleasant odour. What is clear is that they undermined South Africa's new coach.

De Villiers was the first non-white coach of the Springboks but the fuss over his appointment set him off on the wrong foot. Yet de Villiers would soon prove himself unwise in some of his own public comments.

He was aware I had called for his appointment as national coach. And my request soon after he had taken charge to take me back to Paarl and show me where he had grown up and first come to know and play rugby was greeted with enthusiasm.

I remember it well. This was the article I wrote from that day. I feel it merits being repeated below. It received a lot of positive comments:

The broken beer bottles offer a grim, threatening welcome: the rough pieces of splintered wood lying among old, abandoned shoes, speak only of decay.

Beside one tree, discarded tiles have been dumped, mostly broken and chipped. Underneath the majestic trees that still line the ground, there is evidence of fires.

Out in the middle of the ground, the heat is relentless. A handful of small green shrubs flourish, but the sense of abandonment is omnipresent.

Yet there was a time when entire families, indeed whole communities made their way to this place. Residents of Paarl, they laughed, shouted and smiled and supported their favourite teams. The competition was intense, the spirit uplifting.

Peter de Villiers kicks aside a piece of rough wood. In this now silent, empty place, he is lost among his thoughts, momentarily overcome by the memories of his time here. For it was here, on this now deserted, shabby ground that the new Springbok coach first learned about the game that was to become what he calls the passion of his life.

It is 32 degrees, a brutal, enveloping heat, as we stroll across the ground. He grimaces, not from the strength of the sun but the sad sight that confronts us as we walk around this broken place.

'It makes me sad to see this ground like it is. I don't think people realised what they were doing to us…when they moved us out…'

His voice tails off, silent thoughts briefly replacing the words…

Once, he says, it was vibrant, the hub of a community. 'Other people will never understand but this place has got a lot of memories and history. This is a family park. People would come here as a family, the children would be dressed up. There were four rugby fields and there would be eight clubs playing here each Saturday, back in the 1970s. The games would be staged from 9.30 or 10 in the morning until the sun went down. I played here from about 1972 to 1984 and represented the SARU side.

'The people would arrive and there would be fun, laughter. It was a whole community thing because everyone would turn out. So when you turned out to play, the whole town would know how good or bad you really were. To be one of the best, this was the place to be on a Saturday. We worked hard here to become legends in our own time. There was no love lost, I'm telling you.'

De Villiers played scrum half and had a multitude of sporting battles with foes here. There were shouts of triumph, cries of anguish, cuts and bruises. All in the cause of the one thing they shared, a love of rugby football.

'It was a privilege to be with people who really had a passion for what they were doing in life. Rugby was one of those passions,' he explains.

And the support? De Villiers smiles. 'Where the people live, they will support the team that represents the whole community. It was their team, their town. We had a team called "Young Gardens" and all came from where we lived in the town centre, next to the river bank.

'Everybody who lived there were "Young Gardens" people.'

But the brutality of apartheid smashed this happy, vibrant community, like a fist in the face. The Group Areas Act was brought in and the people were shifted out, scattered to all areas like seeds in the wind. Those throwing them out of the centre cared not a jot for where those seeds blew or finally fell.

To this day, Peter de Villiers bears an expression of anguish when he talks of those times. 'What they didn't realise was that they didn't break up just rugby teams or households. They broke up whole communities. People never, ever recovered from that [enforced] movement.'

And there were other consequences, perhaps even uncalculated at the time, of such a fracture of the community. 'The coloured people were a very religious people,' he said. 'But when they moved us into those places, they just chucked us in those areas like a heap, saying, "Go live there."

'Some built new houses but those that couldn't were left behind. That is why you get these areas where people are squatting and they do all the wrong kind of things, because they are left over from those times of apartheid.'

How much hurt was caused to de Villiers and his family? 'Oh yes, a lot of hurt. I was a teacher for 20 years and I taught in those areas. Once, they were good people but now, that is not the way to live. But people sometimes do things not because they want to, but because they are forced to live that way.

'You had to fight to be a hero in your community then whereas before apartheid, everybody was striving to be good people, to be the best in their community.

'So what we have got now is exactly what apartheid has created. This is the result of apartheid and the movement of people out of the township to other areas. Remember, the churches which are your conscience in any society, were closed. So people moved to places where they didn't feel anything. Therefore, one big part of living, of their lives, was destroyed.'

But if Peter de Villiers represents anything in this life, in this country, it is the air of optimism he exudes. All the hurt he knew, the sad times, the sense of humiliation inflicted by apartheid are overridden by his inner desire to make tomorrow a better day than today.

'Now, we have to try to erase this monster we created,' he says of apartheid. 'I believe that with the help of others we can uplift the people again, give them something to clutch on to.'

One of de Villiers' greatest dreams during his tenure as Springbok coach is to play a key part in seeing this famous old ground close to the centre of Paarl restored to its former state. 'In my mind's eye, I still believe we can have the greatest sports facility here in the next few years and I am really going to see if I can make a big contribution to have this place restored.

'It would be a facility for the whole community like it always was. Maybe we can create an indoor facility too with a big museum where we can bring together everybody in Paarl who has something to offer. By doing so, other people could live those times again.

'That is what I see in the future here. I just hope the principality don't sell this place or use it for something else.'

Much has happened here, as in all South Africa, since those happy times were shattered by a ruinous conspiracy. Barbed wire rings part of the ground, homeowners eager to keep out those who use the place for illicit activities at night.

But even in this state, a majesty exists about the place. Elegant, healthy trees line three sides of the old ground, their branches waving in the hot wind.

Maybe, just maybe this once famous ground, where people knew such happiness, can be restored to something of its former glory. If it were, might it not represent an example, a microcosm of what needs to be achieved in so many other parts of South Africa?

I found de Villiers easy to talk to and good company. He spoke in forthright but honest terms. With me, was my wife and son and they too found what you might call this sporting history lesson, absolutely fascinating. When it was over, de Villiers spoke with my young son, ascertained that he played rugby and promised to get him some Springbok gear to play in. It was, it seemed, a spontaneous and genuine gesture.

The article seemed fine and attracted much interest. Then, not long after, de Villiers took charge of a pre-season Springbok training camp.

I had arranged to call him on a Saturday afternoon and what he said surprised me. There was no doubt this would be controversial stuff if put out into the public domain.

So much so that I interrupted him in mid-sentence and said, 'Peter, hold on a moment. You just said …so and so. Are you sure you're happy for me to use those quotes?'

I read him back the most contentious ones from my shorthand note. But he insisted he was happy for me to use them and so I did. This is the story that I wrote:

SOUTH AFRICAN SUNDAY PAPERS
Peter de Villiers exclusive interview
By Peter Bills
The extent of the private, cosseted world in which the Springboks existed during the Jake White era, was last night (SAT) laid bare.

New coach Peter de Villiers admitted that he has found most of the top South African players to be so hide-bound with conservatism that they are scared to make decisions, fearing it as an alien process after the way the previous regime worked.

In his most revealing interview to date, de Villiers outlined the extent of the problem he has inherited. He admitted it could take most of the remainder of the year to get the Springboks playing the way he wants, with greater responsibility.

De Villiers said, 'I am not very happy in terms of where we want them to be at this moment. The players have worked pretty well but the fact is, they were so spoon-fed...by the previous regime...that now we are asking them to think a bit, it is a cult shock for them.

'They are scared to make decisions because they have been so spoilt. Everything was there, they didn't have to decide on anything. They didn't take the blame for anything and that's the hardest part.'

De Villiers is insistent that the Springboks expand their game from the cautious, tight approach seen at the World Cup, however successful that was. But to do that, the players must take on far greater responsibility, make decisions and be responsible for them. It is a far cry from the way things were done previously.

But how much better can the Springboks be if they adopt this new creed? De Villiers' response is fascinating. 'Let's be clear, they are all very good players but they are not the best they can be at the moment. This is what we are trying to do, to improve them.

'But they have to change their mindset. They are talented people but they definitely have to take more responsibility. In percentage terms, I believe we can get another 40 per cent out of these guys. For instance, Bryan Habana touched the ball only once in the World Cup final. Imagine what he might do with much more possession and far greater opportunities to make his own decisions.

'We will push them very very hard to get there, to that extra 40 per cent. But add that amount to what they already have and you can see the potential of these players and this squad. If they are able to do these new things, then this will be a side that will really go places. But this could take up to six months.'

De Villiers hinted at the other elements of the comfort zone in which South Africa's leading players have existed. He talked of the luxury cars the players drive, the plush homes they have bought and the money they earn. None of which he decries but he insists that they focus their minds on only the game and the future. 'If we get their minds tuned to the game, I can be sure they will improve and succeed.

'What they must strive for is improving their own game and integrating that into the team. For a player is only as good as his team-mate.

'We don't expect the players to move mountains but we won't allow mediocrity.'

De Villiers promised he won't ask his players to do anything he wouldn't. 'I will be hard on myself and do my best. I am a very competitive person; I can't play a card game and not be competitive. There is nothing friendly about what I do.

'But the pressure doesn't concern me. I had the same pressure with the Under 21s. I know this is the 'Boks and it is more intense at this level because you have a nation to satisfy. I try to be the best I can and sometimes maybe I put too much pressure on myself. But that's me.'

Players like Victor Matfield, Bryan Habana, Peter Grant and Luke Watson have most impressed the new coach thus far. 'These are the guys that are on top at the moment. They still have that urgency to be better and they work hard to achieve it. That impresses me.

'Victor Matfield is a genius of a player, an expert in the line-out and on top of his game. But he still works very hard. That is the kind of attitude we need.

'In overall terms, I don't know how good we are. But I like this challenge and I want to be among the best in the world. I am not scared by that; I accepted the challenge and I'll do my best. The players have to be the same. They must have the same hunger to achieve as me and they have to perform.

'If they do that to the full extent of their capabilities, then we will be unstoppable.'

ALAS, it wasn't very long before de Villiers made it quite plain there was no longer a working relationship worth the name between him and me. The story had obviously caused deep discomfort in the Springbok camp and de Villiers wouldn't have been the first public figure in history to cite that old scapegoat about being misquoted.

But the truth was, I had reported his remarks with complete accuracy.

I found it disappointing, especially when I had given him the chance to retract his most controversial comments long before publication. That method, by the way, was one I used throughout my entire career.

As for the kit, it was a good thing my son never held his breath in anticipation.

But another strange twist in that South African story came some time later with an extraordinary call from Hoskins, still president of the South African Rugby Union. Clearly excited for some reason about something, Hoskins came on the line, wildly accusing me of demanding kit from South Africa's players and coaches, an utterly preposterous allegation that had no foundation whatsoever.

To this day, I possess not one item of Springbok kit. Yet I have international rugby jerseys given to me personally by players from Australia, France, Fiji, Scotland, Wales, Ireland and England. Nothing from South Africa, even though I personally knew so many Springbok players and coaches.

So much for going around demanding kit! But of course, wires get crossed and human beings get cross.

As for journalism in general terms, I could not for the life of me see the value, as some did, of seizing upon controversial comments perhaps uttered unwisely in the heat of the moment, and plastering them all over the nearest newspaper. Don't get me wrong, this was no holier than thou attitude and sure, I looked for a story as hard as anyone. After all, it was my job.

But I always followed a philosophy of wanting to make contacts and keep them. I wanted the people with whom I worked, who gave me interviews, to have confidence in talking to me. I could see no value in the subject of an article being incandescent with fury at what he was reading, either because he didn't mean it to be reported that way or he'd said something over the top in the heat of the moment and immediately regretted it. In either case, you could say goodbye to that particular contact and what was the point of that?

I'd rather ignore something that would clearly cause unnecessary offence or trouble in the short term, but enhance a long-term relationship with that particular person. You might, as I found, have a working relationship with guys around the world all your career if you were honest and aware of pitfalls they might tumble into. The contrast was to write one sensational story and lose their friendship and assistance for life. I wasn't interested in that.

I sought to build a reputation as a guy anyone could talk to without finding themselves the subject of screaming newspaper headlines the next day. When I wrote the story in *SportsWeek* magazine in the UK back in the 1980s that Welsh rugby star Jonathan Davies would professionalise himself and go to rugby league, I made sure Jonathan saw the story long before it was published. He read every word of it and approved it. He might not remember that now but it is fact.

Likewise, when I interviewed New Zealand star Dan Carter during his sojourn in France for the Perpignan club in 2008/09, the lengthy exclusive article for the *New Zealand Herald* was read by Carter before it ever left Europe. He didn't ask to see it, I told him he would. I wanted to guarantee I'd got it right in tone as well as accuracy.

I remember doing the same with an article concerning Springbok lock Victor Matfield.

In truth, hardly anybody I did potentially controversial articles with (and showed them to the person before publication) ever came back and said, 'Cut this, drop that, don't like this.' But I saw it as a security. I wanted the working relationship with those guys to continue and I wanted them to pick up the article when it was finally in print and think, 'Yes, that's exactly what I said and that's how I said it.'

They had agreed to do exclusive interviews on topical issues. I felt the least I could do was make 100 per cent certain I'd reported the story the way they wanted it reported, not with, even unintentionally, the wrong slant or anything like that.

Speaking personally, such a policy was an outstanding success for me all my career. In essence, it came down to one word. Trust. I wanted people to feel they could trust me to report accurately not just what they had said but what they had intended.

To more aggressive journalists, the rottweilers of our business, such an approach might have been naïve. But to be fair to them, you probably couldn't afford the luxury of such an approach if you were a staff reporter on a tabloid newspaper desperate for scandal and banner headlines each and every day.

But in my situation as a freelance, it was different. I could take a long-term view. And maybe, just maybe, the fact that some of world rugby's leading names asked me to write books with them about their lives might have had something to do with that philosophy.

After all, the likes of Gareth Edwards, David Campese, Willie John McBride, Bill McLaren, Corne Krige, Ashwin Willemse, Dean Richards, Jean-Pierre Rives and the former Australian cricketer Allan Border can't all have been wrong.

Krige, the former South African rugby captain, wrote in a copy of the book we worked on together in 2005, 'To Peter. Thank you very much for helping me write my book. It has come out exactly the way I wanted it.'

I appreciated that comment and was proud of it.

⁊⁊ ⁊⁊ ⁊⁊ ⁊⁊ ⁊⁊

VERY often, top class sportsmen cannot see the wood for the trees. Or, in this case, can't see what is best for them and their own future.

In September 2010, during the Peter de Villiers years as coach of South Africa, I wrote an article in the South African Independent group newspapers urging the Springbok coach to leave at home many of his top players ahead of the November tour to the northern hemisphere.

I'd spent most of that year touring with the Springboks and covering their Test matches. They'd had a hectic programme and by the time we reached the end of September, I was exhausted, even just writing every day, sitting in press boxes and aeroplanes flying around the world.

As for the players, training almost every day and enduring the extreme physicality of their job (not to mention the searing mental pressures of playing Test match rugby), well, some of them looked out on their feet.

It was no wonder. The schedule had been incredible. I went to Cardiff at the start of June to cover a one-off Test agreed to by the South African Rugby Union, against Wales. It doesn't matter in the context of this story, but the Springboks edged home 34-31.

One week later, on 12 June, the Springboks were back in Cape Town, beating France 42-17. The following week, 19 June, they played the first of two warm-up Tests for that year's Tri-Nations Test series, against Italy, in Witbank. The next weekend, the 26th, they played them again, in East London.

That Tri-Nations series began in faraway Auckland against the All Blacks and the South Africans had flown across the southern hemisphere just seven days after the last of the Italian Test matches. In Auckland, on 10 July, they got heavily beaten, 32-12. They then went down to Wellington to meet New Zealand again one week later, 17 July, losing this time 31-17.

From there, the Springboks flew west across the Tasman Sea to Brisbane where they faced, and lost to Australia (30-13) just seven days later, 24 July. If you think this was a schedule from hell, then keep reading.

They made the long journey back to Johannesburg from Sydney, 14 hours non-stop, and after a week or so of rest, began preparations for the return matches in the Tri-Nations. This cluster of games started with the visit of New Zealand to Johannesburg, where they beat the Springboks 29-22 in Soweto, on 21 August.

One week later, 28 August, the South Africans played Australia in Pretoria, the Boks winning 44-31. A week after that, on 4 September, in Bloemfontein, the Wallabies won, 41-39.

Not long after that, the weary South Africans began to prepare for their northern hemisphere tour. They would meet Ireland, Wales, Scotland and England within the space of four weeks, starting on 6 November and finishing on the 27th of that month. Another gruelling schedule loomed, with all the flying and other travelling involved.

But before the squad was selected for that tour, I wrote a strong article in the Independent group newspapers, saying that the senior Springboks, players like John Smit, Victor Matfield, Bakkies Botha, Bryan Habana, Jean de Villiers and others should not go anywhere near the northern hemisphere. The whole lot of them should stay at home and be told not to think about rugby until the following February when the Super 15 began. At least that would give them a reasonably lengthy break from the game.

The reason they needed such a break, I contended, was not just because they had already played so many Test matches in such a brief period of time. The following year, 2011, was Rugby World Cup year. I said that if the South Africans wanted to have a realistic prospect of defending their World Cup crown, their senior players had to get a good rest before the tournament. They would never do that in 2011, we all knew that.

So missing the northern hemisphere tour at the end of 2010 was their only chance of an extended break.

To strengthen the story, I called Professor Tim Noakes, a specialist in the scientific preparation of sportsmen and women from the Sports Science Institute at Newlands, Cape Town, to ask him whether he agreed with my prognosis. He did, 100 per cent, and endorsed my views publicly.

Part of my story contained the following words, 'Others have become weary, mentally and physically. John Smit and Bryan Habana have buckled under the weight of expectation. Neither should go anywhere near the northern hemisphere in November and the marvellous Victor Matfield, even though he somehow kept up his impeccable standards, should also have a lengthy break.'

The outcome was that my warning was totally ignored. John Smit, the Springboks hooker and captain, didn't make the tour because he was injured. Noakes, in fact, told me later that he had spoken to Peter de Villiers and the Springbok medical management some weeks earlier and suggested they rest Smit, ideally with another 12 senior players. Just after, it was announced that Smit needed surgery and could not tour anyway.

By then, Noakes reckoned, even Smit had come to realise how exhausted he really was. But it was probably only when he actually stopped training and playing, that he discovered the true level of weariness within his body.

But as Noakes said to me, there were a number of exhausted players who did not see it. They just wanted to keep playing. One of them was Victor Matfield.

With Smit missing the tour, the onus of leadership fell on the big Bulls lock forward and he never let his country down. When the Springboks flew to London in late October that year to begin their northern hemisphere tour, Matfield was not only on board, but the key man.

Given all this as a backdrop, was it therefore surprising the Springbok tour was disastrous (by their standards)? They beat Ireland and Wales, just, 23-21 and 29-25 respectively. But it then fell apart. Scotland beat them in Edinburgh, 21-17, and England won at Twickenham, 21-11.

It was no wonder. Individual engines had just run out of gas. Here's the killer statistic. From 5 June to 27 November of that year, a period of just over six months, South Africa played 14

Test matches. Victor Matfield, at the venerable age of 33, played in 13 of those 14 Tests. When it was all over, when broken bodies had been put together again, the South African Rugby Union announced an inquiry into the Springboks' disastrous Tri-Nations season. Doubtless, a thought or two was also given to what happened on the northern hemisphere tour, too.

Presumably, the inquiry quickly identified the culprits for this public flogging of young rugby men's bodies. The South African Rugby Union? Surely not, surely they would not be among the suspects?

Surely they would not have agreed to send the Springboks to Cardiff in June for a one-off Test against Wales? And for what reason, anyway? Disingenuous allegations circulating at the time that the SA Rugby Union had made about £1m from that Cardiff Test, were surely incorrect. They could not have been true. Could they?

The key battles of that rugby year for South Africa would be the Tri-Nations games against New Zealand and Australia. You wouldn't prepare for matches against those southern hemisphere countries by playing Wales.

Then there was the question as to who had agreed to play Italy twice. What value was that to the Springboks?

Presciently, even before 2010 was out, Professor Tim Noakes told me that in his view, the Super 15 tournament, which is of high intensity and high travelling fatigue especially for the South African teams, had extinguished any hope of the Springboks winning the 2011 Rugby World Cup. It will now take more than a miracle, he warned at the time.

Furthermore, he said that if Australia and New Zealand did not keep their best players out of a considerable number of Super 15 matches in 2011, they would also not have a hope of winning that World Cup. At that stage, in late 2010, he said he would put his money on a northern hemisphere country, probably France, winning the World Cup.

So what happened? France reached the 2011 World Cup Final and dominated against New Zealand, losing by a single point, 8-7. The better team clearly lost that match.

And the Springboks? Well, 21 high-profile players were left at home when the Boks went to Australia and New Zealand for the away Tri-Nations games of that year, just a couple of months before the World Cup began.

Coach de Villiers had finally bought into Noakes's advice which had proved so successful for the 2007 Springboks under Jake White and in which leading Springboks were excused from the end-of-year European tour and the away leg of the Tri-Nations competition.

But it was too little, too late. No miracle occurred. Even allowing for a shocking refereeing performance by New Zealander Bryce Lawrence in the quarter-final against Australia, South Africa lost 11-9 and went out. Their world crown had gone.

Yet the players still struggle to see the reality. Smit later criticised Noakes for supporting my story. Well, Noakes was guilty of one crime. He signed up to the truth which he had already stated himself, anyway. But it seems too many players prefer to avoid facing that.

Rugby union circa the 21st century likes to call itself professional. But in the view of those who know a thing or two, it is definitely not professional to flog your leading players so that they end up physically and mentally shattered.

If the players themselves are oblivious to the potential damage they are doing to themselves and their careers by wanting to play in virtually every game, the respective rugby unions and coaches of the world have a duty to remind them of the realities of such a situation.

Manchester United do not play Wayne Rooney or Robin van Persie in every single match. Liverpool sent Raheem Sterling away to the Caribbean for a holiday in the middle of the 2014/15 season.

Professional outfits like those know that players need rest. They are not machines. Sadly, rugby union does not yet seem to have grasped such a context. Play them until they drop appears to remain the mantra in certain countries. This alarming state of affairs simply has to end.

In March 2015, in a conversation with me at the Sports Science Institute at Newlands, Cape Town, Professor Tim Noakes made the following observations:

'AT that time, we did tests on the leading players and assessed exactly how much rugby they had played in the previous season. Sharks hooker Bismarck du Plessis played a total of 2,400 minutes through the 2009 season, John Smit 1,400 minutes. Danie Rossouw [then with the Blue Bulls] always played 1,400 minutes in a season for almost his entire career and his level of performance was very consistent. It was always level and he never got seriously injured.

'Others like Bismarck, Schalk Burger and Andries Bekker would play progressively more in successive seasons until in the third season they would inevitably suffer a season-ending injury. And then during the next three years they would follow exactly the same cycle. So we learned that if you want the players to play more than 2,000 minutes a year, they can do that for two seasons but in the third season they will very likely be injured and out for six to eight months.

'So why not rest them more during those first two seasons so that you get full value in the third season without serious injury? And of course in the third season before the injury, they will not play as well as they should in the key moments, in the important games when you need a 100 per cent performance from your key players. If they are too tired they won't deliver because they cannot.

'That is why we always struggle on the end-of-year tours. The players are exhausted and cannot do themselves justice even against less competitive teams as occurred in the 2010 November tour. Anyone watching those games knew that the Boks would not recover in time for a 2011 World Cup victory.

'So we found that each player had an ideal duration of play each season. But once they went over that time period, they were in trouble. But the Boks today have not learned this lesson. That was my advice to Jake White before the 2007 Rugby World Cup. Pull the top players out of the away leg of that year's Tri-Nations. Save them the travel and the matches. So he took 25 players out of that trip, saving them for the World Cup. And look at the result. Indeed, in his book Jake wrote that this was one of the key reasons why his team won the World Cup.

'Jake also wanted to take them to Poland in May before that 2007 RWC for specialised fitness work. I said no way; you will simply kill them. So he ditched that idea. I had no agenda; I just knew these guys needed a rest.

'But the Boks have not learned this lesson. I know it was discussed before they went to the UK in November 2014. But they didn't do anything in the end. They took them all. And the outcome was highly predictable. They lost Test matches and Jean de Villiers suffered a major injury. Was that coincidental? Who knows? But I have my own views.

'What is certain is that constant exposure increases the risk of injury. Ultimately, the coach has to have self confidence in himself to be able to do that (leave players out to rest). You have to have the philosophy of not minding losing some games when you have confidence in winning the big prize down the road.

'Jake White had that but neither Peter de Villiers nor Heyneke Meyer has had it in my judgement. And it will hurt them in the end.

'Still the lesson hasn't got home, it's so sad. They give their hearts to the game but they are so tired these players. And when you are tired the brain doesn't work as fast or as efficiently in transmitting messages to the body and the muscles. This is when you get injuries.

'When I spoke to the Boks in January 2010, one senior player stood up and said he was exhausted. Yet he was a vital player in the 2011 RWC. I said to him, "Why can't you be honest and tell people you are exhausted?" Victor

Matfield intervened and said, "We can't say we are tired. Springboks cannot make excuses for when we play poorly and lose."

'But I wonder whether it is that or whether the players cannot take a step back because they are linked so closely to the money and want that to continue without interruption. At that meeting only one out of 30 was prepared to say he was exhausted. It was like an Omerta.

'When I finished speaking to the players, John Smit said, "This info from Dr Noakes is not of value to us. It is a value to our employees. The people that need to hear this are SA Rugby. We are contracted to play and we have to play if we are selected."

'To which my answer is that I have given similar talks on at least three occasions to the leadership of SARU. So it is not as if the employers are completely ignorant of what is going on.

'But I continue to wonder. Is it the union and the coach who need to learn these lessons? Or is it the players who cannot step back, let go?

'The thing is, the margins in professional rugby are so tiny. You have to have people who are absolutely fresh and so motivated to do it on the day. Bruce Fordyce [the Comrades marathon runner in South Africa] used to say that there is a big one and the other races don't matter. You have to save yourself emotionally for the big one.

'I always wonder: Why do Australian teams so often win the key games particularly in cricket and are sometimes quite ordinary in the games that don't matter. Because they understand this concept – you peak for the games that are critical, not for the ones that are irrelevant – like the matches on the European end-of-year tour.

'The fact is, the Boks didn't win the World Cup in 2011 even though they had the players to do the job. John Smit was tired and Bismarck [du Plessis] should have started at hooker. And there were other players who had not had enough rest going into the World Cup. I still believe if we had followed Jake White's method in 2007 we would have won the 2011 World Cup as well. I told the players that in January 2010 – but they thought differently.

'Victor Matfield? He is a complete freak, the sort of guy that comes around once in every 100 years. There are just a few of that ilk in South African sport: Graeme Pollock, Barry Richards, now A.B. de Villiers. You can't explain it. He is so far out of the normal pattern. What he has done is absolutely unbelievable. If he goes to the RWC again this year it will be freakish.

'Mentality clearly matters, the fact that he is motivated to do it, to go on and on, is crucial. Ryan Giggs, Sachin Tendulkar are others like him. They have all had this incredible desire to keep playing because they believe they can still improve. And they are prepared to do whatever it takes to keep improving.

'They are guys that have done everything and keep going. In a physical game like rugby, Matfield has needed an incredible personality but also a remarkable physical resilience. I watched him play cricket, I couldn't believe it. He scored about 60 off 40 balls against the Proteas about three months ago.

'But sportsmen of that type are one-offs. You cannot take their standards and apply them to everyone else. Nor can you expect geniuses like Matfield always to give you the winning edge as he did in the 2007 World Cup Final. Rather play with 15 sub-geniuses who are properly rested.'

AT a time when rugby union has never been as brutally physical in all its history, young men playing too many games and playing when they are not fully fit, mentally or physically, are dicing with dangers. The consequences down the road in their lives may prove not worth the rewards they see at this stage.

IRELAND

Diary Notes: Ireland, oh Ireland. Now don't get me started on that place.

WALES is supposed to give you a welcome in the hillsides before giving you a right kicking in the gulleys (or should that be goollies?) if you happen to be a visiting rugby player.

As for the Irish, they don't bother too much about the singing and they don't care whether they welcome you in the hillsides, gulleys or graveyards. Wherever they meet you, they'll drag you off to the nearest bar so that you eventually end up in the same sort of state as if the Welsh had mugged you near the corner flag. Except that, you sort of enjoy the descent into physical ruin a lot more.

A rugby weekend in Dublin is the absolute epitome of what the great old game was always about. Friday afternoon tea at Bewley's in Grafton Street, join the post-work throng at any of the city centre pubs (preferably one with a real fire on a winter's night), a few pints of Guinness or Murphy's and the chance to chew the cud with some locals and then off for dinner somewhere.

On the Saturday, priorities are established: enjoying the match, meeting people, making new friends some of whom will probably last a lifetime, sharing a good few beers, maybe a meal later in the evening, and then losing your trousers.

I know opera has its advocates but please, how can you compare an evening of Tosca with a night in a Dublin pub in the company of Irish friends? The only way you can be laid low the next morning after an opera is through earache from all that high-pitched screeching. At least in Dublin if you are laid low, it's self-inflicted and therefore the ruination of choice.

It's no wonder the Irish used to be a deeply religious people, until those naughty boys in the Catholic clergy discovered that choirboys had some kit under their cassocks. Of course, that had the rather unfortunate effect of exploding the whole *raison d'etre* of religion in the country. But before that, the Irish worshipped endless images of the Virgin Mary.

And I could understand that, even though I was never a Catholic. As a visitor to Ireland, I, like a lot of red-blooded males, also worshipped Mary, plus Cathy, Sinead, Ashling, Caitlin and Grainne, to mention just a few. Mind you, I was far from convinced they were all virgins. That notion seemed to be verging on the ridiculous.

Fun, feisty, fabulous – Ireland has some wonderful women, that's for sure. They launch a party like a rocket and break hearts at every turn. And if you get to spend any time with them and they become true friends, you'll never forget the experiences.

But then, you make friends in Ireland in the strangest places. What's more you see characters at every turn around the place. Or at least you used to, before they filled the country with Poles, Latvians, Lithuanians and Estonians. Nowadays, if you order a cup of coffee in an Irish café chances are you'll be served a dish of borscht. Ask for some wine and you're as likely to get a mug of tea or hot chocolate from people making a complete Horlicks of the order.

Nevertheless, you can still find a few of the old characters.

%. %. %. %. %.

Diary Notes: 19 April 1958.
France 11 Ireland 6, Stade Colombes, Paris.

NO, I wasn't actually there. After all, there was a far more important game going on in my neck of the woods and I wasn't missing that for anything, Parisian Can-Can girls or anyone else. Blackheath were playing Rosslyn Park and that mattered far more to your budding future correspondent.

Besides, the Irish didn't take rugby matches seriously in those days. Tony O'Reilly and Andy Mulligan, the 1950s/1960s Irish version of Morecambe and Wise, once went to Paris with an Ireland team for a Five Nations international and took a very good look around the city on the Friday afternoon after training. And then some more in the early evening over a glass of something very elegant and distinctive.

What they saw helped them arrive at an important decision. When the Ireland team went home on the Sunday morning, they would stay on for a few days. Well, the girls were so pretty and so friendly.

By some manner of miracle, Ireland managed to arrive with everyone in attendance that Saturday at Colombes, the old stadium out in the suburbs of Paris, a short train ride from Saint Lazare station, which had been painted so beautifully by the Impressionist master, Claude Monet, in the 1880s.

Among the full complement of players was a man who had a sense of humour about as dry as a flinty Chablis.

Michael Anthony Francis English played for Lansdowne and the Bohemians club of Limerick during his career. Nor was yer man any duffer on the rugby field. Oh no. In fact, even though he won only 16 caps for Ireland in a comparatively short career from 1958 to 1963, he was good enough to go on the 1959 British & Irish Lions tour of New Zealand.

No fool then, Mickey English, on the field but he loved to raise a smile and have a laugh off it. Nor did it matter who was in the line of fire.

English gained renown down the years for his old joke about once playing against the English fly half Phil Horrocks-Taylor in an England–Ireland Five Nations game.

'I went to tackle him, Horrocks went one way, Taylor went the other and I was left holding the bloody hyphen,' he joked.

Not a bad line, but it wasn't Mickey English's finest hour in terms of jokes. That came deep in the bowels of the old Colombes stadium in 1958 when the Irish were in Paris on their biennial French girl hunt. For some odd reason (and the point to remember is that the Second World War had been over for 13 years) the guest of honour was none other than General Bernard Law Montgomery, Monty of El Alamein fame.

If you ever had to nominate THE quintessential boring old fart of an Englishman, Monty would probably top the thinking man's list (closely followed, no doubt, by a bloke called Geoffrey Boycott who used to play cricket).

His father, the Reverend Henry Montgomery, was an Anglo-Irish Anglican priest who inherited the ancestral estate of New Park at Moville, in County Donegal. Alas, his offspring was to become insufferable to most people during the war and an even bigger bore after it.

However, it's unlikely he ever forgot the day he ran into one M.A.F. English, the Irish fly half, at Colombes.

At some point before the game, Monty slipped largely unannounced into the Irish changing room, one of those squalid, dimly lit concrete cabins they had built under the main stand at Colombes for the 1924 Olympic Games. There was a certain hrrrmph, hrrrmph as he stood there, so as to gain everyone's attention.

'Now men,' he said, throwing off the years as if still about to assault Rommel's Afrika corps at El Alamein, 'this is about giving your absolute best and having complete confidence you can prevail. Never doubt your victory but doubt neither the effort required to achieve it.'

Or something like that.

The players hung around sort of listening, some bollock-naked, some clad in no more than a jock strap, others already fitting a scrum cap on to their head and others still trying to tie up broken bootlaces.

Indeed, no sooner had the great man finished his rendition, than a cauliflower-eared Irish prop wandered back into the dressing room from the toilet area and exclaimed to anyone willing to listen, 'Would any of you lads have some hairy twine for me boots? Oi've broken me laces.'

Montgomery apparently ignored this intrusion and stepped forward briskly to shake hands with the men. He liked to do that; Monty always did formal.

So he reaches English and presses the flesh, with the accompanying words delivered from behind a crisply cut moustache, 'Montgomery of Alamein, how are you?'

Bohemians' finest did not hesitate. 'English o' Limerick,' he shot back, 'how's yerself?'

Even Montgomery was rendered speechless by that.

%%% %%% %%% %%% %%%

Diary Notes: October 1986, Dublin.
Ireland 60 Romania 0

I am here for a curiosity, an oddity. Ireland v Romania is not going to be a close encounter. It's probably not going to be any sort of encounter at all.

It's all the International Rugby Board's (IRB) fault. A few years back, Romania had a very decent side. They beat Scotland in 1984, the year the Scots won the grand slam in the Five Nations Championship, and they beat Wales in 1983 and again in 1988.

As for France, the Romanians knocked them off, like modern day tourists get mugged in Bucharest, winning in 1974, 1976, 1980 and 1982.

It should have meant the Romanians were fast-tracked into an expanded Five Nations Championship (like Italy would be in 2000). But the only time the IRB does fast-tracking is when it comes to booking five-star hotels and first or business class airline flights around the world for themselves. They're like Usain Bolt for pace when it comes to those details.

But of course all those victories for Romania did, was ring alarm bells among the stronger nations, especially the Celtic mafia. They didn't want the Romanians exposed to a regular higher standard of rugby, getting stronger and showing up the likes of Wales and Scotland for their inadequacies.

So the IRB, where, just by chance, Wales, Scotland and France all held crucial votes, never quite got around to offering Romania a step up to a higher level of competition. And of course the obvious happened – rugby in that country withered. Wales much preferred that. By 1997, they were cheerfully flogging the hapless Romanians 70-21; four years later they topped that with an 81-9 win and in the next three years, they beat them 40-3, 54-8 and, in 2004, 66-7. They haven't played them since.

It's a good job the South Africans didn't treat the Welsh as the Welsh treated the Romanians. For until November 2014 when Wales beat the Springboks in Cardiff, Wales and South Africa had played each other 29 times in their history.

Wales won once, one match was drawn and the South Africans were victorious on the other 27 occasions. If the South African rugby board had applied the same argument as the Welsh in their dealings with the Romanians, the Springboks would have dropped the Welsh fixture long ago.

As for the French, they won all 14 matches against the Romanians between 1991 and 2006. At that point they too quietly decided, 'No more.'

So all that had just about seen off Romania as a proper rugby nation.

Therefore, the sight of the courageous but outclassed Romanians at Lansdowne Road today won't have people on the edge of their seats. Unless, that is, they have itchy backsides. But you work where you work, at whatever game. And besides, those days in Dublin had other attractions.

It became a tradition – sadly long since extinct – that on the Friday night before an Ireland rugby international, the mighty Distillers group would host a function for the media, both local and overseas, plus visiting officials. In truth, anyone else who would pass muster as a) not someone already completely blotto (which deleted a large segment of the potential gathering) or b) not a wino from the Dublin streets (which ruled out most of Fleet Street's finest, sadly), could often gain entry if they had a reasonable appearance and smiled sweetly at the girls on the door.

ROMANIA being Romania, they arrive at Dublin airport in some old Soviet aeroplane which resembles one of those Air-fix model kits as opposed to a proper aircraft. The ground workers stare in disbelief as this old thing lumbers up to one of the arrival gates. It looks like the sort of craft Lenin once flew in, but certainly not as far as Dublin.

Of course, it is so old that it has had to refuel at just about every filling station on a straight line from Bucharest to Dublin. So it's taken most of the day to get here which hardly strikes you as ideal preparation for the game the next day. Worse still, the eyes of the Romanian players bulge at the goodies in the shop windows as the bus drives them through the city centre to their hotel. They can't wait to get out and tour the streets and shops to see some life, compared to dreary Bucharest. Training? Who wants to do that when shopping in a western city beckons?

It's probably a good thing the players don't know about the Distillers do later that evening. Otherwise we'd have no game on the Saturday.

It's a traditional Irish early winter's night. Office workers scurry for cover from the rain which falls on the Irish capital like stair rods. The saturating showers are blown in on a gale from the Irish Sea which laps up on the capital's shores. If taking a cold outside shower is your idea of fun then this is the place for you. But help is at hand.

Close by the Liffey, the river that flows through the heart of Dublin out to the sea, stands the Distillers brewery. It has been located at the St James's Gate site since 1759, its products as much a life blood to the capital's residents as the great river itself. Not for nothing are those famous wrought iron gates known locally as the Pearly Gates.

We are ushered inside and the famous brew is poured. There is straight Irish whiskey, whiskey on the rocks, whiskey with water or a snug blend of warm whiskey with cloves and lemon. Now this combination alone is a mix able to reduce strong men to silly, gibbering wrecks.

Out of the cold and wet, in this warm room, faces become florid, eyes glazed. For sure, there are nibbles and lots of them. But you know how it is at these events: the drink always has a greater appeal than the food. Especially for the Romanian officials.

These swarthy, big moustachioed beasts from eastern Europe take to the beverages on offer like ducks to water. Only difference is, this lot don't want any water diluting the precious brew.

So we sip our drinks quietly and watch the performance. It is both amusing and revealing. Strong, normally reserved men brought in from the cold, of the weather and their lives in general, become talkative, chatty even and then silly as the drink and warmth combine in a seductive embrace. They laugh ludicrously loudly at tame jokes from the official speakers and begin pushing each other amid the jollities.

Back in Nicolae Ceausescu's security police ridden land of Romania, they are unable to let their hair down. But in faraway Dublin, where Irishmen and women are friendly and the whiskey is flowing almost as fast as the Liffey just outside the door, a warmer world exists. And the Romanians, a people you have to feel desperately sorry for in the nightmare of their Soviet-style existence, just go on and on enjoying themselves. And why not, for heaven's sake?

%, %, %, %, %,

Diary Notes: To Dublin, February 1991.
Ireland 13 France 21
Between 1984 and 1999, Ireland met France 17 times in international rugby matches. It was what you could safely call a one-sided contest. France won 16 of those games, with one, in 1985, drawn.

IT reminded me of that lovely old story about the Irish second row forward of the 1950s, Tom Reid, who was not only a very decent player but a wonderful baritone singer.

Reid went to Twickenham with Ireland in 1956 and suffered a stuffing for those times. England won 20-0 which, given the fact that a try was only worth three points then, was some mauling.

'Ah Tom,' said a colleague as they trudged wearily off Twickenham at the end. 'What did you think?'

Reid sighed the sigh of a tired, exhausted man and replied with wondrous simplicity, 'Twenty-nil, and lucky to get the nil.'

When the French came to town there was always a special buzz. For some strange reason, Frenchmen do not seem to have much of an in-built resistance to Guinness, or the black stuff as it's known in non-PC circles.

It's a bit like a five-year-old playing with a stick of dynamite: it thinks it looks fairly harmless and it can handle it. But it invariably descends into a horrible mess.

The French are an odd people. They go all the way to Ireland for a rugby weekend and the first thing they try to find is a pet shop where they can buy some strutting cockerel to release on the pitch at Lansdowne Road the next day. It's a bit like the Welsh getting off the train at Paddington en route to Twickenham and asking for the nearest farm selling leeks.

Once they've done that, the French disappear for most of the evening into some appropriate hostelry in Dublin city centre. It's not as if there's a shortage of such places. Some fool once suggested a pub crawl around Dublin, drinking half a pint of Guinness in each place he and his pals visited. Far from going right around Dublin, they barely got out of the one street such was the number of pubs on either side of the road, before predictably disappearing into the nearest gutter.

I can't remember the exact time of the evening we met up, but let's just say it wasn't early. How did I know they were French? Well, how many locals in an Irish pub wear a black beret, reek of garlic and are decked out in red, white and blue coloured trousers? And to think they call France the couture capital of the world. Dear me.

Anyway, we were becoming well acquainted with Arthur Guinness's finest and the evening was progressing well. Too well for some.

Sometime later, beyond the bewitching hour, a group of us repaired to the nearby apartment of some girls in the group. By that stage of the evening, you could categorise the Frenchmen fairly easily: those out of their heads with Guinness, those six parts gone and one other who looked as though he had set out from the start to prioritise his evening and was about to make an investment pay off.

The trouble was, one or two of *les frogs* didn't seem quite sure where they were or which town they were in. Still, we got back to the apartment all in one group (as far as I can remember) and some of us just crashed out. The floor wasn't uncomfortable especially when you are so tired and I drifted off to sleep.

I was awoken sometime in the early hours by someone pulling at me and shaking me violently. What was this, an earthquake or someone's stomach in trouble? You never quite know at that time of the morning.

It quickly became apparent that there was another reason for this violent intrusion into my slumbers. L'amour, true love.

'Will yer wake up, wake up,' said yer woman with growing impatience. 'How do I tell 'im I love him?'

Oh dear, few had foreseen this particular Franco-Irish liaison. But then passion is a bit like Guinness – you can't stop it frothing at the surface. So picture the scene: a bleary-eyed Englishman is rubbing the sleep out of his eyes as he sits half propped up on the floor, and an Irish girl is crouching close by, face studiously set and trying to remember the words and accent required to communicate with her new-found beau. C'est incroyable, non?

At the time, when the shaking and shoving had finally subsided and she had retreated to her room with the crucial words locked into her brain and I was preparing to drift off back to sleep, I remember thinking it is always nice to be helpful in such situations, to smooth the path of true love. Or should that be true lust? Anyway, some hours later, the story took another twist. A Frenchman came wandering out of a bedroom. To say he looked dishevelled would be kind. Torn through a hedge backwards might be more accurate.

He seemed in a state of only semi-awareness, as if he didn't really know where he was, what he was doing there and what time it was. He ran his fingers through the tousled hair, yawned expansively and glanced at his watch. In an instant, a look of calamity transformed his face as though it were a mask.

'Mon dieu,' he gasped. 'Eet is so late. Where are my trousers?' And then, glancing around the lounge and seeing only the faces of strangers, he exclaimed, 'And where is my wife?'

Back at the club where we'd all met up the night before, presumably. Or maybe in some Irishman's apartment, searching for her dress and, mon dieu, 'my 'usband'.

% % % % %

Diary Notes: October 1991, Dublin.
The second Rugby World Cup

Now this is a jaunt to be on. We have been in Dublin to cover a couple of Ireland's pool matches at Lansdowne Road in the World Cup tournament. But before the next game, on a day off in midweek, we have been invited to a grand golf course somewhere outside Dublin in County Wicklow by one of the sponsors. Oh dear, do they really know what they are letting themselves in for?

IT'S not unusual, sang Tom Jones, and it's not unusual for rugby's media men to be invited on freebies like today. Nor is it unusual for most of us to make complete clowns of ourselves once out on the course.

Most of us with a golf club in our hands are proficient chiefly in the following: a) destroying the local fauna and flora, b) imperilling the lives of any small mammals or birds within the vicinity, c) doing so much damage to the turf that pristine courses are rapidly turned into something resembling a farmyard and lastly d) imparting a sense of shock and horror in the minds of any members who might be unfortunate enough to witness the goings-on of the media crazy gang.

But to start at the beginning. And therein lies a tale.

Unwisely, I'm the one who has volunteered to drive the four of us out to this course somewhere in the country. I've had a car for a few days and it makes sense to keep it and then drive myself and the boys straight back to Dublin airport afterwards. Only trouble with that is, we have been invited to lunch with drinks after our round of golf. So yours truly won't be drinking.

Anyway, we make our way out of the city heading south-west into County Wicklow. Someone is supposed to have directions to this place but they either can't find them, have left them behind or have eaten them. Who knows?

The point is, we're lost. We drive up this narrow, twisting lane and there's no sign of a golf course anywhere in sight. So we do what you do in such circumstances. We find someone to ask.

Only trouble is, it turns out we've found the very man all Ireland jokes about when it talks of directions. Well, he appears amenable and so it proves. He pokes his head inside the car near the front passenger seat and checks where we want to find.

'Do you know **** golf club?' we ask.

'Ah sure, I'd know it, that's for sure,' he says helpfully.

'So which way should we go?' we ask, adding, 'We don't know this part and we're a bit lost.'

He scratches his chin for a brief interlude, starts to lift an arm in one direction then swivels his body around 90 degrees and briefly puts up the other arm in the opposite direction, before thinking better of that too and putting both down by his side. He looks a bit like one of those airport workers guiding the plane to its parking stand with his arms waving around.

And then he offers that immortal line beloved of all people having a laugh at the expense of the Irish.

'To tell you the truth,' he says, all dead pan serious, 'I wouldn't be starting from here if I was you.'

Well, no thanks to yer man but we eventually stumbled upon the course sometime later. And the usual mayhem ensued.

Someone stood on the men's tee at the fourth, a driving location almost directly behind the ladies' tee 20 yards or so further on. He picked up the most fearsome looking club in his bag, took a horrible swipe at the ball and sent it off like a low, scudding, misfiring rocket straight into the metal box sitting minding its own business in a corner of the ladies tee, like some innocent bystander.

From there, the ball ricocheted up into the air and came spinning down just a few yards in front of where we stood. Frankly, this might have been some notable feat but no-one in the group was in any fit state to appreciate it. We were all doubled up with laughter.

The sight of water seems to induce a total lack of what you could call common sense among shocking golfers. We see a lake and are instantly convinced we're about to play a sublime, soaring shot over it which will plop down gently on the faraway green and trickle up to the hole before dropping in. Of course, the reality could not be more different.

Someone sent a shot so low across the water that, for a moment or two, you were reminded of the Second World War and that bouncing bomb invented by Barnes Wallis which was used on the RAF's Dambusters raid in Germany's Ruhr valley.

The likeliest recipient of this particular missile was a moorhen, out and about on an autumn morning doing no-one any particular harm. As the ball threatened, the savvy bird sensed the danger and flapped its wings for a few moments, taking it out of the flight path. Happily, it was just the ball that died a watery death.

It began to rain, not an unusual occurrence in Ireland. If you're out in it on a golf course, you just play on and get soaked. So on the 16th tee, about 130 yards to the green, it was getting visibly harder to see the flag due to the rain. Someone took an iron out of their bag, heaved a great swipe at the ball – and sent it straight up into the air. The club, that is.

It turned in mid-flight and came to rest on the branch of a tree close by the tee. The rest of us were still laughing as its owner climbed the tree in the rain to retrieve it. And the ball? God knows where that went.

After a few hours of this knockabout stuff with a pretence of golf as an excuse for the ribaldry, the lads began to get thirsty. Funny thing that, journalists so often seem to.

So we repaired to the clubhouse where they counted the number of clubs we were returning – presumably reasoning that half of them would doubtless be stuck up trees or at the bottom of a lake somewhere out on the course – and led us to the calm and warmth of the clubhouse.

Then the serious business of the day began. There was Guinness, whiskey, wine, water (wasn't a lot of call for the latter, I have to report, apart from in my case) and just about anything else you wanted. There was also a cooked lunch.

Some of us had lined up a 5pm flight out of Dublin back to London and, as with all things, it looked eminently gettable when we booked it, allowing several hours for golf and lunch. But when you don't sit down for lunch until 2.30pm it starts to look a touch problematic.

Problematic then turned into probably impossible which then became completely ridiculous. At which point, we all bundled into the car with the cry 'Let's go for it.'

The lanes swept by and a motorway approached which was good news for a mile or two until a traffic jam set in. Then we sat and seethed.

Eventually, at some impossible hour like 4.35pm, we drove into Dublin airport.

'Where's the car hire drop off?' I asked with a sense of urgency in my voice.

'Don't be bloody silly, we haven't got time to go there,' said someone.

'No problem, we'll leave it at the main entrance,' said someone else. And we did.

You could just say the lady on the car hire desk inside the airport terminal had a bit of a shock as four guys pounded past her desk, one of them lobbing a set of car keys at her, like a soldier on manoeuvres with a hand grenade, and shouting, 'It's outside the front door,' as we raced past.

But no worries, as the Australians like to say. We got the flight.

※ ※ ※ ※ ※

Diary Notes: Dublin, March 1993
Ireland 17 England 3

GIVEN the lean years Ireland went through in the second half of the 1980s and the decade of the 1990s and 2000s until 2009, what happened at Lansdowne Road on Saturday 20 March 1993 was little short of miraculous. Men talk about it to this day.

England went to Dublin for that year's Five Nations Championship game seeking a third successive grand slam. And why not? England had won the coveted slam in 1991 and 1992 and had beaten Ireland in their last six meetings, with a tasty 38-9 thumping the previous year at Twickenham.

Now most things considered, that gentlemanly group of men known as Dublin bookmakers are usually among the most cheerful, optimistic souls on the planet when it comes to persuading you to part with your money.

'Ah Sir, you'll be safe and sound there on that one,' they'll tell you as you invest next month's mortgage money on some old three-legged nag. Alas, the late, great comedian Tommy Cooper got it spot-on when it came to backing duff horses. 'I backed this horse today, I did; it ran in the 12.40 at Kempton Park. Didn't come home until 20 to five.'

Yet despite that innate optimism, even the Dublin bookies were confronting stark reality on the morning of that 1993 Ireland v England game. After all, there was no reason on earth why Ireland should get anything but another stuffing. They hadn't won anything for 11 long years, had just been through a barren period of eleven successive defeats and it was the small matter of 45 years since they'd lifted their one grand slam.

So the bookies' odds of 1/10 on England that morning looked about right, until Ireland won 17-3 and turned the whole of Dublin into one enormous party for the rest of the weekend.

Just by chance, one of Ireland's top businessmen, Sir Anthony O'Reilly, had been at the game and afterwards, had entertained his clients in a hospitality suite at Lansdowne Road. He finally left about two hours after the final whistle.

Now two hours' drinking time represents a vast opportunity to most celebrating Irish men or women. Thus, as O'Reilly's chauffeur-driven car nudged its way through the city centre, it came to a stop outside a public house amid the bedlam of the evening traffic.

As O'Reilly sat in the back of the car, speaking on the telephone to his secretary in America, two lads burst out of the saloon bar of the pub and proceeded, albeit a touch unsteadily, down the path to the street.

Their glazed eyes and Guinness-soaked minds tried to focus upon a sleek, black Mercedes, darkened windows in the rear with a chauffeur, complete with cap, in the driver's seat.

Without so much as a hesitation, one of the lads staggered brazenly up to the car and banged firmly on the back window. Now Tony O'Reilly was and remains one of the most famous men in Irish 20th and 21st century history. He was, before financial ruination caused by the great crash of 2008 set in, far and away Ireland's most successful businessman, head-hunted by the H.J. Heinz Corporation in America at a young age and eventually becoming their chief executive based in Pittsburgh for almost 30 years.

He then returned to Ireland and built up the Independent News & Media stable of newspapers which included publications around the world such as the *London Independent, New Zealand Herald, Belfast Telegraph, Irish Independent* and the major English language newspapers all over South Africa.

Throughout his career, O'Reilly has been a feverishly busy operator. Yet he's always found time for small courtesies. Interrupting his phone conversation to America, he wound down the back window, surveyed the two young lads and politely enquired of them, 'Can I help you?'

The pair took in an intriguing scene. There sat the great Irish rugby man, there were his and her telephones beside the back seats of the car and in front, more deep leather seats and a drinks cabinet.

But Irish lads, God love 'em, are not fazed by much. Accepting with alacrity O'Reilly's invitation of assistance, the elder youth stammered out, 'Er, yes, yer can. 624 8593. Phone the wife and tell her we won't be home for three feckin' days.'

%% %% %% %% %%

> ### Diary Notes: September, 1994. To Kinsale, for an interview with chef Keith Floyd.
>
> You could call Keith Floyd a lot of things and a lot of people did (especially his ex-wives). Let's just settle on celebrity cook, television personality, restaurateur, raconteur. Alas, he died from a heart attack shortly after being given the all-clear from cancer. He was 65 and somehow managed to leave just £7,500 in his UK estate, despite years of high earning from TV shows and books. I hope that paltry figure reflected his canny tax avoiding arrangements. But then, he was declared bankrupt twice.
>
> Clearly, it's an expensive business dabbling in wine, women, divorces (he was married and divorced four times) plus failed restaurants.

TO say that Keith gave life a real shake would be to seriously underestimate the man's capacities. A few hours in his company set you up for the next six months of living.

He'd bought an enchanting cottage near Kinsale, alongside one of those creeks up which the waters of the Atlantic Ocean surge on every tide. Somehow, you envisage images of inviting inns on cold nights, days on a boat with a line somewhere out in the water and a relaxing yarn with a few locals when you finally return to shore. And I don't imagine the day we arrived was much different to any other in the Floyd household.

I was editing *Rugby World* magazine at the time and trying to bring it, albeit kicking and screaming, into the 20th century. That was no easy task given that, when you departed ever so slightly from a format probably settled upon before Prince Obolensky scored his famous try at Twickenham back in 1936, you risked the wrath of every retired Lieutenant Colonel and Wing Commander in the English shires.

Honestly, some of the letters I copped when I commissioned a cartoon for one front cover. And then there was the time we had Floyd on the cover, clutching a knife and fork and about to carve a rugby ball, with a bottle of wine standing sentinel beside it.

Anyway, our photographer and myself had flown into Cork airport early and hired a car to reach Kinsale. We knocked on the door of Floyd's cottage at what most human beings would call coffee time but in Keith's household was more like red wine time.

Mind you, the guy had something other than a genius for cooking. He knew a very decent glass of red when he tasted one. Open and half-finished on the breakfast table was a bottle of pinot noir from that renowned Burgundian producer Louis Latour.

'Dear boy, a glass,' smiled Keith.

Well, what could one do except accept, with alacrity?

So, following the creed of the *Mastermind* TV programme – 'I have started so I'll finish' – we all polished off that bottle and then another mysteriously appeared.

When we'd finally drained that one, we went outside for photos. And Keith told me about his rugby times. He never scored a try during his playing career but he did break his nose on the field, attempting that first ever touchdown.

'It was a very rare occasion for me, it looked as though I was about to get that first try. The problem was, I was so excited I ran into the goalpost, broke my nose and the ball squirted out of my grasp so I didn't get the try either. I never again came as close to a score as that.

'I was really too small for rugby and got fed up being bashed up. However, I had an illustrious career at school [Wellington, in Somerset]. We had a wonderful undefeated record for ages. The trouble was, when that ended, we all went off and didn't make it. What we should have done was join minor clubs and play for their colts sides. Instead, we tried to play at clubs like Taunton and we couldn't do it.

'But once I realised the playing side wasn't for me, I found another outlet. I have devoted the rest of my life to being an armchair expert and sharing times with a lot of rugby folk who tend to enjoy becoming completely confused.

'One of the highlights was downing many pints of beer in a clubhouse somewhere on a Saturday night followed by a mass invasion of the local curry house. After that, the trick was not to be the last one left after everyone else had gone to the lav and climbed out of the toilet window without paying. If you were left, you had to pay the bill.'

He always espoused the virtues of the old game. 'In my view, rugby remains a sport unique in the camaraderie it inspires. It is a sensational way of getting on with people. It is like eating: good food and good people create an ambience which is wholly pleasurable.'

He watched the game all over the world but insisted the old Lansdowne Road, Dublin, was his favourite ground. 'It is a sensational atmosphere and the craic really is outrageous.'

Eventually, we all clambered in a car and drove into Kinsale for lunch. For sure, Floyd knew his food and knew the best place to head for in town. Even from a distance of about 20 years, the memory of hot, oak-smoked salmon with Irish soda bread as a starter still prods the saliva glands into frenetic activity. That was followed by fresh scallops and some very nice Chablis.

We talked more rugby, too, in between mouthfuls of fish and fine wine. Keith loved the game, always had done. But the clock was ticking on. Suddenly, we realised we were getting short of time. But before we left, I wanted to tap into Keith's culinary skills. 'I'll buy something you recommend at the local butcher's and you can give me the recipe,' I said.

He waltzed into his regular supplier in the High Street and announced he wanted the finest joint of salt beef they had in the place. As they wrapped it, I scribbled down in shorthand all the cooking details he dictated. Add carrots, leeks, bay leaves, peppercorns, a little wine vinegar and lots of water. Then cook slowly for two to three hours.

We had it for Sunday lunch that weekend. Fabulous. Even in my decidedly dangerous cooking hands, it was superb.

When Keith Floyd took his last sip of wine and shuffled off this mortal planet, rugby football lost a terrific disciple and one of the great recipes of the world went missing.

※ ※ ※ ※ ※

Diary Notes: Dublin, March 2010
Ireland 27 Wales 12

There's no getting away from it. Fact is, you get an altogether better class of drunk in Ireland than anywhere else.

THERE he sat, happy as a lark in springtime, on a favoured patch outside the famous old Lansdowne Road ground in Dublin, home of Irish rugby. His cheeks were a deep ruddy, Burgundian red, hair dishevelled and he wore a faded white shirt under a woollen sweater that had a couple of holes in it and looked as though someone had used it as a tablecloth to serve dinner at some point in its recent history.

No matter, yer man was smiling and cheerful. True, he wasn't actually looking at anyone in particular. Rather, the eyes seemed to cover a wide field without immediate focus on anyone or anything, not unlike a radar screen.

But the intrinsic quality of the Irish when it comes to humour, shone through. Into sound and then eventually sight came a police helicopter, its rotor blades chattering overhead as it monitored the build-up of traffic and people around the stadium.

And brilliantly, instantly yet apropos absolutely nothing, yer man took a swig from his half-empty (or should that be half-full?) bottle of Jameson Irish whiskey, raised the other arm skywards and announced in a slurred voice, 'Whoever said pigs can't fly?'

Whoever said the Irish have lost the ability to make visitors and even locals laugh? The Celtic Tiger is long since deceased, slaughtered by its own rampant greed and self-obsession. Yet somehow, even in extremity, the Irish manage to go on making people laugh, putting a smile on the faces of visitors and locals alike. It is a wonderful attribute.

Of course, at the height of the money madness which led to the great financial crash of 2008, the land was rife with tales of insanity. And rugby men were by no means removed from the process. Paddy (he'd better remain anonymous) was a grand supporter of his local club, but farming was his game. He'd farmed all his life, his father before him, too.

The family farm was no super-sized affair. They had their nine acres and just enough cows to make a living. But then came a life-changing decision. Paddy went home one evening and announced to his startled wife, 'Yer know, this farming is all right. But I think I'm going into property to make some money. I've decided I will build houses.'

When yer woman had sat down and recovered from the shock, she asked him if he was feckin' mad. But he wasn't. After all, too many others were doing it for that to be the case. So in due time, the bank manager arrived to inspect the site and assess his request for a loan to erect nine houses. 'Course, there'd be no reason Paddy why you can't have the money,' he said. 'But tell me this – why would you want only nine? Why not 36?'

Paddy thought hard and agreed that had to make far more sense. So he borrowed 3m euros. It was apparently a small consideration on the part of the bank that his annual earnings were never more than 40,000 euros. Sometimes a lot less.

And so the great building adventure began, just as the train marked Economy began to roll downhill without brakes towards its doom. Paddy's 36 houses, funded by the bank, went up just as the economy went down. He managed to sell three.

With 33 houses empty and unsold out in the middle of nowhere, the bank panicked. Paddy was bankrupted. But he found a solution, as the Irish so often do. All he had to do, he discovered, was cross the border, go and live in Northern Ireland for two or three years and he could discharge his debts. Who knows, maybe even try again when things got better.

You see, I told you the Irish were smarter than the rest of us.

%% %% %% %% %%

Diary Notes: Dublin, somewhere, sometime.

So what is it I like about the Irish? Well, firstly you never know what to expect from them. And secondly, they always seem willing to help you, they're incredibly kind.

I know all about that former England rugby captain O. Cromwell leading a shocking pack of thugs over to play them at the first Lansdowne Road in the late 1550s and kicking lumps out of the locals.

Course, they'll never let you forget that. A friend once took me on a gentle Sunday morning drive around a local town somewhere out in the country beyond Dublin. 'And this,' I was told as we approached some memorial, 'was where the feckin' English murdered a few hundred of our lads.'

'Yeah, well, times change and all that,' I suggested.

The idea went down like a lead balloon.

Anyway, what's there to like about the Irish? Well, how long have you got? Let's start with their hospitality, their sense of fun, their loathing of cant and prima donnas. With a mischievous, evil sort of grin they take a delight in puncturing pomposity.

Then there's their sense of history, culture, enjoying life, music, literature, art and, finally, the wonderful kindness they show to visitors and a sheer wish to help.

SO it's another international day at Lansdowne Road. The old Lansdowne Road that is, with knee space between the seat in front that would make even Ryanair blush and the grim, grey, forbidding concrete of the main stands. Sure, it had all manner of failings. Internet in the media box overlooking the ground? Please, be serious.

Plenty of space on the press benches and easy access? Yes, sure, as long as you're both a contortionist and a midget.

But kindness, hospitality? Take the guy I ran into outside Lansdowne Road one afternoon after an Ireland v England match. I wasn't staying the night in Dublin; the liver was going to receive a well-deserved rest.

I was on the 1815 Aer Lingus flight to London and it looked a squeeze. Always did, but this one was especially tight.

So by the time I've written my reports for a couple of Sunday newspapers and picked up some quotes for Monday morning newspaper stories, it's getting very late. What I need is some luck – like a taxi cruising around the back of Lansdowne Road with a driver who reckons Fangio or Ayrton Senna were, well, nancy boys who wouldn't dare risk bruising their toenails by putting their foot down too hard on the accelerator pedal.

So I come hurtling out of the ground and fix my eye on the taxi rank outside the Berkeley Court hotel. Wonderful. On a usual day, there are about 450 of the damn vehicles. Tonight? Not one.

So, desperate straits call for desperate measures. I rush into the street and flag down a passing motorist. Literally, I dart into the middle of the road and put my arms out. He can either stop or flatten me. Desperate measures, all right.

By sheer good luck, he stops. And he leans out of the driver's side window.

'What's up, what's the problem?'

'I'm in serious trouble. Can you help?'

'Er, well, what do you want?'

'Are you going to the airport?'

'Er, no.'

'Anywhere near it?'

'Er, no. Er, jump in.'

And do you know what?

He said simply, 'When have you got to be there?'

'About ten minutes ago,' I told him.

What a man, what a drive. He took it as a personal challenge, a task thrown at him he simply wasn't going to miss out on. Mind you, I wasn't expecting to find a driver who was colour blind. Well, he must have been because he certainly couldn't differentiate between red and green lights. They all said go to him.

We overtook on the outside, on the inside; we carved up people like a master chef carved a joint of beef at a Sunday lunch, and we broke every speed limit they'd ever dreamed up in Ireland.

We arrived at Dublin airport in about 12 minutes, which was about 12 minutes less than it should have been. It was even time enough for me to relax and grab a coffee before boarding the plane. And when I tried to press a wad of notes into yer man's hand, he just smiled one of those wonderful Irish smiles, all smoothness like an Irish whiskey, and said, 'Ah sure no, 'twas great fun.' It was ever thus in Ireland.

I once arrived at Dublin airport on a Sunday morning for a flight out after an international the previous day. If you work as a freelance, you invariably have a Monday morning newspaper report to write for some paper somewhere. And on most papers' sports desks, it is always preferred if you can file by lunchtime so they have time to see the report and plan the page where it will sit.

It seemed a straightforward job to me but remember, this was in the days before the internet, computers and a click of a button sent your story straight on to the screen of someone sitting on the newspaper's sports desk. A very different world indeed.

I'd written 500 words before leaving the hotel and just had to telephone it to the paper. In those days, they had banks of typists with headphones, typing it all down as you read it out. Sounds like the dark ages nowadays but in reality it wasn't that long ago.

So I'm through to the paper but the switchboard operator advises me all the copy typists are busy.

'But it won't be long,' she tells me reassuringly. So I hold on and quite soon, one becomes available.

The trouble is, the clock is ticking all the while. I'm close by the boarding gate and have taken the precaution of chatting to one of the Aer Lingus ground staff at the gate to tell her I work for the media and have an important call to make.

They start boarding around the time I start filing. And it's soon apparent which process is the faster. Aer Lingus are filling up their plane a whole lot quicker than the newspaper is filling up its page with my story.

I try to suggest to the lady on the line I'm getting short of time. But her fingers tread a measured stride and she is not to be hurried. I'm standing in an open booth not far from the gate which leads down to the aircraft. And I see anxious looks on the face of my contact. I wave a reassuring arm as if to suggest I'll be right there.

But I won't yet, that's for sure. The copy taker ploughs on bravely, like a long-distance runner into a headwind. Progress may be sure but it's desperately slow.

In the end, she comes hurrying across to the phone booth, urging me, cajoling me to board this moment.

'Just give me two minutes and I'll be there,' I say.

Two turns into five and the spirit of willing understanding is clearly starting to fray. But I finish, drop the phone and run. Last on board again? This is becoming a habit I must quit.

But at least I'm on the right plane, which is more than could be said about one of my former Fleet Street colleagues one year as he prepared to depart for an England Five Nations match against France in Paris.

Delayed at Heathrow and distracted by a visit to a bar as he waited for the plane, our confused correspondent eventually made his way to what he thought was the right gate and subsequently, despite his ticket stating PARIS, was somehow admitted to the jet, seated himself comfortably and began to doze off. Alas, his slumbers were rudely interrupted as the aircraft manoeuvred its way towards a take-off position at the end of the runway by the captain's voice.

'Good evening ladies and gentlemen. We will shortly be taking off to the south-west and our flight time tonight to Istanbul is...'

At which stage a roar of protest came from seat 17B. 'Istanbul? What? Let me off at once.'

Well they did, once they'd landed safely in Istanbul. Sadly, by the time they got there, no more flights to Paris were leaving that night. Worse still, the first direct one out the next day to the French capital didn't leave until nearly midday.

Our intrepid traveller duly flew into Charles de Gaulle airport, jumped into a taxi to the Parc des Princes and arrived at half-time.

%, %, %, %, %

Diary Notes: Stadio Flaminio, Rome.
February 2005. Italy 17 Ireland 28

If all this sounds like every journey to or from an airport was like something out of a Marx brothers film, then there's a reason for that. It was.

Take my Rome fiasco after a Six Nations Championship game in the Eternal City a few years back. Same problem basically: I'd booked on the 6.40pm Easyjet Saturday night flight back to Bristol from Ciampino airport, the final one of the day. Can't remember the reason but I needed to get back to my home in Bath that night for something.

But you just knew it'd be as tight as a pair of leggings on a beer lover. But make plans, young man, make plans. And I did.

ROME on some of those February days is a magical place to be. You spend the morning idly window shopping down the Via Veneto, find a lovely café with the strongest smell of coffee wafting into the street and settle down to watch the Roman world and its citizens outside the door. It never fails to attract.

The winter sunshine is brilliant, alluring. It is a heady cocktail which invokes a sense of just being glad to be alive. And of course then there are the Romans, an entertainment in themselves.

They point, they gesticulate, they puff out their chests like mating pigeons and they have in every human mind a plethora of histrionics. Clearly, most also have a fantastic wardrobe at home. Cashmere coats rub shoulders with exquisite soft leather jackets, angora sweaters are set off by lambs' wool scarves. None look anything remotely resembling cheap but then, the mark-up in Italian shops is nothing like as high as the 300 per cent applied by that organised crime syndicate known as the UK retailers.

You can reach the Stadio Flaminio from the city centre by walking, taking a tram or a taxi. Basically, you cross the Piazza del Popolo and keep going. But I needed to make an arrangement for after the game, so took a taxi.

Roman taxi drivers are like their counterparts in all big cities; wolves in sheep's clothing. They smile and beguile as they fleece you, ever so subtly. Still, at least my man seemed reliable. So we reached a place past the stadium where he would wait afterwards, like the getaway driver after a bank robbery, and we could get quickly on to the motorway.

I told him to wait, whatever happened, I'd be there. And I was. The problem was, I was late.

So we're at the after-match press conferences in a room somewhere in the stadium and you get the feeling that sometimes the locals do this to spite the visiting team and media. You don't want to listen to the locals prattling on in Italian before the team you are covering arrives at the press conference. So what do they do? Send the Italians in first and make you suffer and sweat.

This time, the questions seemed to go on and on. And even when the official Italian press conference ended, coach Nick Mallett then did a couple of TV interviews in the same place, which meant the Irish officials could not start their own press conference.

I've known Nick for years and he's a great bloke. But I'd cheerfully have physically thrown him off the stage where the press conferences were being held if he wasn't so damn big.

At last, at last, the Irish arrived. I looked at my watch and winced. They took questions and I covered maybe the first six or seven. At that stage I slipped out and ran for it.

Would my driver be there or would he have given up, thrown his arms around in a hissy-fit and gone home? After all, I was by now a quarter of an hour late. But miracle of miracles, there he stood, anxiously waiting by the car in the pre-arranged spot. But there was bad news. Well, there always is, isn't there? It wouldn't be the Saturday afternoon of an international rugby weekend if there wasn't some problem somewhere.

A crash had closed part of the autopista down which he had planned our escape route from the city towards Ciampino airport. We had no choice but to take our chance through the city streets.

I don't know whether you've ever driven in or around Rome between 5pm and 6pm on a Saturday but I can tell you, all human life is there. You get people stopping and blocking all the traffic while they wait for someone else to load their shopping into the boot of a parked car, get into the car, take off their coat, re-arrange their hair, put on a seat belt and re-arrange their truss for all I know.

And then, after all that, they need about four attempts to reverse their car into a space into which you could comfortably fit a Sherman tank. And all the while I'm in the back checking my watch about every half minute and seeing a largely hopeless situation becoming diabolical.

I also have something else to do. Before 6pm, I have to file 1,000 words from the press conference, with quotes from the two coaches and leading players, especially the Irish, for a Sunday newspaper in Ireland.

By now, they don't have copy takers any more, the poor creatures have become obsolete thanks to computers, but as I couldn't type a sensible sentence in this car as it swayed and weaved around the city streets, avoiding but more usually hitting the myriad potholes along the way, I have to ad-lib it to my office via a mobile phone.

Ad-lib? That means you have to focus your mind intently and as you speak the words to someone in the office, imagine how the story will look when it appears in the newspaper the next day. All my notes from the press conference were in shorthand, so you have no more than a few seconds to 'read' the shorthand notes, all lines, curves, squiggles, dots and dashes and get the words into your mind and then use another part of your mind (assuming you have one) to think of an intro to the story and appropriate sentences where you can best use those quotes.

It helps if you can do all this in the calm and quiet of an office. It is, let us say, something of an impediment to be doing it in the back of a Rome taxi speeding towards an airport, with people and cars all over the road, the clock ticking down and the driver in front swearing and shouting at pedestrians or drivers at most junctions.

But hey, I signed up for all this long ago so I'm not complaining. For truth to be told, the adrenaline it stirs, bubbling away inside, is a wonder to behold. At times it seems all but uncontrollable, like a tap turned full on and jammed. But the intensity of the focus required gets the job done. A thousand words ad-libbed are soon winging their way from my office to Dublin for the next morning's paper.

Meanwhile, we weave and dart our way around and through the Rome evening traffic until we come to a piazza. And a hold-up. Temporary traffic lights? An accident, perhaps? Cows crossing the street? None of these.

We are treated instead to the classically Italian spectacle of two cars at crazy angles across the road, both with some minor damage and the respective drivers engaged in a fist fight. This scrap is being played out against a blaring backdrop of car horns, blasting away into the night, not least from my taxi driver.

After some minutes, the pugilists are quietly convinced by a bystander that a fist fight in the street with the traffic backed up might not be awfully clever because the Carabinieri will doubtless be along shortly. So arm-waving replaces the fists and the two combatants get back into their cars and resume their journeys. All in a Roman evening.

The journey is slow, the hold-ups endless. And I'm shouting from the back at the driver, pointing at my watch and telling him the world is about to end if we don't make the airport in time. It is then he begins to show those true qualities that mark out Italian taxi drivers from their fellow citizens.

We approach a set of lights at red and he simply ignores them, goes straight through nearly colliding with a couple of cars coming from a side street. Horns roar, arms and fingers are hyperactive. More importantly, he keeps going.

At another set of red lights, he can't go straight through as he has about ten cars blocking his way to the front of the grid. So what does he do? Drive up on to the pavement, squeeze between a lamppost and the fence and drive down the pavement until he's passed the lights and it is clear to re-join the road.

The man must be mad. I applaud generously.

They will close the gate at 6.10pm for my flight and at 6.07pm, he drives into the airport but stops some way from the departure terminal. I shout at him, telling him to keep going and point to where I need to be dropped off.

Euro bank notes flutter around the inside of the taxi as I hurl a pile in his general direction, open the door and run for the check-in desk.

There is one long queue – for a moment, I relax, until I realise that is for the Liverpool flight. Down the other side of that queue, is an empty space leading to a check-in desk which has a sign up for 'Bristol'. I arrive at the desk at 6.09pm.

I don't remember much about the flight home. I think I crashed out after the long day.

※ ※ ※ ※ ※

Diary Notes: The K Club, Dublin. August 2007

You see, the great thing about the Irish is, they don't get flustered if you break the rules. Even better, they never hold it against you if you've done so to get a drink. I suppose they must empathise with someone in such a plight.

WE'D been to a dinner, a big official one at a beautiful estate out in the country, about an hour from Dublin city centre. But the fact was, it was too big a do – about 500 people turned up in the enormous chandelier-draped marquee.

The idea was courageous but have you ever been to a dinner with 500 people and had a meal to remember? You either see one end of the room finishing their meal as you're about to start or by the time the main course arrives it's half cold. Or both if you're really unlucky.

So we didn't linger long. Yet we had been comparatively tardy by the standards of certain others. A car drove us back to the K Club, scene of the 2006 Ryder Cup, where most of us were staying. And when we tumbled out at the famous club, it seemed the perfect idea to find the bar and have a nightcap.

Comfortably ensconced on a couple of high chairs beside the bar were two old journalist friends of mine. But there was a look of concern on their faces.

'Oh we came back a while ago,' they said. 'But the problem is, the barman has disappeared here and we've been waiting ages for a drink.'

What else could a visiting Englishman do but serve two thirsty Irishmen with a drink? It seemed only manners, a matter of courtesy.

You don't need to be a qualified barman to serve a drink if you've served your qualification in the world of journalism. Any journalist worth his salt has probably stood at more bars than any single barman on the planet. So we ought to know a thing or two and hey, besides, it was gone 11pm and who was bothering to count out measures any more?

So I jettisoned my jacket, rolled up both sleeves and took over as the K Club's new barman. With a beaming smile.

'Now gentlemen,' I enquired politely. 'What will it be?'

'I'll have a pint of Guinness thank you barman,' said one.

'Mine's a gin and tonic,' said another. And the lady in the room opted for a glass of red wine.

So the tap pouring the Guinness overruns just a teeny bit but hey, who cares? And I might just have got the mix between gin and tonic water a touch wrong. 'Christ,' said my second customer. 'I don't know where you learned to make 'em like that but I'll have another. Could I have some ice this time, please?'

Why, I even began to juggle little blocks of ice into the air, bouncing them out of my fingers, on to my wrist and then an arm before flicking one into the gin and tonic. In the meantime, I had to be sure the red wine was worthy of my serving it, so I slurped down two or three mouthfuls. Just to be sure, as they say in these parts.

By now the Guinness was ready for topping up, another glass of red wine was poured and handed to the lady and the gentleman tackling the G&Ts looked rather like he'd been standing too close to a hot fire. His cheeks were glowing, at least the ones you could see.

I was even so courteous as to serve two total strangers who approached the bar requesting drinks. Well why not? All on the house, of course. We couldn't be bothering about anything as vulgar as money at that time of night.

The assembled company happy with their drinks, I resumed my seat on the other side of the bar and sipped my own pint of the black stuff. And do you know what? I'd barely had time to finish half a pint before yer man the barman suddenly reappeared with the words, 'Now lads, what can I get yer?'

They sure know how to pour drinks down your throat in that country.

☆ ☆ ☆ ☆ ☆

Diary Notes: To Castlemartin, County Kildare, one of the then homes of Sir Anthony O'Reilly, owner of Independent Newspapers & Media Worldwide (INM). One of several occasions in the 2000s.

ON 23 June 2014, Tony O'Reilly was declared by a court in Ireland to be insolvent after he had lost a legal battle to delay a court order that he should pay £18m to Allied Irish Banks.

O'Reilly had asked for a six-month delay on the action so as to conduct an orderly sale of assets.

Once Ireland's most successful businessman, it is said that O'Reilly lost around 230m euros (with his brother-in-law Peter Goulandris losing roughly a similar amount) trying to save Waterford Wedgwood before it fell into receivership in 2009.

It was also alleged that O'Reilly spent around 350m euros buying shares in Independent News & Media in a doomed attempt to see off the rival shareholder challenge of Denis O'Brien.

At 78, just about all O'Reilly had worked his entire life to create had crashed in ruins.

Now I am perfectly sure – and I'm willing to bet Tony O'Reilly himself would agree with me – that all the jealous, envious, never-haves, downright disingenuous, will have been cheering themselves to sleep that June night.

For the fact is, there is nothing so omnipresent, not just in Ireland but in so many countries of the world, as the tall poppy syndrome. Being successful in life puts you out among the bullets being fired. Achieving is a dastardly crime in many people's eyes. Being rich and successful is virtually a hanging offence.

What is it someone once said? 'The hardest thing about being successful is trying to find someone genuinely pleased for you.' How true.

O'Reilly's sin, if that is what it was in some people's eyes, was to achieve, to work hard, get the rewards from his own initiatives and enjoy them. Was it ostentatious to own a country mansion an hour out of Dublin, with a mile and a half of the River Liffey flowing through its grounds? Sure, if you'd got the money by robbing banks. O'Reilly didn't.

He had a brilliant business career but fatally, he made financial mistakes. One of them, incidentally, was spending so much of his own money trying desperately to stave off the collapse of a company he saw as one of Ireland's finest, Waterford. Again, if that was a crime, string him up. But I beg to differ.

You speak as you find and I have no agenda here. I am fully prepared to say I worked for him for about ten years in all and found him the best proprietor I ever worked for by a country mile. He treated you as a professional, expected you to behave as such and he rewarded you very well for your endeavours.

I went all over the world working for the many newspapers in his group. And I worked endlessly, each and every day into the night. Then I'd get up in the morning and do three new stories for newspapers, all before breakfast. That was how it was, that was how I wanted it.

At the 2003 Rugby World Cup in Australia, a six-week-long slog, I worked all day every day of the week on stories for newspapers in the group all around the world. Starting at 7am, I'd usually be finished by 6pm and have about an hour off.

Then at 7pm each day, I'd settle down to write a book I was doing at that time, the life story of the BBC rugby commentator Bill McLaren.

When I flew home after the tournament, I'd written hundreds of stories for the group and finished a 90,000-word book. Slept well on that flight. But then, others often worked just as hard. But I am not convinced they were as well rewarded.

O'Reilly once called me at home one night and we talked. 'You work so hard,' he told me at one point in the conversation.

'Look,' I replied. 'I've never had a problem working hard. I'm like a lot of people in that respect. But like a lot of others, the only problem I've encountered far too many times is that people don't want to pay you commensurate with the hard work you put in. You do, and you get a hell of a lot back. It's a win-win situation.'

I don't believe it was just our shared love of rugby football that brought us together on many occasions. Once, I found myself at a private dinner on a Sunday night at his home at Castlemartin. I was the only non-member of his family present, a considerable privilege and a lovely evening.

Another time, my wife and I sat up with him until 4am one day in his study, just talking about life and the world. He was never less than hugely stimulating company. His memories, of boyhood in Ireland, his reflections on the many changes in Irish society and of business times across the Atlantic in America, were never less than riveting.

Success? It lay all around you in those days. Whether it was at Castlemartin, where he had a beautiful log cabin built in the grounds beside the river and he would have afternoon tea sometimes or just go there for some peace to read, or in Normandy where his family owned a beautiful chateau on the site of William the Conqueror's castle, he was the most generous of hosts.

He told a wonderful story about the Monet he had once bought at auction in New York. When he was 16, he and a friend took their bicycles on the ferry to Le Havre and cycled down to Rouen to start their holiday. As they sat on the steps of Rouen Cathedral, an old man came up with some pictures of Monet's painting of the cathedral, explaining how the artist had portrayed the building in various stages of the strong, midday sunlight.

The great Impressionist painted several versions and one of them, O'Reilly bought one day.

He was always the best raconteur most people had ever heard and he told this story brilliantly. One of the drivers who worked on the estate was asked to go to Dublin airport to collect a package. He didn't have a clue what it was.

When he got it back, they invited him into the main house at a pre-arranged time, when the Monet would be unpacked and hung on the wall.

But first, they told him how much it was worth.

'Jaysus, I should have had an armed escort,' he replied.

No, they said, that would just draw attention to it.

So they rolled off the packing, got the great work out of its wooden case and put it on the wall. Yer man took on a somewhat puzzled expression.

As O'Reilly said, 'When we want to insult someone in Ireland we tend to start the sentence with, "If you don't mind me saying so..."'

And yer man, clearly bewildered that anyone should pay millions of pounds for this particular work of art, said, 'If you don't mind me saying so, it's very bloody faded.'

O'Reilly's face as he told the tale was as bright as the sunshine on Monet's canvas.

It gives me no pleasure whatsoever to record his disastrous losses. But I am immensely proud to say I worked for him and knew him in good times. He was and remains a remarkable human being.

He has been denigrated and criticised by many. But would those who castigate have given a fraction of the sums he cheerfully handed out to charities and other good causes?

Would they have raised hundreds of thousands of euros, probably millions over the years, to help others? Unlikely. Would they have regularly signed personal cheques to help out friends in their time of need like he did? I doubt it.

Financial adversity late in his life does not mask one factor about Tony O'Reilly, or Sir Anto as his long-time driver used to call him. He is one of the most generous men I ever met, not just financially but with his time and consideration for others. And that needs saying because he would never mention it himself.

FRANCE

Diary Notes: Heathrow airport, Friday 1 March 1974.
The trouble with this job is that everyone thinks it's a fantasy. When I was hired by one newspaper publisher and told my closest pal some of the terms, he exclaimed, 'But this isn't a job, it's a gift.'

It might appear that way. Business-class trips upstairs in Qantas to Australia, visits to South Africa and the alluring Cape for rugby internationals, weekends in the south of France in a rugby-mad town. It might evoke some mental images of a fantasy for rugby-mad men. But there are plenty of trips that prove to be a pain in the backside or just plain dangerous.

I MEAN, take this shambles. God, it is horrendous. You would never exactly nominate Heathrow as your favoured venue for a quiet little soiree or family supper. But this is ridiculous.

Outside, frequent snow showers are being blown around on a strong, ice cold wind. Inside the hot, cramped terminal, there are thousands of people and mountains of luggage stacked up everywhere.

Friday night flights out of Heathrow or most London airports for that matter are really only for the sadistic. Tonight, there are two problems: the weather and a strike by British Airways workers.

Much of northern Europe is engulfed by the snow and ice which doesn't help. I'm trying to get to Paris for the France–England Five Nations match tomorrow afternoon. It is England's first visit to a new ground in the French capital, the Parc des Princes. But how to get there?

The queues are endless and stultifyingly boring. Eventually, we are told there is only one option (apart from packing up and going home).

Air France is attempting to take up the slack but you can only book a guaranteed seat either going out to Paris or coming back, not both ways. I opt for the return because I'm working on Sunday afternoon at Richmond and need to be sure of arriving on time. So, like thousands of others, I have to take pot luck on any old airline going over to the snow-swept French capital. And my luck is out.

For a start, no-one knows what they will be on because they're bringing planes from the US heading direct to Paris, into London to collect this abandoned army of passengers.

Now I have to concede, flying Saudi Arabian airlines has never exactly been top of my 'Most Wanted Experiences in Life' list. This intends no disrespect to what I am sure is a thoroughly worthy airline, but the opinion was cemented on concrete, as it were, a few hours later when we approached Beauvais airfield in the dark, swirling snow, bounced down on to the runway, took off again, bounced down a second time and then slithered clearly out of control for hundreds of yards down the runway until coming to a God-decreed halt a few yards inside the airfield's perimeter fence.

The pilot was presumably no more than an interested observer, just like the rest of us.

I have to say, I've had funnier experiences in my life.

But that said, at least I'd made it to Paris and could cover the match. It turned out to be a 12-12 draw, one try each with England's coming from that elegant centre (or wing) David Duckham.

It was that sort of night too, nothing dramatic, certainly not for me because I had to be up and out at the crack of dawn to reach the airport for the early Air France flight back to London. There are colleagues of mine who'd be up all night and go straight to the airport. And good luck to them, they had some great times. But with work the next day that's not always the best preparation.

The airport was again as crammed full as a tin of sardines. And as chaotic as Heathrow had been 36 hours earlier. But at least the weather was a bit better, although those travellers who hadn't booked a guaranteed seat for the return leg, still had to take their chance for the flight back to England.

I checked in, boarded the Air France plane and dozed off. Very soon, we were gliding into Heathrow on a cold but bright Sunday mid-morning. Bags collected, I made my way to Richmond to report on a club match for *The Times*, which they had ordered on the Friday.

There seemed no rush to get home afterwards, either. I'd filed my report and a long, tiring weekend was finally over. So I headed for the warm, welcoming bar at the Athletic Ground for a couple of pints and a bit of relaxation. That was a whole lot more pleasurable than just missing a couple of trains home, which then happened. Eventually, I rang the bell of my parents' house, where I was staying, around 9pm on the Sunday. An extraordinary scene then unfolded.

The door opened and my parents, my mother with tears in her eyes, gaped and gawped at me, at first unable to say a word. They then both fell on me.

I grinned. 'I've only been away for the weekend, what happened?' I joked. 'Did you miss me that much?'

'But haven't you heard?' they said, almost in unison. The grin began to freeze on my face.

'No, what?'

'A Turkish airlines plane leaving Paris for London crashed on take-off. England rugby fans, everyone on board is dead. When you didn't come home earlier, we thought you were on it.'

It transpired that 346 people had been killed, the highest ever death count of any single plane crash at that time. It happened because a ground crew worker failed to close a rear door properly. As the jet took off, it blew open and brought down the whole plane, sending it diving into the forest of Ermenonville, north of Paris.

Many of the victims were rugby fans, a few rugby writers too, who had been unable to book a guaranteed return flight to London but had managed to get on the Turkish airlines jet which made a special stop in Paris en route from Istanbul to London, to collect some of the stranded passengers.

It transpired later that it was the next plane out after my Air France jet had left.

%, %, %, %, %,

Diary Notes: To Paris, early 1985.

Jean-Pierre Rives, legendary figure of French rugby these last ten years, retired at the end of the 1984 season. Sought by every publishing house in France to pen his sporting autobiography, suddenly a rogue Englishman has entered the field of runners and riders. Much to the chagrin of the locals.

I was talking to a pal of mine, a publisher in London, about some projects. A few ideas were discussed but he admitted 'The book we would really like to do is Jean-Pierre Rives' autobiography. But the French will have it sewn up.'

'Well I know him well enough, I'll ask him,' I replied. A day or two later, that familiar soft voice, almost sluggish and dreamy in tone, came on the line. 'Yes, Peter, we can talk about it. Come to Paris and we will see.'

So I went, and he agreed, which set off a series of petulant hissy-fits among the rugby-writing fraternity all over France. It was as if Josephine had deserted Napoleon and gone off with some lord from the English shires.

One night, Rives and I dined with one of them. At first, I thought the garlic cruncher was about to plunge a Gallic fork up my nostrils. After that, he just sulked. Which I assumed was wonderfully French.

We agreed to do the book together but that was the easy part. For a start, Jean-Pierre had a memory like a sieve. Ask him about the three tries he scored in one match and he'd smile. 'No, not me, Peter,' he would say charmingly. 'When was this? I do not remember this.' And it went on.

It wasn't a wind-up – he genuinely couldn't remember much about his career because it no longer interested him. He'd long since jettisoned all those memories.

Anyway, with the publisher's advance banked and probably spent by now, we had to do something. So we planned a series of meetings at his Paris apartment.

SOMETIMES, I would set off around midnight from southern England to journey through the night to Paris. It was a whole lot easier than fighting the morning traffic in Paris and I'd arrive by 7am. Invariably, the lovely Jennifer, Jean-Pierre's American model girlfriend, would welcome me at the door. God, those Californian girls. What was it The Beach Boys sang? 'I wish they all could be Californian.'

We became very close, Jennifer and I. So close we almost married one day. But I'll tell you about that in a minute.

So I've parked the car in Jean-Pierre's side street near Republique in Paris this particular morning, gathered piles of reference books and such like to work with him for much of the week and banged on the huge wooden door. Eventually, it is opened, furtively, and a small head peeps around it.

'Bonjour Jennifer,' I say but the words freeze in my throat. For whoever this fabulous creation of a female is, she certainly isn't Jennifer. But she is equally charming and the black nightie she is wearing on a cold autumn morning certainly isn't any disincentive to the caller. It's a tragedy for French males they don't have milkmen in France.

A peck on each cheek is followed by a soft purr of a sentence, 'Bonjour Peter, Jean-Pierre zed you would be 'ere. Come in.'

He's completely calm and relaxed when he and I are alone inside the apartment. 'Peter,' he says, a broad wink from one eye. 'Jennifer is en vacances; 'zees is la nouvelle Jennifer.' So that's all right then. Glad we've cleared up that little source of possible misunderstanding.

Jennifer, mark one, came to stay with me once in England. Drop-dead gorgeous as ever, she was going to a wedding in London the next day and I offered her a lift into Chelsea, as I was going close by anyway.

But what with one thing and another, we were late and the 11am start was perilously close. She thought it was at Chelsea

Town Hall, so we stopped outside and rushed in, all breathless and excited, to check it was the right place.

An elderly gentleman with pince-nez glasses perched on the end of a long nose, peered up from his sheaf of papers. 'The wedding,' we said, in unison.

'Ah now, don't be worried. It will all work out in the end, you will be married,' he said. It's probably fair to say I looked hopeful and Jennifer looked alarmed.

Back in Paris, long days would be spent attempting to fire Jean-Pierre's faltering memory. Trouble was, he liked to talk about anything except rugby. Those Gallic eyes began to droop, and he'd stop halfway through a sentence. But talk to him about his art and it would be as if you had given him a couple of bursts of 220 volts.

We were sitting there late one afternoon and he announced suddenly, 'We must go to the airport. We have dinner tonight in Geneve.' Well, why not?

The problem was, he had left it absurdly late to get to Charles de Gaulle airport. Boring day-to-day events like traffic jams held no interest for Rives so he never considered them. But as we set off, with me driving, he got more and more edgy. 'Faster, faster,' he urged. Extricating yourself from the snarl of a Paris rush hour traffic jam would have required the skills of Houdini, not an English sports writer. We even tried a couple of diversions up pavements which brought an instant, warm rapport with pedestrians. At one point, I received the ultimate compliment for some wild, improbable manoeuvre which nearly cut short the lives of a couple of passers-by.

'You are a crazy driver, just like the Parisians,' beamed my companion. It was a badge of honour.

We then tried a short cut. That was a disaster waiting to happen. It reached its apogee when we found ourselves out on a country road and had to ask a farmer for directions. We could hear the planes, see them climbing into the sky but could we reach the airport? Could we heck?

We did in the end, but of course far, far too late for the flight to Geneva. That was probably halfway there by the time we rushed into the concourse. But when you travelled with Monsieur Rives in those days all was never lost.

With my help, he has dragged not only an overnight bag but a huge golf bag and full set of clubs up to the check-in desk. Now under normal airline rules, you have as much chance of getting a set of golf clubs on to a plane under the aegis of cabin baggage as trying to manoeuvre your recently deceased grandfather on to the jet and settle him comfortably beside the window into seat 8A.

But this was Air France, this was Jean-Pierre Rives and this was a young lady at check-in having a public orgasm in front of the great man. They cosied up close together, blond hair (his) brushing blushing cheek (hers) and a few shy smiles and soft words later, we are dragging the enormous golf bag up the steps on to the plane. Would they fit in the overhead locker? Yes, if you'd drilled holes in three lockers so they could lay flat. As it was, they had to lay down on the floor in front of us and anyone rushing past to the loo had to be careful they didn't trip over them, go flying forward into the flight deck and end up with their head stuck out of the front window of the plane.

Honestly, you couldn't make up this stuff.

So to Geneva: city of bankers, cuckoo clocks and a shocking war record.

We climb into the chauffeured car and head out of the city, up into the hills. By now, it is dark and from our increasingly elevated viewpoint, we can see the lights twinkling all around the lake. I don't have a clue where we're going and Jean-Pierre, as per usual, is asleep beside me on the back seat. Never mind his rugby prowess; this guy could sleep for France.

In about an hour, we come to an inn and tumble out. Inside, we enter the quintessential Swiss chalet; wooden floor and beams, wooden seats beside tables, red and white check table cloths and cushions and a roaring log fire on a cold and increasingly wet autumn night. And there waiting for us is our dining companion, the French Formula 1 motor racing driver Alain Prost. Another quiet day in the life of Jean-Pierre Rives.

He once took another player's passport when they were about to fly overseas for a tour to Romania. Rives, travelling with the French Universities party, had forgotten his own passport. But another player decided at the airport he could not travel due to injury, so Jean-Pierre borrowed his. The fact that the other player was a tall man and had very dark, short hair compared to Rives's long, flowing blond locks, made not a fig of difference.

And when he got back to the airport at the end of the tour, his team-mates were astonished to see him wearing only shorts, a T-shirt and flip-flops without any of his bags. 'These people are so poor I gave them all my clothes,' he explained. 'They need them more than me.'

That was Jean-Pierre down to a tee. He would give you the shirt off his back if you wanted it. And he has never changed. He's still one of the nicest men who ever played rugby football.

But if you wanted to write a book about his rugby career, I quickly realised it was pointless staying in Paris. So with my brilliant girlfriend, who was conveniently fluent in both French and Spanish, we set off for the great rugby lands of the south – Perpignan, Narbonne, Lourdes, Beziers, Toulouse, Dax, Tarbes, Pau etc.

And there we tracked down just about all Jean-Pierre's mates to elicit the real story of the man and his times. Jo Maso in Perpignan, Michel Palmie in Beziers, Didier Codorniou, that prince of centres, in Gruissan near Narbonne, Walter Spanghero in Narbonne, Jean-Michel Aguirre and Philippe Dintrans in Tarbes, Jacques Fouroux, Roland Bertranne in Bagneres de Bigorre, Jean Salut and Jean Claude Skrela not to mention Rives's mother, father and other relatives, all in Toulouse, Jean-Pierre Bastiat and Claude Dourthe in Dax and the late, great Robert Paparemborde in Pau.

Great men, great game, and the passion for rugby in the towns and villages of France in those days crackled like the local electricity supply. When a provincial club reached the final of the French Championship, the whole town was decked out in the club's colours. Butchers had the heads and carcasses of pigs festooned in ribbons in their windows; almost every shop had some special display to support the team.

Back in Paris, times with Jean-Pierre were invariably mad, manic and muddled. But then, in the France of those times, just about anything seemed possible.

※ ※ ※ ※ ※

Diary Notes: To Paris, 3 February 1990.

France 7 England 26 in the Five Nations Championship at the Parc des Princes.

Now officially, 49,370 people crammed into the Parc des Princes for this humdinger of a game. What was more important was that it was a miracle anyone got there safely.

A vicious storm with freak winds had dominated Le Weekend, in both the UK and northern France. Ferries across the English Channel had been delayed for hours due to the gales, the sea was boiling. Of course, the lumbering ferries are usually delayed anyway. But at least this time they had an excuse.

When we finally arrived in Calais, driving down the motorway to Paris was like gripping the wheel of a car in an engineer's wind tunnel. A couple of people were killed by flying roof tiles on the Saturday morning in the French capital. In all, about five people died.

In fact, the weather was bad everywhere. My great pal Clem Thomas, then rugby correspondent of the London Sunday paper *The Observer* had taken eight hours (instead of the usual four) to drive from Swansea to my home in Tunbridge Wells, Kent, on the Thursday night where we were hosting him and his wife, Joyce, for dinner.

Clem played in the days when fun was synonymous with rugby. Whether he was playing for his beloved Swansea and physically manhandling some opponent from Cardiff or Newport, proudly wearing the three feathers of Wales against New Zealand or causing chaos with his chums for the Barbarians on the Easter tour they used to make of South Wales, Clem enjoyed life. Hotel managers and their staff generally went in fear and trembling when one of those rugby teams came to stay.

Who else would have managed to tie one chambermaid's panties to the top of the hotel flagpole, fluttering proudly above the town of Penarth in South Wales, one Easter night? Clem and his pals were back in town.

Cliff Morgan, who played with Clem for Wales and the British Lions in the 1950s, once memorably described Clem Thomas as 'the only man I ever knew who took his work on to the rugby field'. Cliff's comment might have sounded amusing but contained an element of deadpan seriousness.

Clem Thomas was a butcher by trade.

So we'd given it a lash, as they say, that night (and I don't mean the weather). But when the burglar alarm was set off at 3am on Friday by the high winds, it wasn't exactly ideal preparation for Clem's next day. The whole house was awake and Clem had to leave at 6am to drive to Dover to catch an early ferry. The Channel Tunnel would not be open until May 1994.

In the event, we fell asleep and couldn't wake up in the morning. But Clem and Joyce, who did, battled through pouring rain and high winds to reach Dover, only to sit for hours in the port as a succession of sailings were postponed or cancelled.

I always wondered, years after, whether that night and the next day was a contributory factor in what was to happen in Paris that dramatic Saturday.

IT just so happened that the A international between the two countries had been played at the Stade Jean Bouin, just across the road from the Parc des Princes in south-west Paris, on the Saturday morning. I wasn't covering it for anyone specific but thought I'd go along to watch. It was a good thing I did even if I never took a single note.

But this was a reminder about the need for a journalist always to be prepared.

Once the morning match was over, we adjourned across the road to the Parc des Princes in anticipation of the main event, for which I was writing. You climbed several flights of stairs to reach the press room at the Parc and when we got there, a delectable sight greeted us.

Filling fully one side of the vast press room was an enormous spread of food, above which was strung a banner. It read 'Produits Artisanals de la Charente'. It was a promotion of all the great culinary delights of that French region and you could climb in.

Baskets of oysters and prawns lay plonked next to plates full of foie gras. Bottles of cognac stood beside others of Pineau des Charente, as well as red and white wine. Plates of meat, cheeses and salads plus copious amounts of bread and some small, delicate patisseries for a dessert, completed the feast. It knocked into a cocked hat the usual plate of half-stale sandwiches, with ends curling up, which were to be found in the press room at most English clubs at that time.

But if this was an aesthetic delight, a sight close by was by no means as appealing. Sitting in a chair was Clem Thomas. He was sweating profusely, short of breath and looked grey. I thought at once he must have eaten a bad oyster or something like it.

'Clem, what's the trouble?' I asked.

'Pete, I think I'm having a heart attack. You'll have to do the match for us. A thousand words on the final whistle. Oh, and 500 on the A game this morning.'

With that, he slumped back on his seat, waiting for the ambulance that had been called.

Now, some very famous people have had heart attacks in the French capital, many of them from the world of music. Georges Bizet, Maria Callas, Jim Morrison and Robert Palmer all suffered attacks there. I was never a budding opera singer or composer but even so, I nearly joined them.

Scrabbling around among my fellow writers for the details of scorers from the morning match, I was still dictating that report to the copy typist back in London as the French and English anthems blared out across the ground.

When you cover an international rugby match, it's as well to prepare properly. Acquiring a sound knowledge of the players appearing in that particular match is always important.

Bill McLaren, the BBC TV rugby commentator, used to start his preparatory work for internationals on Mondays at his home in Hawick, up in the Scottish borders. He was a real professional, Bill.

I'd prepared for this match, but not for writing the back page lead story in one of the UK national Sunday papers. And with the game going on, I had few opportunities to think up specific lines or phrases. All I could do was concentrate ruthlessly.

Eventually, from a scribble of shorthand notes that crawled across the pages of my notebook like an escargot inebriated by Pineau des Charente, I managed to pen a couple of phrases. But the problem was, you couldn't take your eyes off the game. Or the weather.

At one end of the ground, behind a high fence, stood a large sports facility covered in green rubber cladding that housed squash or indoor tennis courts. Or at least it had at the start. By half-time, it looked like someone had taken a giant, unseen pair of scissors to it. A great slash lay across the middle and two huge pieces flapped helplessly in the gale.

At half-time, poor Clem was still sitting sweating profusely downstairs in the press room. 'Pete,' he pleaded, 'if they don't get an ambulance soon and get me to hospital, I'm going to die here.'

We berated the press room officials and got them chasing the medics. At last, they arrived and rushed him to hospital. Clem was lucky. The one they took him to turned out to be one of the top heart hospitals not just in France but all Europe.

He survived.

England, meanwhile, led by Will Carling, had adapted brilliantly to the impossible conditions and were doing a lot more than just surviving. They were untouchable and, incredibly given the conditions, almost error-free for most of the game. France hardly got a look-in but it was the excellence of the English play that stood out.

That was good news for me. In a sense, the story wrote itself. Even so, when I picked up the telephone in the press box with ten minutes of the game left and started dictating the report as the match came towards its conclusion, it'd be fair to say that the adrenaline was flowing as fast as the grey clouds that the gale was sending scudding over the Parc des Princes.

I had no time actually to write anything down. All I could do was digest the crucial lessons from the match, think up a couple of neat phrases and start ad-libbing my 1,000-word report. Or to put it another way, filing straight out of what passed for my brain. You can understand why I was so concerned.

But I was lucky the outcome was already obvious well before the end of the 80 minutes. If a result is in doubt when you start filing a report, catastrophes can occur.

I remembered one night at the Nou Camp, covering Barcelona in football's European Cup. Ten minutes from the end, Barca, who had been in charge throughout, led 2-0. Five minutes from the end, it was 2-1 and I began to sweat. Two minutes from time came the equaliser. It finished 2-2 and I had to throw away everything I'd written for the London daily papers about Barcelona's supremacy and start again. Nightmare stuff when you're working against a very tight deadline.

But this was different. England had won and won superbly. And you pour your life into a report like that. No ifs, buts or maybes. You do it, you crack it. No excuses are possible. Make a muck of it and you won't get another chance. Hence the manic levels of intensity when it comes to concentration.

The adrenaline flowed, sweeping with it my report. Throughout, I was checking with the copy typist in London how many words I had written. If you write 50 or even 30 too many, the sub-editors, under huge time pressures themselves, will go ballistic, wasting time cutting your story to fit the slot. I filed the teams on the bottom of the report, plus the ubiquitous list of scorers. And that was it.

You can't change it, not for that first edition of the newspaper, anyway. What is there is there; the wrong phrases, mistakes, misinterpretations, the whole lot, you have got to live with them.

My call to the sports desk in London about the possibility of re-writing for the later editions, those distributed closer to London and the Home Counties, brought the sound of surprise.

'Only if you really want to,' was the response. 'We're very happy with it as it is.'

That sounded good so I left it at that. Sometimes when you write from your inner soul, it's a whole lot more piquant. And they really were happy. When I got back to London the following week, the sports editor told me, 'Yours was the best report of all the Sunday papers.'

There was just one problem. At 4am the next day in Paris, as we entered another nightclub in the French capital, my appetite for more action insatiable, my weary travel companion moaned, 'Just when on earth is that adrenaline going to stop flowing?'

%% %% %% %% %%

Diary Notes: To Auch, south west France. September 1990

So the question in the forefront of our minds this particular day is where to go for a weekend break. We've had a diet of non-stop sport; it seems like forever since we didn't have a weekend working.

So I ask the lady where she fancies. Milan, Madrid, Lisbon, Paris? You have to be careful here 'cos she's wary about anywhere in France. Been dragged around too many French rugby towns down the years not to bear the scars from those shocking late nights and ending up knee deep in mud, red wine bottles and discarded Gauloises.

Madrid and the Prado? I'm not sure. Would have been a stone-cold certainty if Real had been at home in La Liga that weekend. But they weren't. Milan? Well, Inter are home but only to Cesena. Small fry. So we go on.

'I know,' I say. 'What about Auch?'

'What about Auch?' she says, coldly. 'We went there a few months ago for that France match against Romania. Don't you remember?'

Do I remember? You try driving a car all the way from London to Auch one-handed, because it felt like your guts were going to fall out the whole way, then spending most of the weekend ill in bed at the hotel, while the lady went out to swish dinners in places like a 15th-century town hall, and a Michelin chef's restaurant. Never forget Auch.

So why Auch? 'Well,' I explain gently, 'it looked a nice place, I didn't see much of it before and it is full of history. Old capital of Gascony, statue of D'Artagnan: Musketeer Country as the guide books say. And barely an hour by hire car from Toulouse airport. So, easy to get to.'

Her facial expression alters. 'Who are they playing this weekend?' she asks threateningly, her face darkening like the sky before one of those almighty Pyrenean storms.

'No-one. Look, we're going for the culture, the history, that superb cuisine. It'll be a great weekend.'

But then, perhaps she ought to have considered that Napoleon invited the youth of France to share a nice autumn walk from Paris to Moscow in 1812. And Hitler forced his young men to make a similar journey 129 years later. Like the trip to Auch, they ended up physically shattered too.

AUCH boasts an impressive list of attractions for the tourist. The Archbishop's Palace, the Cathedral of Saint Marie which dates to 1489, the Musee des Jacobins in a former monastery and the 14th-century Tour d'Armagnac, used as a prison down the centuries.

You can also see the railway station where the French police corralled thousands of terrified Jews in 1942, stuffing them on to trains that took days to reach the death camps in Poland. Hardly France's finest hour.

By a sheer, extraordinary coincidence, Auch was also the home town of one Jacques Fouroux, French international rugby player and coach. Pure chance that, I swear it.

So we fly to Toulouse, pick up the hire car and make our way south-west through the pretty countryside to the town. The hotel is great. Soft sofa in the room, inviting bed, nice view. The clock on the old cathedral booms out 6pm and on a sunny evening, we stroll down the enticing, twisting streets, the ancient houses of the old quarter towering over the narrow cobbled streets, like some giant over a child.

A bar is located, two glasses of kir arrive and we settle down in the warm sunshine, a quiet, pleasant night ahead of us. This is la vraie France, this is what you don't get in Swindon or Coventry on a September night.

And then I think I see a familiar face. It disappeared into a shop in a trice, but I thought it was…no, it couldn't possibly have been…no, no, of course it wasn't. I look again. Its owner re-emerges, peers down the street and sees me. Mon dieu, it is. Monsieur Jacques Fouroux.

'Peter', he cries, 'what are you doing in Auch?'

One look at my wife's face tells me that she suspects a stitch-up. I feel as guilty as a bloke wearing a striped top, black face mask and carrying a swag over his shoulder, outside the town jewellers.

'A weekend in the country, away from rugby, Jacques,' I reply briskly, with the PC words of some politician's PR sidekick.

At 1.62m and 65kg, there wasn't a lot of Jacques Fouroux. But then, France seems to specialise in producing little men with big ambitions – Napoleon, Petain, Fouroux, Sarkozy.

Jacques Fouroux first played rugby for France in 1972 and he instantly appeared an oddity. In an era when France had huge, brutal forwards built like brick outhouses, 5ft 3in Fouroux could be seen barking at the behemoths up front, shouting, cajoling and urging them on. Sometimes, he'd give them a whack on the backside, like farmers do to meandering cows, just to remind them who was in charge.

Bill McLaren once took one of his peppermint Hawick balls out of his pocket, sucked it thoughtfully and pronounced Jacques as 'the pocket Napoleon'. It's true, he was always a leader in waiting. Alluding to Bonaparte's nickname, the French dubbed him 'the little Corporal'.

He won 27 caps for France, 23 as captain, including the 1977 grand slam. He then coached his country to the Grand Chelem in 1981 and 1987 in the Five Nations Championship. He would have become president of the French Rugby Federation had he been patient. But Jacques, impetuous and impatient, was always in too much of a hurry for everything. His premature coup against the steely incumbent Albert Ferrasse ultimately failed and Fouroux (or Foo-roux as the people of the south called him) fell off the rugby stage. He would be dead prematurely, too, at the ridiculously early age of 58.

There might not have been a lot of Jacques but by God, did hospitality and kindness ooze from his every pore. If he liked you, there was nothing he wouldn't do for you.

He'd invited my wife and I to be his personal guest for the France–Romania match at Auch in May 1990. When Romania won 12-6, their first victory on French soil in 66 years of trying (and the last time they beat the French), I thought it might ruin the evening. How wrong could you be?

He'd wined and dined us in his own inimitable way. On the Saturday night, we were invited to sup at the fabulous Hotel de France, the top place in town where the chef, Andre Daguin, was one of the best and most renowned in France. Jacques' welcome was fulsome, his smile warm and his wicked sense of humour as vibrant as ever.

The word was, Andre Daguin's place was always heavily booked. And on a French rugby international weekend, it would be heaving. But you see, these details never bothered Jacques. There was always a way around such trifling, inconsequential difficulties.

So we had got dolled up, all finest bib and tucker, and walked into the dining room. We walked through it and out the other side and there wasn't a spare chair in the vast place, never mind a table. My wife and I looked blankly at each other. 'Where to now?' she said. 'Ssh,' said I, 'this is Jacques' town and he'll deliver. I'm sure of that.'

And he did. Of course he did.

We were shown to our table, a garden table with wooden chairs, all set for four, in the middle of the kitchen. All around us, flambés flared, stews simmered, foie gras was cut and lightly grilled, steaks sizzled. Chefs shouted, waiters rushed and bustled. In terms of the bustle, it was like setting down your dining table in the middle of rush hour in Chatelet-Les Halles metro station in Paris.

We sat entranced, watching this manic demonstration of French cuisine on the go. And when we'd had two or three courses, the sommelier having been summoned to our table to select the best wines, we upped sticks almost in mid-mouthful and moved seamlessly into the dining room where a table had become available.

We had started with drinks on the terrace of Jacques' home outside the town at 6pm, the view like a painter's canvas of a Pyrenean mountain scene. We finished in the restaurant in town, the last people, long after 1am. The evening had been extraordinary and quintessentially Fouroux-ian.

He'd taken me down to the cellar of his home and unearthed some fabulous bottles. Jacques once worked for the Hennessy cognac company and he must have had the finest selection of post-prandial bottles in the entire Pyrenees. He pulled one out of its rack and thrust it into my arms. 'For you' he said, as I looked at the vintage; 1950-something. Typical Jacques, but then again, we just seemed to gel as people. It can be like that sometimes.

Whatever the reason, it was extraordinary what it led to. Team buses and dressing rooms are private sanctuaries barred to all-comers. Bruisers straight out of gangster films guard the entrances. Yet I once found myself inside a French international dressing room before a match, and of course, Monsieur Fouroux always hustled me inside when he saw me in the corridor waiting to go in after games as a press guy.

Once, after an international in Paris, he invited me on to the team's official bus for the ride through Paris from their hotel to the after-match dinner. I'll say this, those gendarme outriders don't half make crossing Paris on a busy Saturday night a piece of cake. And the fun and games going on down the back of the bus, orchestrated chiefly by Monsieur Fouroux, was a wonder to behold.

So four months after our first visit, here we are back in Auch. We've taken the precaution of not informing Monsieur Jacques we are coming, oh no. My life wouldn't have been worth living if I'd done that.

So imagine my complete surprise (and doubtless the sinking feeling in my wife's stomach) when Jacques pops his head around the corner of a shop and spies us. We finish our drinks and are hustled off down the street, almost like a couple of naughty schoolkids caught drinking down at the town bar during lunch break. But of course, Jacques has a plan. He always has a plan.

In Rue Pietonne, one of the narrow, twisting little alleyways to be found in the old centre of Auch, stood Restaurant Claude Laffitte. This was not a place for the faint-hearted. Portions of foie gras as big as building bricks were routinely served while steaks half the width of a cow arrived on your plate. Then there were the pommes de terre – they were cooked in goose fat.

Of course, being someone always greatly concerned about consuming a healthy diet, I knew the only way to alleviate such a rich dish was by attacking the red wine. But if you got out of there having downed less than two bottles per person, not to mention assorted aperitifs and finished it all off with a couple of Armagnacs, poured as liberally as if it were Coca-Cola, you would consider it a fairly quiet night.

So you get the picture – anyone with a serious weight, alcohol or heart problem would be well advised to steer clear of the place. In fact, McDonald's down the road almost certainly had less calories per mouthful.

So we enter the restaurant with a sense of foreboding. And rightly so because on this warm night, a giant ice bucket is standing on the table filled with what was euphemistically called fruit cocktail. The only thing you could say about that was bananas.

It was a warm night and an ice cold long drink seemed the way to go. Alas, about halfway through the third (or was it the fourth?) glass, I began to study this brew. For sure, there was rum lurking somewhere but I suspected Cointreau, white wine and a couple of other devilish ingredients were involved. Whatever the cause, suddenly I detected a problem with the floor in the place; it seemed to have started moving. I never knew Auch was in an earthquake zone.

And the strange thing was, the more I supped, the more it appeared to sway, seemingly slipping from one side to the other. Eventually, after a gargantuan plate of foie gras (with a large glass of Jurancon, of course), I staggered upstairs, clinging to the banister rail like a mountaineer on Everest hanging on to his rope for dear life, and reached the bathroom. There, that age-old remedy for a grossly overloaded stomach was duly enacted.

Ten minutes later, I retraced my steps, feeling (and apparently looking) a whole lot better. But this was a mistake. No sooner had I retaken my place at the impromptu dinner Jacques had arranged than a bulbous red wine glass was set down before me and a hearty Cotes du Rhone poured. I wasn't sure this was likely to be the ideal remedy for my condition but imbibed liberally anyway, as you do when you're a fool.

An enormous plate of coq au vin and several glasses of red later, not to mention desserts, it seemed like a smart act to send for the huskies and try to locate the hotel. But we then made a gross error. 'Why had we really come to Auch?' asked Jacques.

'Ah,' said I, conspiratorially, 'a secret which I will tell. It is a late celebration of the lady's birthday.'

I thought maybe, through the haze of alcohol, I'd just said something indecent, like asking the pleasant blond waitress to loosen her blouse or something. But whatever the reason, Jacques almost immediately vanished.

When he came back, he ordered coffees and Armagnacs all round, presumably in case we were still thirsty. The hour was ticking towards midnight and the restaurant had by now closed. We were about to go when there was a knock on the door. Customers, this time of night?

No. But another Jacques Fouroux fiendish plan was about to be revealed. Led by France's coach and followed by the owner, the diminutive, balding and red-faced Claude Laffitte who wore an expression of pure mischief on his chubby round face, the pair of them entered the dining room with their trouser legs rolled up to the knees, each man with a chair slung over one shoulder to signify the bagpipes and lustily singing the Gay Gordons. And behind them followed a local patissier, carrying a birthday cake.

No ordinary cake this, though. Iced on top in white, out of the centre arose an enormous pink phallus, complete with turned down, overlapping icing around the top. The rest I'd better leave to your imagination.

So we found ourselves at midnight tucking into a cake that had been ordered and baked specially no more than an hour earlier, and with one of the great men of French rugby putting a knife through the phallus and roaring out 'ooooh, aaah' as he cut. Honestly, some people's imagination.

% % % % %

Diary Notes: To Bordeaux, 30 October 1993 for France v Australia.

Now this looks like a top weekend. Fly to Bordeaux to cover the touring Australians' Test match, the first of two internationals they are playing on a short visit to France.

Alas, tours like this are not what they used to be. Years ago, countries like New Zealand and Australia used to go all over France playing local teams. They would play a Provence-Cote D'Azur XV somewhere like Toulon, move around the Mediterranean to meet a Languedoc team at Narbonne and then a Centre-Limousin combined side at Brive. No tour of France was complete without a game against a Basque XV which was always as spicy as a piment d'Espelette pepper for which the region is famous. Then they would play the French Barbarians on some regional ground, like Agen.

The French selectors used these games as virtual trials for the forthcoming internationals in November in the northern hemisphere. Thus, every single match was potentially a mugging up a dark alleyway waiting to happen. If a touring team reached Paris or Bordeaux for the Test match at the end of their trip without broken bones, smashed teeth and shins bashed to the colour of midnight blue, something was wrong.

And years ago, it was always hit and miss with injuries. In 1977, when France played the touring New Zealanders in Toulouse, beating them 18-13, the All Blacks wing Bryan (B.G.) Williams took a heavy blow on his hip.

'I think it's dislocated,' he told the French medic on the sidelines. 'Oh no, Monsieur,' came the reply. 'You can run on it still.'

When he tried, Williams felt so searing a pain he thought his leg was coming off. It was dislocated but by the time he was eventually operated on, arthritis had set in. Six years later, when I stayed with him in Auckland during the 1983 Lions tour to New Zealand, Williams was still suffering agonies. He'd had a hot tub installed in his home and only by spending an hour in it every morning could he get any movement in his body. Later, he had a hip replacement.

These days, it's all a lot more clinical. Teams just fly into a city for the Test match, play the game and fly out. They never see anything of the country except one training ground and a hotel. Those great nights being hosted by a local club are things of the past, more's the pity.

SO we disgorge from the plane from London and there is the usual race for the car rental offices to be head of the queue. I'm not quite sure how he managed it but the wily Clem Thomas has his keys while I'm still in the queue. But then luck enters the equation.

Because I was late, held up waiting for baggage, I'm well down the back. And by the time I get to the front, there is a problem. No more cars in the bog-standard intermediate group which I have booked. It might still be seven weeks to Christmas but I swear it arrived tonight.

'We have a Mercedes we can give you,' suggests the pretty young lady at the desk, helpfully. 'Eet ees a good car for you, oui,' she cooes. Oh yes, no doubt about that.

I hardly like to ask which model because after all, a Merc is a Merc. But joy behold, when I get outside and look, it's an E Class turbo. Now this is a car that can shift; no arguments about that.

And it's ideal because I haven't come just for the match. On Sunday morning, together with photographer Dave Rogers of the Allsport agency, we have planned to meet French centre

Philippe Sella, drive him back down the motorway to his home at Agen, and do a photo shoot with him and his family for *Rugby World* magazine, of which I am the editor.

It might have been a touch daft trying to squeeze the great French centre, his 1.81m, 86kg frame plus all his kit and Dave's photographic gear into a Citroen with baggage space really only big enough for a takeaway pizza.

But before that, we cover the match and France's 16-13 win. Test matches come and go and sometimes you recall an incident or two from them. But you're just as likely to remember some other event from the weekend. Which is exactly what happened this time.

We were invited to the after-match banquet attended by the two teams. Now this can either be torturous or tremendous. I once went to a banquet at the London Hilton after an England–Wales Five Nations match and got stuck next to some Lady Curmudgeonly who had long since perfected the art of speaking with a mouthful of plums. Exciting night, that was.

It was reminiscent of the time when that great Australian player David Campese played for the Barbarians one Christmas at Leicester. Afterwards, at dinner, he was seated next to some former Colonel whose disintegrating human frame was being held together these days chiefly by regular, large infusions of whisky.

Turning conspiratorially to Campo at one point in the evening, he conceded most generously of himself, 'I played once, don't you know.' It wasn't very often Campo was rendered speechless but that was one occasion.

Anyway, we're seated at this long table in a former wine warehouse overlooking the great Gironde river in central Bordeaux. And a most strange scenario is about to unfold before our eyes.

The players have had a tough day physically and want to unwind. The media boys, likewise. As for the officials, they always want to unwind and refuel. After all, it's free.

So when the first dish is served, together with copious bottles of wine, most of the assembled throng move at once. In fact, the rush to grab the bottles is more reminiscent of a Bulgarian shop selling fresh meat in the Soviet era, than some trendy, swish private dining room in elegant Bordeaux.

I watch carefully as everyone starts pouring this stuff down their throats, except one French player, whom I am sitting next to. He doesn't move a muscle towards the wine, and I find this odd. For sure, he does drink – I've spent quite a lot of time in his company down the years. But he apparently isn't interested this evening. Or so it seems.

Three more dishes are served, each with a different bottle of wine. And each time, he scorns all offers of a glass. By now, I am becoming fascinated with this fastidiousness. Or is it that? Is there some cunning plot afoot here?

It's true; the first wine served was probably bottled for the purposes of cleaning out a car engine's interior. It hit your throat like a 6ft 7in rugby forward. The next one was better, but no classic. The third a little better still but again, we're hardly talking Chateau Lafitte 1961.

So when the boeuf is finally served, I am watching my fellow diner intently. And I am not disappointed. No sooner has the waitress plonked down markedly fewer bottles of this wine, than my friend moves with the cunning and speed of a crocodile. Of the four bottles deposited, he reaches an arm across the table and seizes two, both of which are immediately deposited in a bag under his chair.

Now most people, having filled their gullets with the first four wines, neither see this smash and grab nor remotely care about it. After all, the evening is by now in full swing. So my fellow diner's act goes largely unnoticed by the mob.

I raise an eyebrow and pick up one of the two remaining bottles to study it. And I understand instantly. Château Haut-Brion. A Premier Cru Classe served at an event like this? No wonder my friend moved so adroitly.

For this is a wine of very serious dimensions. As early as the 15th century, the name Pontac was associated with wine trading in the Pessac suburb of Bordeaux. Jean de Pontac (1488–1589), the son of Arnaud, was the original founder and builder of

Château Haut-Brion. At the age of 37, he married Jeanne de
Bellon who brought a part of the Haut-Brion domaine in her
dowry. A pity my missus couldn't match such largesse.

During the course of his three marriages, the last begun at
the age of 76, 15 children were born. So what with wine, women
and doubtless the occasional song, he was a busy boy was our
Jean.

Haut-Brion's fame and notoriety went far beyond those
times. At one stage, the French were becoming so appreciative
of the Vin de Pontac that the Duke de Richelieu introduced the
King to Haut-Brion.

In charge of foreign affairs under Napoleon, Charles-
Maurice de Talleyrand-Périgord bought Haut-Brion in 1801. For
sure, a very distinguished history and an equally distinguished
wine...

My fellow diner smiled at my expression of curiosity. 'Ze
best wines are always served last at zees dinners, Peter,' he
explains. 'Eet ees not every day people hand out bottles like
zis for nuthin.'

It's no wonder my pal won more than 50 caps for France and
today runs a multi-million euro business based in the country.
With cunning and predatory skills of that nature, he was bound
to achieve in life, as he did in sport.

So the next morning, some of us in chipper mood, others less
so, we pack up at the hotel. Dave and I drive the short distance
to the French team hotel where Sella has asked us to meet him
at 9am on the dot. We get there to find trouble.

Far from clambering into the car for the 125km journey
down the A62 Autoroute des Deux Mers to Agen, it appears
we are not going anywhere for some time. The French coach
Pierre Berbizier was so displeased at the performance the
previous day he has ordered an extra training session this
Sunday morning. But excusez-moi Monsieur, I thought the
French won. What would he have done had they lost? Guil-
lotined half the side?

It gives us a problem. We are on the 2.30pm British Airways
flight to London Gatwick and time now looks very short. We

wait and wait until eventually, sometime after 11.30am, we collect Philippe and head for the motorway. As soon as we filter on to it about ten minutes later, I ask him, 'How fast can we go?'

The great man pulls his coat lapels up around his neck, shrugs and says matter-of-factly (why is it all Frenchmen shrug?), 'No problem. I know all ze police 'ere.' And with that, he goes off to sleep.

An invitation of that nature is like gold nectar to a thirsty Australian. We hammer down the autoroute at 180km per hour, a liberal interpretation of the advised 130 speed limit. In a tiny Citroen, it would have been next to impossible and closer still to death. But not in the Mercedes.

To cover that journey in just over 40 minutes, was not exactly a normal sight on the autoroute, unless the Formula 1 boys happened to be in town. But the truth is, we're still in serious trouble time wise.

We reach Philippe's home, find his charming wife and adorable young children and set off for a short walk beside the canal. Dave wants some shots, close up and long distance, showing the autumn colours and we sure have the right day weather wise. It is crisp and cold but beautifully sunny. Agen looks regal in the early winter sunshine with colours of red, gold, yellow and green on the trees beside the canal.

Sometimes with the snappers of this world you think they can never be satisfied. If it's hot and sunny the light is too bright; if it's dull and wet, too dark. If it's too cold cameras can malfunction.

So getting the right climatic conditions can be tricky. But judging from the purrs of delight coming from behind Dave's camera, there won't be much wrong with these pictures. There wasn't: they proved to be stunning images.

Just one thing was wrong; the loud ticking of a clock in my mind. It's already 12.45pm and the flight goes at 2.30pm. Worse still, Bordeaux airport is on the far side of the city when you approach from Agen and the A62. It has to be the best part of 150km away and it's going to take us at least an hour and

15 minutes to get there from Philippe's family home, even disregarding the fact that they advise we check in at 1.30pm. Some hope of that.

It's fair to say that the French and the English have never quite fully understood each other. The French, well until more recent times, regarded burgers as a meal suitable only for dogs, and couldn't begin to understand why every Englishman did not enjoy a seven-course feed every time he sat down to the table. Nor can they begin to comprehend how the English don't share their love for a two-hour lunch break every working day or frogs legs for an afternoon snack.

But in the interests of the *entente cordiale* sometimes a man has to do what a man has to do, even if every fibre in his body is straining against it.

We'd taken our last pictures, stuffed all the gear in the car and profusely thanked our host and his family for their time. We were about to launch the grey coloured rocket in the direction of Bordeaux airport when the bombshell hit.

'But before you go, my family would like to invite you for champagne at my father's house,' said Philippe. It hit us like a blow in the solar plexus. The choice was stark – rush off like a couple of rude, ignorant Englishmen or smile, resign ourselves to a later plane (there wasn't another that day and we knew it) and accept humbly and with good grace the invitation.

Of course, we did the former. No, only joking. But there was a definite sense of inevitability about our fate as we returned to the house and sipped champagne. A reason to celebrate? For sure, if you counted the friendship of this great man of French rugby and his charming, welcoming family as something to be treasured. But not if you feared you were confronting chaos through the missed flight.

So we smiled and sipped and chatted. Then, we said we really must go and so we did. We rolled the Merc out on to the A62 heading west at 1.17pm, 73 minutes before take-off…150km away.

'I tell you what,' I said to Dave as we picked up speed. 'I think this could still be on.'

I glanced sideways to see an expression of alarm spread across his face. 'Well,' I said trying to be reassuring, 'we could at least have a go at it.'

There was nothing in our favour, except for one very considerable factor. It was Sunday lunchtime and all France was eating and drinking. The roads were absolutely empty. The great car accelerated and accelerated; far beyond 130 (80mph), up to 180 (111mph), Sella's preferred cruising speed, now at 200 (124mph), then to 220 (136mph). I pushed it up to 240 and then we hit 250 (155mph) before I wound it back a touch.

At that speed, motorway signs flew past so fast we could barely read them. The odd car we did see and overtake disappeared so quickly into the distance it was as if we were in a jet aircraft. If we'd hit a radar trap, I reckoned I'd be spending the next six months sweating it out with Papillon and his mate Louis Degas on Devil's Island off the South American coast.

But on we went, and incredibly we had no *bouchon* (motorway hold-up) to concern us. We approached Bordeaux still at high pace and maintained most of it even on the huge Peripherique which winds its way around the city.

With a scream of halting tyres, we roared into the airport's car rental depot at precisely 1.56pm. The 150km journey, which officially should have taken an hour and 24 minutes on the autoroute, had taken us 39 minutes.

We ran for the check-in desk, made it with barely a couple of minutes to spare and picked up boarding passes. 'Time for a coffee,' I suggested and we repaired to the cafe.

'Billsy, that's the last time I ever travel in a car with you driving,' said a voice not far from our intrepid photographer.

'Hang on,' I shot back, 'what's that brown liquid on the seat beside your trousers?'

He looked down, and then smiled.

〽 〽 〽 〽 〽

Diary Notes: Assorted rugby nights out in Paris.

Don't know why, but Paris always seems to be the scene of the best rugby stories, albeit perhaps on a par with Dublin. I love the one about that iconic Irishman Willie John McBride captaining Ireland there in 1974 and making it his business to keep an eye on the new cap that day, a certain Maurice Ignatius Keane of the Lansdowne club.

Now Big Mossie, as he came to be known, had already made quite an impact the week before his debut for Ireland. He'd played for Lansdowne on the Saturday afternoon in a club match in Dublin and the Irish selectors had announced their team to play France the following weekend, at 6pm on that Saturday. He was awarded a first cap.

Cue wild celebrations in the clubhouse round the back of Lansdowne Road. And yer man, all huge hands, massive forearms and thick neck with his famous shock of dark hair and ruddy complexion, was at the centre of the fun as it unfolded.

It didn't look quite so rosy a picture at 2am the following day. Unlike a great many, Big Mossie was still standing; well, just about. He made his way slowly and unsteadily to the gents and then re-emerged. A pal shouted, 'Now Mossie, you're in here; there's another pint for yer.'

But Mossie had had enough. 'Ah no, I'm off home meself.' And with that, he somehow found the stairs, stumbled down them and unearthed his car keys from a pocket. Not perhaps the best idea in the world.

A short time later, a vehicle was to be seen heading unseemly slowly in the wrong direction up a Dublin one-way street. The gardai saw it, caught it up and stopped it.

Big Mossie wound down the window and beamed at the policeman. 'Ah now Mossie, we'd heard tonight you'd won yer first cap and you've probably had a glass or two to celebrate. Is that right?' said the officer.

An expression of complete incredulity appeared on Keane's face.

'Are yer mad officer?' was his slurred reply. 'Oi've had 22 feckin' pints and I'm away home now.'

'Ah Mr Keane,' said the officer in utter exasperation, 'I wish you'd not told us that. I wish yer hadn't.' But he reputedly got away with it anyway.

So the next weekend, in Paris, a dinner-jacketed Keane is offered copious glasses of champagne at the after-match banquet. He looks around in hope of a proper drink, Guinness, but sees nothing on the silver trays but this damn Bollinger, or whatever they call it.

A long time later, after the fine wines and cognacs they serve you at the French dinners, Mossie is on the loose in Paris, albeit with McBride close by. Around midnight, they find themselves in Montmartre and Mossie decides he is hungry.

Willie John parks him against a wall outside a kebab shop and goes inside to order. Alas, Big Mossie's curiosity not to mention his hunger gets the better of him.

Stumbling into the shop, he spies McBride at the top of the queue and sidles up to him. There, sitting on the bench in front of them, is a sausage, nicely cooked and just oh so tempting. Big Mossie can't resist. He picks it up, encloses it in one giant paw, turns his back and heads out of the shop, completely oblivious to the fact that it is attached to 49 more sausages.

The trail of sausages across the floor of a Montmartre shop is a sight to behold around the midnight hour.

A sight, you might consider, to rival that of a taxi screeching to a halt in the early hours of a Sunday morning somewhere in Paris, and a blond haired young man stumbling out to find the nearest lamppost to deposit the contents of his night's celebrations.

To the astonishment of three Welsh rugby fans, making their weary way home after a night out on the town following a France–Wales Five Nations international in the 1970s, this was no ordinary diner who'd had one over the top. They stood there bemused as Jean-Pierre Rives tumbled out of the cab, closely followed by the great Gareth Edwards.

And did Jean-Pierre get any sympathy from the bystanders? Did he heck. 'Well done Gareth,' they chorused. 'We might have lost the game but we've beaten them in the drinking stakes.'

THE nights in Paris seemed long and legendary. Once, during a Five Nations game in the late 1970s, the mighty French lock forward Jean Francois Imbernon of the Perpignan club, a man built rather like a double decker bus and about the same height, broke his leg and was despatched to hospital.

Later, much later that night, I found myself searching through various floors of a chic Paris nightclub, Castel, to where the French players had repaired. I needed to find one of them for a quote for my story for a Monday morning newspaper but at three in the morning my chances were not great.

They were most certainly not helped by what happened next. With the place virtually pitch black except for some soft, muffled lights, my right foot suddenly connected with something extremely hard barring my way. At the moment of impact, there came a huge, angered roar from the owner of this barrier.

Peering down at the chair from which the roar came, I saw a certain Monsieur Imbernon. To say he didn't seem terribly pleased to see me would be like saying the French do not exactly welcome the sight of a plate of English baked beans and sausage placed before them at breakfast time.

As Imbernon ruefully rubbed his broken leg and felt the heavy plaster which I'd just given a good kicking, I decided to call it a night. There might have been plenty wrong with Jean Francois's leg but his enormous fists still looked in rude health.

※ ※ ※ ※ ※

Diary Notes: To France, firstly to Toulouse, to cover the 1986 New Zealand tour. The All Blacks play, and win, the first of two Test matches on this tour they are making of France. The following week, the second and final Test will be played in Nantes.

I am struck by the thought that someone else made this journey a long time ago. We have set out from Toulouse the day after France's conclusive defeat in the first Test. Nantes, a city on the great Loire River, is our destination.

We'll take a good couple of days to get there because the final Test isn't until the following Saturday.

But at least we are making the long journey in comfort. About 42 years earlier, the Das Reich regiment of the German army, stationed at Valence d'Agen, near Toulouse, had been ordered to march through France, right up to Normandy to help try and repel the Allied invasion.

But the Das Reich's progress was to be slow and frustrating. At every opportunity, brave members of the French resistance did what they could to impede the German regiment's progress. With the Allies fighting to avoid being thrown back into the sea, time was critical and the resistance knew it.

Bridges on their route were blown up, snipers felled individual German soldiers as they marched. By the time they reached the rural Limousin, the brutal Germans had had enough. At a small, sleepy village a short tram journey outside the regional capital, Limoges, the Das Reich soldiers gathered together all the townsfolk they could find. Most of the working men were away, either at the war or employed in Limoges.

Those men the Germans could find, mostly elderly, were herded into barns. There, they were first machine-gunned in the legs to prevent escape and then soaked in petrol and burned alive. Somehow, six men escaped.

The women and young children were hurried into the church which was then set alight with incendiary devices. When they tried to escape, they were shot. In total, 190 men, 247 women and 205 children died on 10 June 1944.

The village was named Oradour-sur-Glane and it remains today as it did when the Germans left it late that night. By the time they departed, they had blown up every house, destroyed just about everything. It is haunting to see the remains and items like rusting bicycles and old cars outside the wrecked houses of the village. We diverted close to Limoges to visit Oradour. Then we continued north to Nantes.

Now the French are particularly partial to a good battle. Places like Verdun are revered as part of French culture. How little we knew that a simple rugby match that was to be played at the end of that week would go down in French sporting folklore as the 'Battle of Nantes'.

Until 2015, it had been a closely guarded secret as to what the French did in preparation that week after they'd lost the first Test 19-7.

Some said that national coach Jacques Fouroux had them fighting each other, on the training ground, in the boxing ring, anywhere.

Whether that was true remains unknown. But what is certain is that this rugby international would be one of the most brutal ever seen in the northern hemisphere. For sure, it was one of the toughest games I ever witnessed in 50 years of watching top-class rugby.

Grown men shuddered visibly at the collisions, players found their bodies increasingly resembling those of animals in the abattoir.

Allegedly, the reason for this extreme physicality by the French was revealed recently by the French team doctor at that time. Speaking to the respected French investigative journalist Pierre Ballester, Jacques Mombet alleged, 'Amphetamines always existed in rugby.' He further alleged that in the 1970s, entire teams took them. He called their use 'systematic'.

Mombet is quoted as saying to Ballester, 'They [the French team] each had their little pill in front of their plates for the meal before the match. The All Blacks realised that their opponents, unrecognisable from the previous week, were loaded. The players were free to take them [the pills] or not.'

Whether the allegations were true or untrue, what is certain is that from a convincing defeat, seven days earlier, France so turned the tables that they won the Test match 16-3. They did it through sheer brutality. I doubt any New Zealand side had ever encountered such a ferocious physical assault launched against them.

Evidence of the violence was everywhere to be seen, all over the field. Just sitting in the press box watching, you felt bruised and battered.

The All Blacks' number eight, Wayne 'Buck' Shelford, lost four teeth and then was knocked out in another incident. But those were not the worst of Shelford's injuries.

When it was over, the wrecked bodies removed from the field of battle, we gathered in the corridor under one of the stands, to await the media interviews.

As we hung about, a door used by the medics opened and for some reason, remained open. It was like a casualty clearing station in a war scene. Inside, lying on a simple, plastic covered bench was Wayne Shelford. He was stripped naked from the waist down and a doctor was inserting stitches – in his scrotum.

A rogue boot had apparently torn Shelford in that impossibly sensitive part of his body, as he lay trapped in a ruck. It was the sort of sight that never left you if you were a male observer.

※ ※ ※ ※ ※

Diary Notes: May 1998, to Paris for the French Rugby Championship Final, one of the great nights of the northern hemisphere rugby season.

The French club championship final is nowadays always held in Paris. There was a time when it alternated between Bordeaux, Lyon and Toulouse. But the great lure of a weekend in the capital to climax the long domestic season (not to mention the greater riches on offer there) was too strong, so from 1974 it has always been held in Paris.

IT is the weekend when the provinces invade the capital. To see thousands of Perpignan fans pouring off the TGVs that have raced up the Rhone from Catalonia on the Mediterranean carrying fans to the final, is one of the great sights. It is a similar experience with the Toulouse supporters or the highly passionate Toulon fans. Then there is the sea of yellow and blue that denotes the Clermont Auvergne supporters.

But here's a strange thing. When they have gone past, shop windows are still miraculously intact. The bodies of old ladies do not litter the gutter; local hospitals are not on a state of high alert to receive the casualties. Vive la difference between rugby and soccer supporters.

The final has nothing to do with winter. It is usually held in early June, by which time Paris can be seriously warm. To allow for this, the match usually kicks off at 8.45pm. In 1984 at the Parc des Princes, the two teams, Agen and Beziers, completed the 80 minutes with the scores level.

After a short break, half an hour's extra time was called for, by the end of which the scores were still level, 21-21. A major conflab then followed before it was decided that someone would have to be the winner, and penalty kicks at goal were ordered.

As the clock ticked closer towards midnight and the penalty competition drew to a close, it was eventually settled by Beziers' steelier reserve. They won the shoot-out by three penalties to one to take the trophy.

In 1990, Racing Club de France met Agen in the final. This wasn't just a clash of rugby players but a collision of cultures.

Racing included players like Frank Mesnel and his brother-in-law Eric Blanc, who had created the famous Eden Park clothing range. All they did, the way they dressed and operated as a business, was elegant. The Racing backs wore pink bow ties, the emblem of Eden Park even in the actual match.

Then, at half-time at the Parc des Princes, 45,000 spectators were astonished to see a Racing official appear on the pitch resplendent in knee-length white shorts, the famous light blue and white striped shirt and a navy blazer. He was carrying a silver tray with a glass of champagne for every one of the Racing backs.

The farmers and manual workers among the Agen forwards watched this floorshow and clearly took it the wrong way. They saw an insult and launched a ferocious assault on Racing in the second half. You winced just watching it.

To their credit, Racing held their nerve amid the heightened physical storm. They also endured half an hour of extra time before finishing 22-12 winners.

Anyway, this particular night in 1998, the Paris-based Stade Francais team finish the final in glory by carrying off the famed Bouclier de Brennus, the huge French Championship log. What is even better is that because they have beaten Perpignan 34-7, extra time is not needed. Do not underestimate the importance of this factor. It means that there is a decent chance of sitting down to dinner at a favoured Parisian restaurant, close by the Bourse, by about half past midnight.

Believe me, that's pretty good going because some years, after waiting an hour or more for the two teams to arrive at the after-match press conference and then seeking out and talking to specific players, you don't get back into central Paris from the Stade de France until well after 1am.

You then settle down to your magret or whatever but it's definitely getting a bit late.

But this year, I'm comfortably ensconced at a pavement table outside the restaurant by about 12.30am. And we've had the oysters to start and are tucking into magret, cooked rose as the French say for its best flavours, when my mobile rings. At this hour of the night it isn't likely to be work because it's morning on the other side of the world in Australia and New Zealand where I write for newspapers, night time in London and Ireland and definitely sleeping time in South Africa.

The call comes from a lot closer to home. My journalist pal Serge, a rugby writer for the *Midi Olympique* newspaper, is just across the other side of the French capital.

'Peter, where are you, what are you doing?' he asks.

'Laying in bed making passionate love to a French lady and wondering why the hell you are interrupting us,' I reply.

'Oh, mon dieu, non. I am so sorry,' says a deadly serious Frenchman. After all, such acts are of extreme seriousness to Frenchmen. But I jest.

'Go on Serge, I'm joking. We are eating magret outside a restaurant beside the Bourse. Why, what's the problem?'

'You must come here, to the Hotel de Ville, now. The Mayor of Paris is giving a reception for the Stade Francais team and the media is invited.'

So we finish the duck, down the remainder of the wine and call a cab. Hotel de Ville here we come.

You come upon it and marvel at its imposing, majestic façade, no matter how many times you have seen it. At the top of the

Rue de Rivoli and reconstructed in the 1890s, this particular
night it is floodlit and hugely impressive. As is the red carpet
awaiting all the invited guests to the reception.

We are admitted, partly on the evidence of my media card
but perhaps chiefly because Serge is there to smooth our passage
of entry, especially so in the case of James, my rugby-mad nine-
year-old. With his beard covering part of a face that looks as
though it has been lived in to the absolute full, rather like a well
crumpled favourite suit, Serge is an operator, a facilitator. He's
also one of the kindest men I have ever come across.

If you want to know the best restaurant and who to call for a
table, Serge is your man. If you need an introduction or perhaps
a quote from a rugby man, Serge can help. He is generous to a
fault, cheerfully ready to fight you physically for the right to
pay a restaurant bill. And he has an enviable longevity when it
comes to surviving the long, late nights of our profession.

Once, he went to a grand party of his French journalistic
colleague, the renowned writer and party-goer Jean Cormier
which began at 5pm. They went straight through the night,
somehow came out alive the other side at breakfast time
and kept on going through to 6pm, when another evening's
festivities ensued. You need the constitution of an iron steamship
to plough on through those kind of waters.

So we make our way up the vast, marbled staircase from the
main entrance hall, to a sprawling room with elegant, rich red,
ceiling to floor drapes and a deep pile carpet. My word, these
French politicians know how to look after themselves. Stinting
is not a word in their vocabulary.

We are greeted by an astonishing sight. A series of trestle
tables, joined together, run from one end of this vast room
right down to the other. All but buckling under the weight,
they contain huge supplies of jambon cru, that delicious cured
ham that comes from, in this particular case, Bayonne, the great
Basque port on the Atlantic.

James takes one look at this and starts salivating on the spot.
'Can we have any of it?' asks a small voice. 'Help yourself,' I
suggest, and he needs no second invitation. To call him a pig

for stuffing down so much would probably be most accurate, not to say highly appropriate.

The beef that follows is cooked saignant as the French say and hordes of hulking great rugby men, their friends and assorted guests descend upon this enormous feeding trough. Champagne is served prior to estates full of red wine.

At around 4am, I decide we have to leave because we're due to catch the first Eurostar back to London around 7am. 'But must you go so early?' exclaims Serge, a puzzled expression on his face. 'Surely not.'

A party that ends at such a disgustingly early hour as this is not one worthy of discussion, in Serge's mind.

Of course, nine-year-old boys being nine-year-old boys, we have to find somewhere to buy pain au chocolate for breakfast and a sandwich for lunch before we board the train after our two-hour sleep. But with those chores completed, we can contemplate a pretty successful weekend.

※ ※ ※ ※ ※

Diary Notes: Toulon rail station during the French Rugby World Cup, 2007.

I sometimes wonder what it is about some human beings and speed. Now don't believe, on the basis of the Agen-Bordeaux airport journey, that it's just men who feel the desire to go ballistic in cars with the technical power to match their testosterone. Some women are like it, too.

The 2007 Rugby World Cup held in France was a great event. How could it be otherwise with the whole country en fete, as the French say, at the rugby festivities?

Thank God, too. I'd been writing and arguing publicly for the best part of 20 years that France should host a Rugby World Cup.

'Oh,' sniffed the critics, 'they're too disorganised. It would be a shambles.'

Yes, but even if it were, consider all that passion for the game. That alone would make it a raging success, I would argue.

In the end, the IRB agreed and awarded France the 2007 tournament. What a triumph it was.

You could cover a night match in Paris, cross the city early the next morning to one of those great French rail stations like Montparnasse or the Gare de Lyon, and board the TGV for Montpellier or Marseille for another game that very afternoon. That night, you'd ruminate at length with your working colleagues or friends at the games you'd seen and swop your experiences, while dining under the stars looking at the Mediterranean. I can think of less beguiling locations in the world. Like Port Talbot, for instance.

There is a belief chiefly in the UK that the French rail system is as smooth as the finest oyster. Well, it isn't, far from it. And this particular day, it is living down to my expectations.

I'm on an inter-city train from Nice, the city on the Mediterranean in the far south-east of the country, to Toulouse for a World Cup game that night. You tend to think it won't take long but in truth, it's a six-and-three-quarter-hour journey along the shores of the Mediterranean, across the Camargue and then down the Med to Beziers and Narbonne before turning west and rushing through the great vineyards of the Corbieres to Carcassonne and then into Toulouse, capital of the Haute Garonne region.

We're tootling along, doing fine, until we reach Toulon. To be precise, we start mucking around shortly before the chief city of the Var region. Finally, we labour into the station and shudder to a halt with a finality that suggests the odd wheel or two may have become detached, or the driver has reached retirement age and won't be taking the train another metre further.

A wait of interminable boredom is interrupted by a French woman, probably in her late 40s. Dressed casually, in jeans, T-shirt, light sweater and with a silk scarf loosely knotted beneath a dark leather jacket, she exudes French chic. From her mouth comes a choice of either English or her native language.

Trailing behind her, although quite why I cannot tell at this stage, are two young backpackers of indeterminate origin. For some reason, she leans into the compartment where I am sitting alone.

'Cees train will be 'ere for per 'aps four hours. I will take my car and drive to Montpellier [about 200km further west along the line]. Do you want to join us?' she cooed. 'Eet ees always ze same: today a suicide, tomorrow another problem. Zees trains are terrible.' It seemed a bit harsh on the railway people, but there it was.

Now maybe it's the Union Jack underpants I am wearing on my head or the bowler hat on top of them with the rolled up umbrella, pin-striped suit and red rose in the lapel, but for some reason she seems to know full well I'm English. I mean, I haven't even opened my mouth yet. But she's explaining the situation in her broken English, which in fairness is nowhere near as broken as my French.

It transpires the train will go no further; there has been a suicide attempt further down the line towards Marseille. Well, as Basil Fawlty once remarked about some guests who cancelled their table on gourmet dinner night due to illness, let's hope it's nothing trivial.

But the lady has the answers. Her car is here outside Toulon station and she can drive us to Montpellier, where we can find another train to Toulouse. It seems a thoroughly reasonable proposition. Until we clamber aboard and she turns on the engine.

HER adventure party on the platform comprises a French student, an English journalist and two of the ubiquitous travelling Australians: a veritable pot pourri of humanity.

What the experience would do was remind me of the intrinsic characteristics of the French. Truly, these are a different people.

But first, we have to arrange refunds for the premature termination of our journey. The leader of our group thrusts her way to the front of the queue with the aggression of some SS guard outside Berlin station. Once there, she remonstrates with a woman behind a window with a large sign Ferme.

The conversation becomes heated, arms waved and voices raised. 'She sez she cannot open zis window, eet ees not time. Incroyable, these people don't care.'

Given that the whole station has been paralysed with hundreds of people waiting for refunds, she has a point. But French officialdom is not for dissuading. It never is.

And, I muse, there is nothing like a little adversity to study a people, warts and all.

At last we complete the paperwork, gather our bags and find her car. Thank God, I think, a BMW: this should be solid and safe. Well, the car itself probably is but not in the hands of this particular lady.

Here is a woman driver who could loosen up your sphincter muscle from a distance of 50 metres. And although I wasn't actually able to check, you'd have to believe she was the proud owner of spherical objects upon her person.

The three-lane motorway she treats as her personal domain. Why use just one lane with three available? And what is that extra space called the hard shoulder for if you can't drift into it occasionally? And all this is negotiated at a speed to outpace Hamilton or Vettel.

As we sweep down the motorway towards Aix-en-Provence and Marseille, the car weaving around as if on a dodgem track, she performs her piece de resistance.

If you haven't seen a French woman drive a car, answer her mobile phone and hunch her head so that it is jammed between her ear and shoulder, wave one arm in Gallic expression at parts of the telephone conversation and, with the other hand, try to reach into her trouser pockets to find some cash for the toll booth as her knee takes control of the steering wheel, then you haven't lived.

The way the car veers around the road is clearly a touch disconcerting to some but, hey, this is France and the French. Who's getting excited?

As we fly out of Marseille (still by road), the Australian girl in the back inquires somewhat weakly, 'Er, what is the speed limit in France?' It is 130km per hour, but to our intrepid driver, that is no more than advisory. She is up nearer 170 and enjoying the view.

'Ah, look at all these boats, they go to Corsica,' says our tour guide, one arm directing our view to the port while the car drifts alarmingly sideways, narrowly missing the crash barrier.

Speed cameras? We actually hurtle past one; happily, the glass frame has red paint sprayed all over it. The French don't take kindly to rules and restrictions.

And then, mon dieu, someone has the temerity to try to get past.

'Oo 'ees this – a crazy person?' she asks no-one in particular, studying the rear view mirror and waving both arms this time. It takes one to know one, I guess.

As for patience, that's a game for card players, not French drivers. Her other favourite party trick is to get within touching distance of the car in front at high speed and then swing the steering wheel to overtake at the final moment.

Fine, unless someone happens to be in the lane she wants. The consequent deafening blast of horns that accompanies her actions bring forth loud snorts of derision. But then, using the motorway like a rugby field – a side-step here, a weave and rapid evasion there – can present difficulties to others.

By some miracle, we limp into Montpellier still alive, but shaken and most definitely stirred. Profuse thanks are offered and there are warm embraces all round. And then I cross the road to the railway station where, precisely 45 minutes later, the exact same train I had abandoned in Toulon trundles into sight.

Ah, but would I have seen French life in all its glory had I sat forlornly at Toulon awaiting the train's eventual departure? Another day lived to the full.

Part 3

AROUND AND ABOUT

I'M not saying rugby union is the only sport where you can find qualities of such camaraderie and friendship. Far from it, in fact. What an arrogant remark that would be. I am certain the devotees of hockey, men's and women's, basketball, cricket, soccer, golf and myriad other sports could offer a long list of enjoyments, people to meet, moments to treasure, special places where their sport is played. I have enjoyed writing about many of them during my own career.

But then there's rugby, the King of them all!

And joy of joys, most often the places where you find the real beating heart of the game is nowhere near Murrayfield, Lansdowne Road, Eden Park or such exalted venues.

When the 1983 Lions tour had finally dragged us all around New Zealand in a losing cause for 13 and a half weeks and spewed us out in Auckland ready for the long flight home, I took a small diversion. And why not? I was perfectly equipped for a week in Tahiti, what with all the New Zealand winter weather clothes I'd been lugging around for more than three months.

So wearing a couple of pairs of trousers, three shirts, two thick sweaters, a jacket and a sheepskin coat (I couldn't fit any more in my overloaded suitcases), I arrived at about 3am at a sweltering airport at Papeete, the capital of Tahiti. Whether the customs official thought I was a drug carrier because I was sweating bucketloads from fear, I don't know. But the sweat from all those clothes on a hot night made me target No. 1 coming off the plane. It took about a day to go through all my gear, notebooks, papers, clothes, shoes, boots etc. before they finally accepted I wasn't trying to import a few tons of heroin.

The customs men were especially intrigued by one thing, a sculpture cast in solid bronze which I'd bought from the highly talented New Zealand sculptor Ken Kendall. I'd never heard of him before I went to Tauranga to interview the All Black wing Grant Batty. On his desk sat this handsome sculpture.

'Who created that, it's superb,' I said.

He gave me contact details and Ken and I became friends for the rest of his life. A very talented man was Ken Kendall.

Yet even all that profound hassle was worth it. The morning paper in Tahiti announced a humble club rugby match would be played on the main sports ground in Papeete. So I pitched up.

Whole families lined the touchline and surrounding areas, people picnicked and kids ran everywhere. If ever you wanted to see the quintessential image of a sport that traverses social classes, financial standing and such like this was surely it.

Compared to a Lions tour of New Zealand, it was like the other end of the rugby spectrum. But what made it special was what makes club rugby special the world over – the simplicity of it all and the warmth of the welcome offered to any strangers.

I got talking to an English guy who was married to a Tahitian. And in case you wonder, no, his name wasn't Fletcher Christian. Wasn't even a descendant. But he shouted me and my girlfriend a beer or two and then we shared a feed. And just talked. This is what rugby does the world over: welcome to its wondrous ways.

In the mid-winter of 2015, I stood on a rugby touchline in the south-eastern suburbs of London, watching a match at the Dartfordians ground in Crayford, Kent. The temperature was about 2°C and the rain, when it came, was driven horizontally at the few idiots standing forlornly on the touchline, by a gale tearing across the barren, mud-covered ground.

When one of the wings, half frozen to the spot and soaked by the rain, came shivering to the side, I joked, 'Hope they're paying you well for this. Either that or you deserve a medal with your tea.'

His reply was straight out of the pages of the *Coarse Rugby* manual. 'Actually, I have to pay them for the privilege,' he grimaced.

The mud was so thick, the rain so heavy and wind so strong it took me 20 minutes to recognise my own son who was playing. And even then, because the mud and rain had so disfigured his face, I could only be sure he was out there somewhere because someone shouted out his name.

All over Britain, all over the world each and every week of the year, men (and an increasing number of women) young and old are enduring these kinds of barbarities and indignities in the name of rugby union. May they please the gods.

And it's at grounds like Dartfordians, a strip of mud lying beside the A2 bypass on which cars rush by towards London or down towards Kent and the English south coast where the real rugby people are to be found.

It's at clubs, too, like Tunbridge Wells in Kent, Avonvale at Bathampton just outside Bath and many, many others where husbands and wives stand in foul weather on a Sunday morning, trying to encourage their offspring or teach the rudiments of the game to a handful of seven-year-olds who often can't remember which direction they're supposed to be running in, can't remember to pass and certainly can't understand why their parents and other grown-ups are standing effing and blinding on the touchline and cursing the referee.

And it is people like Chris Hobbs, lifeblood of the small Avonvale club for years as player, coach of the juniors and others, general go-to man and heartbeat of the club who epitomise what this sport is all about. Wouldn't you like to be married to Chris, ladies? Out training himself two or more nights a week, out taking training for the youngsters another two, out all day Saturday either playing or taking a team somewhere and involved at the club on a Sunday whenever special events were held to raise funds.

Every club has a Chris Hobbs and the whole darn lot of them are heroes down to their mud-caked socks, boots and jock-straps.

Together, these wonderful people comprise the rich tapestry of rugby.

You see, if you asked me to put into words the essence of the game, I'd say it was people like this and the friendship they offer to anyone, especially new faces. Sure, you have the sporting and fitness elements of the game. They're both important, especially these days with increasingly sedentary lifestyles.

But not as important as the lifelong friendships this sport goes on and on bestowing upon any soul who cares to pass through its doors. I found just such a welcome once at the Santa Monica club in California.

Mind you, to find it, you have to negotiate about 2,000 blocks coming out of the city of Los Angeles. No good asking for directions, either.

Just pass the 2,000th McDonald's after Sunset Boulevard, hang a left and we're down there on the right, sort of thing.

And you ask your girlfriend, 'Now was that the 1,999th McDonald's or the 2,000th?'

'Must be the former,' she says, ''cos there's another one right down the street. Look.'

But once you get there, you find just the same thing. People offering a warm handshake in greeting, a drink and finding the time to chat with you. And then, in this case, after we'd watched the game that weekend, being invited back to the home of rugby devotee Kilian Kerwin, one of the club's officials, for a barbecue with the team and everyone else.

Some might snort with derision and say rugby in America is no more than a precocious child, a little upstart with so much to learn and a lot of living to do. Rubbish. Clubs like Santa Monica know exactly the key ingredients of this sport. They prove it every time a stranger walks through their gate.

But of course, the more traditional locations for rugby do excel. Take Wales. My dear father went to Rydal School at Colwyn Bay, North Wales. Some distinguished alumni ran on those rugby fields, future Welsh internationals Wilf Wooller and Bleddyn Williams among them.

'Go to Wales to watch and learn the game,' Dad always said. 'They know the game down there and you'll get the reception of your life.' He wasn't wrong.

In November 2014, Sir Stanley Thomas, for so long the lifeblood (not to mention financier) behind the Cardiff Blues, hosted a lunch for guests before the Wales–South Africa Test. My son and I had been invited by Gareth Edwards.

Gareth arranged, firstly, a prime parking spot behind the Arms Park stand, morning coffee, lunch courtesy of Stan, two prime seats for the game, afternoon tea and drinks when it was all over and, well, just about anything else you might want.

And the friendship and hospitality throughout the day was exceptional. You found yourself engaged in some delightful conversations with total strangers. Rugby, the language that heals, that crosses borders and seals divisions.

Some years ago, for an article wanted by the *London Sunday Times*, I tried to bring together for a unique one-off interview, those legendary men of the Pontypool, Wales and 1977 British Lions front row, Graham Price, Bobby Windsor (The Duke) and Charlie Faulkner. Pricey was my contact, my go-to man and a guy I had long respected as a great figure of the game.

Marvellous man, and the subject of a marvellous story about the aftermath of his debut for Wales, against France in Paris at the Parc des Princes in 1975. A French backline move broke down around the Welsh 22 and the ball was booted way downfield. A chase ensued, with the unlikely figure of Wales's new tight head prop, one Graham Price, lumbering along in pursuit of the more fleet-footed members of the French defence and Welsh attack.

Of course, the impossible happened. One Frenchman slipped, another fell over completely and a third probably just gave up. And a wicked bounce of the ball meant it eluded the first Welshman arriving on the scene only yards from the French line.

But up it sat, like an egg dropping safely into the straw in a hen coop, into the arms of Price. He staggered a few yards and fell over the line for an astonishing try. Nigel Starmer-Smith's words on commentary went down in the annals of the game, 'They'll never believe it in Pontypool.'

Alas, it turned out the following Monday night when Pontypool reported for club training, not everyone back in Wales had been impressed. Ray Prosser, legendary hard man of the Pontypool club and a stern coach, walked into the dressing room as Pricey was relaying the story to some chums.

'Pooh, couldn't have been much of a French scrum, could it,' scoffed Prosser, a Lion himself back in 1959. 'How the hell would you have the energy to run 75 yards for a try? Real tight-heads don't do that.'

Anyway, on this particular night, Pricey promised to turn up. Charlie would too, he said.

'But you can't expect Bobby to be there. He'll say he'll make it but then something will turn up and he won't come. He's always busy, doing something, going somewhere.'

So I set off from Kent, drove down the M4 and in pitch darkness drove over some mountain in South Wales, past lots of sheep (couldn't see the shaggers, it was too dark) and even passed the odd house or two. Then I found it in a small hamlet, the pub in which Pricey had suggested we meet. Talk about the back of beyond.

I walked in to find a full house of cards, the full set of the Viet Gwent as they were also known. Bobby had made it.

We settled down and I ordered pints, Bobby lit his pipe and we talked rugby. For hour after hour.

After a while, I noticed every local in the place had filled a spot in a sort of semi-circle around the table and back to the bar. They were as intrigued as I was, just sitting there listening to the tales of rugby days and times, opponents, team-mates, referees, the lot. They talked of an era, a particularly special one for Welsh rugby when the national team was pre-eminent in the northern hemisphere (challenged only seriously in most of those years by the French).

The stories, the sense of fun and friendship just poured out of them, like fresh pints poured from the tap. It's true that later in my career I interviewed Nelson Mandela, elicited some quotes from Prince Charles at a Buckingham Palace rugby function and met some other world-famous people.

But none of them could begin to match the rich seam of stories we mined that particular night. I doubt I ever did a better rugby interview in my life.

And when it was all over, when Bobby had puffed the last of his pipe tobacco and supped the last drop of his final pint, they stood up, shook hands, cracked a joke or two with the locals and we all headed off into the night.

There were no PR people around to hurry them up and shut down the conversation after four questions, no demand for money from them or agents, no thought of any of them playing the 'I'm special, don't you know who I am' role. Everyone else in the place would have roared their heads off at them if they had, and they all knew it.

Just simple, great men of rugby football who gave their time for free and enjoyed the stories and companionship, plus memories of times, past and present.

This has been the legacy handed down through the ages to followers of this exceptional game. And I can tell you, so many times, most of us seated in the press boxes of the rugby world have thought to ourselves we must have won a Lottery of Life ticket actually to be paid to go and write about this game and, in that era, make friends of so many people attached to the sport.

These were remarkable human beings, strong, outwardly tough, occasionally gruff men who would faithfully take the lottery tickets around the tables of their local club on a Saturday night to raise funds. It didn't matter whether they played for the fifths, the Extra A's or the first team (or were Welsh internationals).They did it because their club was very often the heartbeat of the local community.

And as Bobby Windsor, The Duke, said, 'You don't get ahead of yourself when you come from roots like ours. You'd cop it from everyone, not least the Missus, if you did.'

You'll find a welcome such as this all over Wales. And anywhere else where rugby is the topic of conversation.

Working with the BBC commentator Bill McLaren on his autobiography which was published in 2004, was a joy. I'd fly north from Bristol airport, not far from my home at the time in Bath, landing at Edinburgh airport before 8am. I'd make my way past the bar (where some hardy souls were already halfway through their first pint of the day), pick up a hire car and head south, down to the Scottish borders. The gently rolling hills and mountains around towns such as Hawick, Selkirk and Kelso offer a beguiling backdrop. It is a wonderful part of the world.

Bill and his lovely wife Betty would welcome me like the son they never had, Betty fussing about what I'd eat for breakfast and how I'd like my tea. Bill would hover, smiling benignly at his wife's kindness and friendliness. And then we'd get to work and Betty would quietly melt into the background, letting us talk rugby for hours at a time.

By the time I returned to Edinburgh and flew south, I had enough material for several weeks' worth. And so it went on like that until we'd finished the book.

Sadly, Bill's memory began to go. I drove down to see him one morning before a Scottish international match I was covering one afternoon at Murrayfield. 'Aye, it's grand to see ye, but why are ye here today?' he asked.

'Oh I'm covering the match at Murrayfield this afternoon,' I said. Moments later, he seemed perplexed. 'Aye, but why are ye here in Scotland?'

When Bill McLaren passed away, Scotland didn't lose a son. It lost a legend, not to say a lovely man.

Whenever BBC commentary duties permitted, Bill spent many hours of his later life watching his beloved Hawick. And in the autumn glow, with a strong sun dipping in late afternoon behind the hill above the historic old town and the golds, yellows, soft greens and reds of the leaves tumbling silently from the trees like soldiers falling quietly on the battlefield, you could see why he so loved that part of the world.

Watching rugby, wherever it is, is invariably a delight. An afternoon match watching the Blues team at either Oxford University's Iffley Road ground or Grange Road, Cambridge's home, is another special pleasure. And one of the joys from past times was the sense of never knowing who you might see. In 1985, while I was travelling across the south of France with my girlfriend interviewing many rugby colleagues of Jean-Pierre Rives for the story of his life, we arrived one Saturday in the Catalan town of Perpignan, close by the Mediterranean.

'USAP v STADE TOULOUSE, Samedi 1500hrs' announced a poster somewhere in the town. So we bought tickets and sat at the back of a stand. Within the first ten minutes, I turned to a supporter of Toulouse sitting next to me. 'Excusez-moi Monsieur but this number 13. Who is this player? What is his name?'

'Denis Charvet,' was the answer. 'He is young but a good one, I think.'

At that time, Charvet had only played a handful of club matches for Toulouse. But his genius stood out. So much so that when Derek Wyatt, in charge of choosing a team to comprise the Major R.V. Stanley's XV to play Oxford University in the annual pre-Varsity match fixture at Iffley Road phoned me to ask if I knew of a good centre they could pick, I named Charvet.

'Denis who?' asked Wyatt. 'Yes, but can he play? Is he any good?'

I managed to get both Jean-Pierre Rives and Charvet over to play in that Stanley's team. And was the kid any use? Well, he scored a hat-trick of tries himself, made a couple more for others and dominated every UK national paper's rugby page headlines the following day. What a player Charvet was, a creative, attacking genius with electric feet.

It's tempting to claim I discovered him. But it would be a bit wide of the truth. I'm sure Toulouse already knew they had a gem on their hands, as his subsequent international career, which began one year later, proved.

Calamity so nearly befell that French trip. We went to just about every rugby town in the south, finding someone to talk to about Jean-Pierre. By the time we had got back to Paris, I had a bag of about ten or 12 cassette tapes from the interviews. We parked up somewhere near the Eiffel Tower, left the tapes hidden in the locked glove compartment and went for dinner.

When we came back, glass from a shattered window lay all over the ground beside the car. My mind pressed the 'Panic' button. What had happened to the tapes? The glove compartment had been wrenched open and there lay the tapes.

'Merci Monsieurs, for not taking them,' I thought many times subsequently.

℔ ℔ ℔ ℔ ℔

I ONLY toured Argentina twice. I'd got off the round-the-world jet the season before the Pumas were admitted to southern hemisphere rugby's elite in 2012, in a new Four Nations Championship. But I went there with the Springboks in 2005 and found it every bit as challenging and fascinating as in 1978, my first visit. Great country, intriguing culture. And as for the steaks and wine, well, you have to go a long way around the world to find better.

The South Africans, to their credit, tried to play Argentina most years. Unlike some other rugby nations I could mention. So in 2005, working for the Independent News & Media group which owned most of the English language newspapers in the major cities of South Africa, I went to Buenos Aires for the game.

The match itself wasn't anything terribly special. The Springboks won 34-23, their customary victory over the Pumas. Mind you, the Boks' biggest problem on the day had come before they even reached the Velez Sarsfield stadium. An inexperienced police motorbike outrider, sirens blaring, hustled the South African team bus down a strangely narrow street on the journey from the hotel to the ground.

I don't know what the Spanish is for a short cut but the focused Boks largely ignored it, until they realised the problem. It was a one-way street with a dead end. The only way out was to reverse the bus a couple of hundred yards back up the street with cars parked on both sides. Not easy.

They made it eventually, to the humour of most on board.

In 1978, I went to South America at the time of the FIFA soccer World Cup which was hosted by Argentina. It was a nasty, difficult time in the country. A military junta, led by General Jorge Videla, was in charge. It had abducted and killed unknown numbers of political opponents, some, allegedly, by throwing them out of aircraft as they took off over the River Plate. Or just torturing them to death and stealing their children.

You would make an international call from a Buenos Aires hotel and know someone was listening. There were strange clicks to be heard on the line; at one stage, a stifled cough. Not something you're used to when you file your story from Cardiff or Dublin.

I'd gone partly to see the football – it was a real privilege to be in Buenos Aires for the weekend of the World Cup Final – but especially South America per se. So at one point, I embarked upon a five-week overland tour of the continent, starting off in Rio de Janeiro and initially heading down via Paraguay to Montevideo, capital of Uruguay, before crossing the River Plate to Buenos Aires, then the Argentine pampas and climbing up the spine of the Andes to Salta in northern Argentina, across Bolivia and on to Peru, Cuzco and the magical Machu Picchu.

But it was in Montevideo that I encountered a problem. I was filing a weekly column for the *Manchester Evening News* and needed to telephone it, on an international reverse charge call, from the hotel where I was staying on the Uruguayan coast. The first surprise was the telephone, one of those you used to see in war movies which had to be cranked up by means of a handle on the side.

'Heinz, get me ze Obersturmfuhrer, ja,' sort of thing.

I seriously doubted whether anyone at this hotel had even heard of Europe or Britain, never mind Manchester. To say it was rudimentary would be kind.

No matter, after a lengthy wait, I heard the familiar dulcet tones of the lady copy taker in faraway Manchester.

'Alloo Peter, 'ow are yer luv,' she said. I almost felt back at home.

'And where are you calling from today?'

'On the Uruguayan coast, near Montevideo,' was the response.

'Oo, never 'eard of it,' said she.

We got about halfway through the story and quelle calamite. The line began to fade. No amount of frantic handle turning to crank it up made any difference. We lost the connection and then received a stark message from the Uruguayan operator. Calls to Europe are delayed by 48 hours.

Oh dear. Another chapter which wasn't included in the *How to be a Journalist* textbook of life.

Where do you go, what do you do? It's a bit much asking carrier pigeons to fly that far with your precious copy.

But if you think about it, it's obvious isn't it? The British Embassy, that overseas sanctuary for UK travellers in distress. Or in this case as it turned out, an overseas watering hole.

I caught a bus into Montevideo and knocked on the Embassy's front door. I showed my press card, explained my predicament and was invited into the hallowed halls to wait.

Presently, a figure straight off the set of a *Carry On* film came bounding down the stairs with a jaunty stride. Slicked back hair, elegant curled moustache set comfortably on a slightly florid face, he wore a suit that was straining at the leash under the pressure of a burgeoning stomach and a military-type tie that looked as though it had witnessed close up too many good lunches.

A hand was proffered in greeting. 'Carruthers-Smythe,' he smiled expansively. 'How can I help?'

I looked around for the arc-lights; I was convinced it was the actor Terry-Thomas reincarnated.

I explained the problem, to which our man abroad all but scoffed in derision.

'Oh, no problem old boy. We have priority on lines. I tell you what, why don't you come upstairs to my office to wait for the call?'

We did, and even at 10.30am found time for a G&T. A large one, at that. And then another arrived. By the time the call came through, I reckoned I'd stumbled upon a friend for life, someone who treated me like a long-lost brother. Here he was, that scion of the British Establishment, pouring drinks courtesy of Her Majesty's faithful taxpayers like you'd pour milk into a bowl for a thirsty cat.

Eventually, I finished filing and stood up, face doubtless flushed, to shake hands and depart. But I'd made a mistake. The British Embassies of the world in those days didn't do half measures, when it came either to their drinks or hospitality.

'Well old boy,' said my man in encouraging tones, 'time for a spot of lunch, eh what?' I accepted with alacrity. Well, what was a poor UK taxpayer to do?

So we crossed the street, headed down a couple of side alleyways and arrived at a restaurant. In either window of the double-fronted entrance, a roaring brazier with vast chunks of wood was cooking huge pieces of meat on metal skewers.

I wouldn't know how many animals had been sacrificed for our benefit that day. But if you order JUST a steak in such parts of the world they look at you as if there is something wrong with you. 'What is wrong with our parrillada?' their faces enquire.

Now the parrillada is a big boys' lunch. Sure, there's a steak on the plate but that's only part of it. You'll likely find a vast chunk of pork, some gargantuan cut of lamb, kidneys from God knows what type of animal and half a dozen sausages. Oh, and don't forget the *entranas* – entrails.

And that's not to share – it's just yours.

Of course, it goes without saying that you couldn't possibly eat all that amount of meat in a single sitting unless you had copious amounts of red wine to wash it all down. But with Her Majesty's Foreign & Commonwealth Office budget looking after the necessaries, I hereby put hand on heart and make a damning confession. We did not stint in the wine stakes.

In fact, the bottle suggested by the sommelier was so good, it didn't seem to last any time at all. Odd that. And that was before the food even arrived. When it did, we discovered another strange thing: it seemed to go down so much better with the red wine. Hence, further supplies were ordered by our man in South America.

This thoroughly congenial gathering was so pleasurable that time simply seemed to float by, like flotsam down a river. The bottles of red had long since been consigned to history when mine host happened to glance at his watch.

'Good gracious me, it's four o'clock,' he cried with horror. 'I have a meeting, I must go. So nice to have met you.'

He stood up, gave a cursory glance at the bill which was dismissed with a handful of notes and departed. I made my way unsteadily back to the Uruguayan coast – or was it Bognor or Bangor, I wasn't really sure by that stage – marvelling all the way at that timeless institution known as the British Establishment.

Part 4

I HAVE loved this profession all my life. It's not been a duty or a right to be involved in journalism. Just an absolute privilege, nothing less.

Sure, the disingenuous say some wicked things about it and its participants.

Try this witticism from Oscar Wilde, 'There is much to be said in favour of modern journalism. By giving us the opinions of the uneducated, it keeps us in touch with the ignorance of the community.'

And Samuel Clements added, 'If you don't read the newspaper you are uninformed. If you do, you are misinformed.'

But seriously, journalism has been my profession, my life and that of a lot of other people around the world. For anyone fortunate enough to have made a career out of it, there have been handsome privileges attached to this business, especially in the world of sport.

For example, I have been to every Rugby World Cup ever staged. There are comparatively few of us journalists who are members of that particularly exclusive UK club. Stephen Jones of the *Sunday Times*, Chris Jones of the *London Evening Standard*, BBC radio's Ian Robertson, freelance Chris Thau, the BBC's Cardiff-based Huw Llywelyn Davies and photographer Dave Rogers qualify. There may be one or two others but not many.

In the world of golf, I was asked to fly to West Palm Beach in Florida a few years ago to interview Jack Nicklaus at his private office. What a host. He just couldn't have been more open, pleasant and objective, not to mention humble. And the pleasure of sitting down to interview greats of the golf world like Gary Player, Arnold Palmer and Nicklaus in the opulent surroundings of the Augusta National clubhouse during the week of the majestic Masters, is a pleasure on a par with a venerable single malt. Roll it around your memory in your later years and just enjoy, enjoy.

It's a fascinating place, Augusta. As a media person, you are allowed access to the exalted Augusta National clubhouse. Climb the oak, carpeted staircase to the first floor and you can sit down for breakfast or lunch at any table. If Jack Nicklaus and his guests, or former Masters champions like Fuzzy Zoeller, Ben Crenshaw or Fred Couples happen to be at the table, that's fine. You just sit down and they welcome you. People in golf seem rather good at that.

Before I even got to Augusta one year, I sat beside Peter Alliss, the BBC golf commentator on the nine-hour flight to Atlanta. We just chatted, about life mainly, a bit about golf. Listening to some of his stories was as good a way of passing the time on a flight as you're likely to find. Mind you, I never managed to inveigle myself as a member of the Mile High Club.

I flew into Sydney once, saw Jose Carreras was singing at the Opera House that night and bought a ticket. Afterwards, enchanted by his brilliance, I talked my way into his dressing room.

'You don't know me from Adam,' I told him, 'but you met and sang with one of my daughters at the Three Tenors concert in Bath a year ago. Katie was a member of the Bath Abbey Girls' Choir and she sends her warm regards to you.'

Firstly, he smiled and readily agreed to my request for an interview the next day. Then he came up with a plan. 'I will sing at the Royal Albert Hall in London in four months' time. Please come with Katie and bring her to my room afterwards. I would like to meet her again.'

What a gentleman.

I went to the Sydney Olympics in 2000. Memorable experience, that, especially when I spent an afternoon with the 1936 USA Olympic athlete Louis Zamperini, who was a team-mate of the immortal Jesse Owens.

For me, Zamperini was the one that got away. We chatted for hours, he told me his incredible life story about his athletic feats, meeting Hitler at the 1936 Berlin Olympics, his race and then Second World War exploits which led to his plane crash, weeks afloat in a boat in the Pacific as his mates died and finally, his capture and torture by the Japanese.

At the end of it, I told him, 'Hey, Louis, do you fancy working together on a book?'

You didn't have to be Clint Eastwood to see that story would make a film.

'Hell yes, I'd love to,' he said. 'Only trouble is, I just started working with someone else on the story. Name of Laura Hillenbrand.'

And yes, sure, the book made a movie, directed by Angelina Jolie. Close one, that.

Cricketers? I met Donald Bradman in Adelaide, the South Africans Graeme Pollock, all grace and elegance as a player and a man, plus the wise Ali Bacher, in Johannesburg, the latter someone who has been a sage counsellor on many occasions. Denis Compton was charming, Brian Lara a quiet, thoughtful man. I dined many times at John Arlott's table at his Hampshire home and will never forget those moments. You would finish, maybe, at around 3am on a Sunday, sleep in and then stumble downstairs for coffee around 11am, to be confronted by the sight of John deep in discussion with his sons, Tim and Robert, as to which reds would best accompany the roast lamb lunch. Special times.

One of the guests who frequented Arlott's table was England cricket captain Mike Brearley. He and I once had a feisty run-in shortly after he had been appointed England leader in 1977. A provincial newspaper, the *Liverpool Daily Post*, called me and asked if I could do an interview with Brearley in the light of his appointment. I got a number and rang him.

In answer to my first four questions, he replied, 'No, yes, no, maybe.'

'Mike, can you please tell me what is the problem,' I said.

'I'm bored with this interview,' he replied.

My response may just have surprised him. 'I couldn't care less whether you are bored. You have accepted the post as England captain and talking to the public, supporters who pay good money to watch England matches, through the media is part of the job you've taken on. Or are you too arrogant to do that?'

With that, I slammed down the phone. There wouldn't be any interview for the paper but I wasn't prepared to be insulted just for doing my job.

Except that about 15 minutes later, the phone rang in my office. It was Mike Brearley. He certainly didn't have my number so he'd called the Liverpool paper to ask for it. His words marked him out as a big man, in the true sense of the word.

'I wish to apologise for my behaviour. I was out of order and I can only apologise. It was a difficult time for me when you called but I shouldn't have said that. I am sorry. Let's continue the interview.'

He gave me the best part of half an hour and the paper got a very good interview. But the most revealing thing had been his action and apology. Few sportsmen would have the cojones to do that. It earned him a hell of a lot of respect, in my book at least.

In rugby, I was fortunate to work with the likes of Gareth Edwards, David Campese, Willie John McBride, Andrew Slack, Corne Krige, Jean-Pierre Rives, Bill McLaren, Victor Matfield, Dan Carter and Dean Richards to mention just a handful.

I loved the modesty of those guys and Edwards was typical of that. I called him one day and suggested writing a book together.

'Oh no, I did one when I retired,' he answered. That was in 1978, more than 20 years earlier.

'So you've done nothing in your life since?' I replied.

'Oh yes, plenty.'

'Right then, let's do a book.'

It sold so well the publishers insisted we did another. They came out with that immortal line to sports stars, 'You must have loads more stories to tell.'

Gareth looked at me and I looked at him. We didn't say a word to each other, but knew. Yet somehow, we did do another book and that sold well, too. Just showed the enormous popularity of the man, really.

He is a credit to his sport and much the same goes for Willie John McBride in Northern Ireland. Incidentally, alongside both men are wonderful women, Maureen and Penny, such down-to-earth, delightful people.

I loved the story McBride told about one time on a Lions tour of South Africa.

Bored by the long, official dinner after a match, he and a fellow Lion slipped outside and wondered aloud where they might find a car. A complete stranger came over, handed them some keys and said, 'Borrow mine.'

That was the sort of thing that happened in those days.

So they drove out into the Johannesburg suburbs (as you could do safely at that time) to find a party, or at least some fun. They spotted a house with several cars parked outside and down the street, figuring this was where the action might be.

The front door was unlocked yet there seemed no-one around. By now it was late, after midnight and it had been a long, tiring night. McBride's pal slumped down in a chair and fell asleep.

McBride felt hungry and decided the answer was to raid the fridge. Inside it, he spied bacon, eggs and sausage. Just the thing for a true Ulsterman – an Ulster fry!

The great Lion was happily turning bacon over in the pan when a lady clad in her nightdress and dressing gown appeared at the foot of the stairs. 'Who on earth are you and what do you think you are doing?' she demanded.

At which moment, her husband reappeared at the front door (he had been taking friends home), took one look at a crumpled figure wearing a Lions blazer asleep in an armchair and then saw Willie John McBride attending to a frying pan on the stove. He burst out laughing.

They stayed for 'breakfast' and remained friends for years.

Rugby is like that. What a game it is that forges friendships that last a lifetime. Note to those who run the world game – do NOT forget this and do not, by your carelessness and preoccupation with the vast finances pouring into the top end of the sport, let the grassroots wither and die. The game at that level, and especially the people who administer it through their generosity of time and effort, is the true lifeblood of the sport, far more than the elevated levels of Test match rugby.

‰ ‰ ‰ ‰ ‰

JOURNALISM was my life and it gave me life. In so many ways. Above all, anyone handed this press ticket to life ought to be down on his knees each and every day, thanking the Almighty for his generosity.

That is why I find it sad to survey the world of newspaper journalism today. Everywhere you look, retrenchments rule, cuts collide. Oh sure, newspapers are still printed and a lot of their workers are battling courageously to try to turn the tide that threatens their entire futures.

But there is no denying that the heyday of newspapers is long gone. Inexorably, life moves on, different times bring fresh trends. But to watch the decline of a business that has been one of the great pillars of society, almost any society, for hundreds of years does invoke a certain melancholy among those who spent their lives immersed among its labyrinthine ways.

Equally, it would be trite, to say the least, not to mention downright untrue to claim that those in modern day sports journalism no longer have ANY fun.

The characters who write the words we purvey and ponder are too many and varied for that to be the case. From myriad backgrounds of social class and location, they combine to create a powerful unit, setting before us on a regular basis their contentious, opinionated views of the world.

But maybe that's the problem. The world. That's where the fun element has gone AWOL. And missing with it are most of the great characters that hallmarked a profession. You have read about some of them in these pages. I cannot believe it would be possible to have the kind of fun out of sports journalism today that I and my fortunate colleagues had in our era. Too many aspects have combined to blight such a concept.

French rugby writer Serge Manificat put it like this, 'Modern day journalism? It is a time of great transition and mystery. My life as a rugby journalist has been marvellous: rich, exciting, without any comparison. If a rich businessman had offered me millions of euros to become a trader, a banker or a boss in any company or industry I would have turned down his demand right away. I would never have changed my existence.

'For me, journalism was a profession that could instil passion. But now, for those coming into it, it will have to be a labour, just a labour. The worst thing is, they won't get any freedom at all. [Most of them] will never travel, never talk to anyone in the game except through Skype or a smartphone. [Most] will only visit countries…for their work…through a computer or TV screen.

'Big Brother is now the name of their editor. No pleasure to share with colleagues, no excitement to live among supporters in a crowd, no liberty in asking your own questions to players.

'Assembly line is now the nickname of modern journalism.'

In modern day life, administrators rule, the financiers plus Health & Safety tzars with them. You can't do this and you can't do that. Don't eat or drink this because it's ruinous to your health. Don't go swimming in the sea because you might drown. Don't stand near that radio mast because you'll get cancer. And don't dare to use your own eyes and brain to cross a road until some bleeping, bleedin' automaton tells you when to.

I sometimes envisage a kind of Orwellian nightmare future in which every human being in the population will be ordered to hospital in their early teens and their brains clinically removed. In their place will be fitted a computer, programmed so that they are physically unable to cross a road until a signal from a corresponding computer by the pelican crossing bleeps a message that tells them to. What's more, if they eat more than a certain-sized piece of meat or swallow more than one glass of wine in a single evening, some element of the computer will automatically trigger the 'WASTE' button and the excess amount will be spewed out of that 'person's' body.

As for sex, that is sure to be one of the key programmes fitted in the human being's electronic brain. Drop your pants on the floor and a warning buzzer will sound with a message. 'This is the third time this month, the 17th time this year. Be careful. This could raise your heart beat to dangerous levels. Get in a cold shower and then go straight to bed.'

And just for an easy life, you'll go along with it. In fact, you'll have to because you won't be able to turn off the programme. Ever.

Already, you have motor cars that the moment you exceed the official speed limit on a road start bleeping and nagging at you, trying to make you feel ashamed and telling you to slow down. It's like having a fish wife on wheels.

Something of the sort has been happening to journalists in recent years. Like an ivy surreptitiously creeping up the front of your house, the devious list of don'ts has multiplied alarmingly these past few years. In most cases, you can't entertain clients to lunch or dinner and charge the cost to the paper (even though you might get a cracking story out of them) because the owners say reporters are now like anyone else. They can buy their own food.

Some top-notch writers and correspondents go somewhere like Dublin or Paris to report a rugby international match and have to fund their own meals and drinks. All a far cry from the days when expenses were 'invented' and fictitious names applied to the sheet, just to keep everyone happy.

Course, the whole thing has been like a drunkard swaying and veering alarmingly first one way, then the other. What went on in the days when 'Dickens, C.' and 'Churchill, W.' were collecting their 'expenses' from the offices of a Fleet Street tabloid, were insane.

But what goes on today is equally mad. It's a bit like trying to identify the differences between Hitler and Stalin. Both were extremists, nutcases. They just came at their business of butchering from completely different directions.

Today, the newspaper owners of old who agreed almost every crackpot union demand just for the sake of a quiet life are gone. In their place have come adults who presumably all had a fetish with scissors throughout their childhood years. How else to explain a mantra that says, in effect, cut, cut, cut?

But if you keep on cutting, what are you eventually left with?

The decline in health of the patient known as Mr or Mrs Newspaper has been global. From the *New Zealand Herald* to the *South China Post*, the *New York Times* and the *Irish Independent*, sales of papers have been as dented as if the newspaper's building itself had been hit by a large, passing truck.

Sizes have been reduced together with staff numbers. Some bright spark somewhere, thought up the idea of dumping most journalists who were earning anything approaching a serious wage and replacing them with a 20-year-old.

'What a saving, what a brilliant idea,' said the men in suits in the accounts department. 'At a single stroke, by changing just one person, we have saved the owner more than £80,000 [working on the basis that the senior journalist might be on £100,000 and the kid who replaced him, on £20,000].

'Imagine if we do that with almost every senior member of staff. We can save millions.'

Then another clown thought up the idea of not paying even the 20-year-old his expenses for food if he was working in the paper's time. 'Well,' he reasoned, 'the guy would go home and have a meal which he'd bought himself. So why don't we extend that to when he is working for us. We don't have to buy his meals.'

So they saved another bucketload of money. Easy this, isn't it?

Then genius number three came up with a wizard of an idea.

'Why do we have to employ any of these people?' he asked. 'If they are on our books, we pay them even when they're sick, we pay them when they're on holiday, we pay their national insurance contribution and even ridiculous things like maternity or paternity pay. If we close their jobs down and just get them to re-apply for a role of that kind, we can employ them all on a freelance basis and save ourselves millions spread over large staff numbers.'

So they did. And they lived happily ever after.

Well, not quite. You see, not everyone who used to buy one of their products, i.e., a newspaper, is completely brain dead. Some may acquire a daily paper to pore over the financial figures, some to pore over figures of a very different kind.

But what a huge number of people who took the trouble to go and buy a newspaper did want was some opinion and expertise in the columns. They wanted to be entertained and a different, challenging philosophy put in front of them, a view that differed from their own which they could adopt or reject as they saw fit. Quintessentially, they wanted a forum for informed debate.

Above all, and here lies the nub, they wanted someone who had some authority, had experience of times good and bad and could make a reasoned argument one way or the other on a particular topic. The viewpoint from the hill marked 'Experience' can be very different from all others.

Alas, this was where the so-called genius of the accounts managers floundered. This was where their trousers fell down.

As most of the writers of experience and authority were gradually retrenched, so the numbers buying the newspaper dwindled correspondingly. Now wasn't that a strange thing? Who would ever have thought that? Was it a complete coincidence, an utter freak of nature that as senior men departed to be replaced by kids who had seen nothing and done even less in their lives, an awful lot of people stopped buying their paper?

I am 100 per cent certain that the goons in the accounts departments of newspapers across the world all swear allegiance to the view that all that happened WAS a complete coincidence. Or, and this is their usual 'Get out of Jail' card, they all blamed something else. The internet.

'Ah,' they say, 'you can't compete with the internet. Instant coverage of news and sport as it happens. No-one has a chance of matching that sort of service.'

In part, that's true. If the Prime Minister or President is shot, it is unlikely you are going to close your doors and windows, turn off the television and computer and go to bed until the following morning when you can go out of the house and buy a newspaper to read about it. But then, doesn't television provide an instant service of news and sport? And newspaper sales were not falling off a cliff when TV was up and running in the same way they are now that the internet has arrived. It wasn't as if there was no precedent for instant news. Television had been providing that for years.

In general, newspapers survived the advent of TV because they still offered something different. For a start, they provided the intrinsic pleasure of sitting down somewhere, like on a train, in a park at lunchtime or at home in the evening, with something in your hands that you could read at your leisure. It was both an aesthetic and intellectual delight.

Newspapers have clearly not survived the advent of the internet to anything like the same degree. But is that their fault or the internet's?

Confronted with this challenge, what newspapers had to do was enhance the appeal of their product. They needed to provide more, not less entertainment, expertise and authority in their pages. They needed to ensure they had on their editorial staff a group of writers people would want to read each day. They needed to provide not only comprehensive but innovative coverage to an outstanding degree so that many of their discerning subscribers felt they just couldn't find that quality of coverage on the net.

But instead they self-destructed, detonating their product from within by wiping out the ranks of their own esteemed writers or commentators. As an exercise in self-annihilation, it was about as bright an idea as taking a stroll along the DMZ between North and South Korea.

Yet almost all the newspapers of the world had one potentially decisive advantage over the net. Most of the writing on the latter is dire, simply dreadful. Of course, there are exceptions but as a rule of thumb, that is the painful truth. That's what 20-year-olds who are being paid a pittance give you.

If you find a really well-written, creatively argued article on the net it is almost certain to be on a newspaper's own site, written by one of its own journalists. Yes, some do still exist, particularly on the national daily papers of a country or major city. But too many, far too many have been made redundant.

Then there has been the problem of those actually in decision-making editorial roles on the papers. Too often, they have also been sub-standard. There is a reason for that.

In the past decade or so, many newspaper editors in the field of both news and sport have been taken from the ranks of inside men and not, as used to be the case, from those with vast amounts of outside reporting experience. Those sorts of guys instinctively knew how to communicate – but sadly, too many of the current crop of editors and sports editors are nothing more than company men, often with depressingly little outside reporting experience.

What is more, they are led by the accountants who, in reality, now make the decisions.

The argument for continuing to invest in the product by funding reporters to get out there and dig up the stories, and find out what the public was actually saying and what most mattered to them, was lost too easily because the wrong people were promoted into the top jobs.

And the main reason for that – the original sin which led to decline – was the advance of new technology, in the production of newspapers, which led to a real division in the business between the inside and the outside men. This predated the internet by many years but may well have been the true beginning of the problems.

In earlier days, working inside and outside the office was still interchangeable. Indeed, many people both edited and reported on local and regional newspapers. In Fleet Street, most top editor's jobs were taken by former reporters and correspondents, many of whom still had leading writing positions and were visible to their readership. Max Hastings on the *Daily Telegraph* was a classic example. But how many current editors and sports editors now do that?

Because they were seen by the public to be leading the line they were also the ones taking the big editorial decisions. Now, the only big decisions most of them take are budgetary ones. There is surely a case to make that, because of all this, the accountants were allowed to take over the building all too easily, and without any intellectual or journalistic challenges to their bottom line.

Finally, as the nature of newspapers changes from journalism to churnalism (i.e., everyone using the same sources) so the nature of our free society changes. That is the biggest danger of all, that a free press becomes less able to check and challenge

– simply because it does not have the financial resource, or the will to do it – and that therefore our freedoms become less free. These are disturbing thoughts regarding the future.

There is another problem linked to all this. In the world of sport, far too many media organisations cravenly accepted the dictates of the PR men brought in to handle the media affairs of national unions, clubs or franchises. Suddenly, access to players became restricted with, in many cases, some simply hidden from the media representatives.

This was pathetic and, in the case of a sport like rugby where regular access even to the best players in the world had always been available, something that threatened to alter the whole social make-up and structure of the sport.

Suddenly, young players were emerging who had no contacts with media men, no understanding of their needs and no thought that by talking to the media whenever required, they were spreading the message of their sport and potentially drawing in an ever wider audience.

In the professional era, none of that mattered to young players earning handsome salaries and driving sponsored cars. But it hugely damaged the game and bred a different type of player, many of whom crassly lacked the social skills to deal competently with either the media or public.

In the case of the media, in general they just lay supine and accepted these damaging restrictions. Few offered much resistance.

Yet this was not professionalism at work among national rugby unions, top clubs or franchises. What it was, in fact, was crass amateurism. For one very good reason.

Would anyone suggest that American sports, their organisation and structure are amateur? The complete opposite is the case. In almost all they do, in the way they run their whole business, they are the epitome of professionalism.

Yet their philosophy in dealing with the media in the States could not be more different. They go out of their way to cultivate the media, offer them the best facilities and access to whichever players they want whenever the media want them.

Media representatives are allowed in the dressing room of most top sports outfits in America. For the sport's mantra is this: How can we help the media? How can we get more exposure for our sport through them?

Contrast this with certain rugby clubs and provinces in the UK who make no attempt to hide their dislike for the media. They go out of their way to make their lives difficult and block free access to whichever players the media would like to interview that particular week. How should the media in Britain have handled this closing off of access, this obstruction? Simple. By forming a collective approach that told the national union, club or whoever that unless things changed, there would be no coverage of the club or franchise. Furthermore, there would be a total ban on using the names of sponsors associated with the national or local team or tournaments and no free publicity of forthcoming matches, kick-off times etc.

Had a collective approach prevailed, the organisations would have wet themselves with fright and capitulated. Imagine what their sponsors would have said. But instead of this, it was the media who folded. Worst of all, they did so with no thought for their customers who would want to read something of interest.

They used to say the forwards in rugby were the donkeys. Plenty of grunt and grind but no brains. Really? Read these comments from the Toulon and Italian tight head prop forward Martin Castrogiovanni, given to London's *Daily Mail* and you might think differently:

'A lot of the interviews you see before or after the match…I don't want to say it's bullshit but it's all polite and careful.

'I am one of the old fashioned guys and will still say what I think. Not because I want people to like me but because of who I am and what I am. In life, it's good to say what you think.

'We live in a free world, or at least we think we do. But sometimes you get told off for what you say. It's "you can't say that" or "be careful what you say to the media".

'In rugby, we used to kill each other then go for a beer together. But now, rugby is everything that we hated about football.'

This is not just a problem related to the UK. In Cape Town, South Africa earlier this year, the local rugby franchise in the Super 15 tournament, the Stormers, put up for interview one day a first team player notorious for talking in platitudes. He could stand there for 20 minutes, talk non-stop and say absolutely sweet FA. Nothing at all.

So when he was led into the room to conduct interviews this particular day, most media men walked out. The PR guy was furious and complained. But what about? Was he so used to seeing complete rubbish written in papers or appearing in recorded interviews or online that it was an affront to his carefully stage-managed plan when some media guys with judgement said, no thanks, and left?

For far too long, these sports organisations have just taken the media for granted. And the media have meekly accepted their greatly reduced opportunities. It has meant that the person who means most, the newspaper reader, has been fobbed off with the kind of predictable nonsense a child could have written. Is it any wonder so many of them have stopped buying papers?

Let me tell you a couple of stories about how top sports stars deal with the media in America. For a period of a few years, I went to Augusta and covered several US Masters golf tournaments. At the prestigious Masters, by the way, if you are an accredited media person, you can just wander into the players' locker room and talk to whomsoever you want. No restrictions. You don't even have to knock on the door.

One year, I wanted to do a major interview with the South African Gary Player for the newspapers I was working for in South Africa.

His representative asked me, 'When would suit YOU? You'll be busy during the day at the course. What about seven in the evening at the private house where he is staying?'

I turned up at this palatial pile, was warmly received and had an hour with him. He could not have been more helpful.

Another time, at the 2007 US Open at Oakmont Country Club, near Pittsburgh in Pennsylvania, I desperately needed to see the South African golfer Rory Sabbatini as he completed an early round US time. Problem was, Johannesburg is six hours ahead of Pittsburgh and as it was already around 1pm at the course, it was 7pm South African time and I had only a few minutes before deadline for that night's first edition papers.

Then came the worst news of all. Sabbatini, already a guy with a reputation as someone with a fuse that regularly shorted, marched on to the 18th green his face the colour of thunder. He was about to sign for a round of 84, an absolute nightmare. By his demeanour, you could tell that doing a media interview was about as ideal a suggestion as jumping into the nearest lake, golf bag and all.

But you do what you have to do and as he came off, the steam almost pouring out of his ears, I introduced myself. 'Listen,' I said, 'you won't want to do this but I really need you to tell me about that round for the South African papers. And I've got a very tight deadline.'

He said, 'Give me two minutes, I'll sign for this pile of shit and I'll come out and talk.'

Right, I thought, I know the guy's game. He'll take another exit from the scorer's cabin and disappear.

So what happened? He signed, came back out and said, 'What do you want to know?'

In the end, I had to stop him, I was so short of time before deadline. But it told me a hell of a lot about the sheer professionalism of guys like that. Most people would have run from an interview at such a time. But not Sabbatini. Showing up was not just a credit to himself and his own character but to his sport.

Going back to newspapers, another crass mistake made for so long by most of them was to offer all its editorial coverage for free on the net. This was, and remains, suicidal. Of course newspaper sales plunged if people could turn on their computer in the morning and read a whole paper without going anywhere near a shop to buy a copy. You had to wonder why on earth they didn't have more faith in their product.

Wouldn't the same happen to any commodity if you could get it for free on the net? Marks & Spencer or Morrisons didn't offer free food to online customers. Had they done so, their sales in store would have gradually collapsed.

Newspaper proprietors were too frightened for too long to bite the bullet and charge for their product on the net. Yet a few that did, like *The Times* in London, now has increasing numbers of online subscribers through its Times Plus package. This package offers a copy of the paper delivered to the subscriber's door, plus access online (which is otherwise barred) and access also to internet offerings, such as special events. It is like joining a club and although we don't know the exact breakdown of numbers between those just buying the paper and those joining Times Plus, overall subscribers are said to be around 400,000.

By contrast, papers like the *Daily Telegraph* and *The Guardian* continue to give their content away for free. It makes no sense.

Just 15 years ago, the *Daily Telegraph* was selling in excess of one million copies daily. Today, that figure is around 490,000 and continuing to decline. The *Daily Express* has fared even worse, dropping from just over a million in year 2000 to 457,000 at the start of 2015. In the same period, the *Daily Mirror* has slid from 2.2 million daily to 990,000.

Yet one newspaper, based on invention and adapting to the changing demands of public opinion, has bucked the trend. The Independent Group's *i*, a greatly slimmed-down newspaper from the usual and offering just a brief coverage of the world and its events each morning, started off in 2011 with sales of 133,000. Earlier this year, it was selling 280,000.

The cover price, 40 pence, was nowhere near the cost of its UK national rivals. But it was providing a niche in the market that clearly increasing numbers of readers sought.

But the examples of such commendable innovation have been few and far between in the media world at large. Like dinosaurs sensing mortal wounds, they have approached their doom with a heavy plod. Shedding parts of the body has not worked.

Of course, to round out the picture properly, you have to say that newspapers were hammered by the world financial crash of 2007/08 and the subsequent collapse in advertising revenue. This could hardly have been foreseen, certainly not to that degree. In a sense, it was the perfect storm: the growing power of the internet allied to savage reductions in advertising revenue.

Sensible economies were inevitable in such a situation. But too much of an air of panic pervaded the newspaper business. The jettisoning of some crucial assets, individuals critical to an ultimate recovery, was a trend that became madness, paranoia. Whether they were writers who could have lured back to their paper some of the readers lost, was never considered. The scrapheap was piled high with many notable literary figures. Their ghosts have haunted their old newspaper offices ever since.

What was perhaps most bizarre was that amid this deafening sound in the journalism forest of chainsaws decimating the business, some newspapers that clearly required pruning were left untouched.

Thus, we might say tongue in cheek, they have left undone those cuts they ought to have done, and they have done those cuts they ought not to have done. And there was no sense in them.

Back in Cape Town, even in 2015, the morning edition of the *Cape Times* is challenged almost the moment it appears on the streets by the morning edition of the *Cape Argus*, the evening paper of, er, the same group. In the early years of the 21st century, this was a policy straight from the madhouse.

The folly continues to be exacerbated by the appearance of a *Cape Argus* evening edition. Yet sales of both daily and evening papers are struggling to get much beyond 30,000, a substantial decline from years gone by. As recently as 2006, the *Cape Times* was selling 56,000 on its best day. In other words, sales have just about halved in only nine years.

Clearly, savings could be made by restricting the *Argus* to an afternoon paper. Yet the madness continues and someone somewhere is digging ever deeper into his pockets to find the money. Unless there is a political element to the equation which has not been revealed.

This is far from the only example of a profession that has given a highly meritorious impression of some poor unfortunate desperately thrashing around but drowning out in the ocean. Setting one part of your newspaper business in direct competition against another is plain daft. In all of this, it is hard to ignore one undeniable fact. Newspapers have also lost sales to a major degree because they have lost their way in terms of what they have been offering their readers.

For example, it is hard to believe that the traditional readers of the UK's *Daily Telegraph*, many of them retired, middle-class people from the prestigious AB1 advertising group, want to read stories about the teacher who ran off with a 15-year-old pupil, or the vicar who was enjoying affairs with some of his female parishioners. Yet too often, the *Telegraph* seems to be stuffed full of such tripe. The paper became so obsessed with Pippa Middleton, sister of the Duchess of Cambridge, that it gave her an individual column. Of course, it said nothing and matched the tripe elsewhere in the paper.

And lo and behold, sales continued to fall. Eventually, someone woke up and applied some common sense. The column was quietly buried. But how much would that lunacy have cost? And did anyone ever stop to think about whether the views of a publicity seeking silly socialite would be compatible with those of traditional *Telegraph* readers, the retired Colonels from Hampshire and such like? It was about as bright an idea as asking Adolf Hitler to pen a column for the *Jewish Times*.

Thus, should we not ask ourselves, is the decline in sales the fault of readers who abandoned the paper in the light of such a trend? Or were the people who decided to take the paper away from its roots the ones really responsible?

It is not an exact science, but one point emerges with brutal clarity in all this. Too many newspapers today, from national dailies to provincial evenings or weeklies, are just not very good products. Might that not have had something to do with this widespread decline?

People generally stop doing something or going somewhere if what they find when they get there is not much good and not to their satisfaction. Especially if they have to pay for it. You can't blame them for that.

There is, I suspect, still a market for good quality, enterprising and inventive newspapers, albeit not to the same degree as 20 or 50 years ago. The changes in social trends in that time have decreed as much.

What there is clearly no longer an interest in, are newspapers that have drifted away from their regular readership and now fill their pages with rubbish, or material that someone else has already had on its internet site for anything up to 24 hours. They continue to do it to save money, yet then turn around and wring their hands in despair at the ever rapid decline of sales. I mean, hello, who is using the family brain cell here? When is someone actually going to think the unthinkable, to go where no human brain has ever gone before and connect the two?

I'll give you an example of this muddle-headed thinking. In late 2014, someone I know pursued a job opportunity on a UK regional newspaper. They made their interest known to the paper and were duly invited for an interview. What they heard when they got there, frankly alarmed them.

A young woman from the paper's Human Resources department seemed to be asking many of the questions, even though there was a senior editorial figure also in attendance. Some of those questions were inane, so much so that my pal quickly realised he wasn't interested in the job, even if he'd been offered it.

One reason for that was a question he put to them. 'If you get much of your news from a weekly press conference which is open to all the media, internet, print, TV, everything, how do you match the challenge of those outlets that can get quotes from the press conference up online or even on screen within an hour? Because there is surely an intrinsic flaw here.

'What value is there in you coming out the following day, almost 24 hours later, with the same story and exactly the same quotes as have been widely seen (and, almost certainly, read by anyone interested) for most of the previous day and all that evening? Why would anyone bother buying your paper to read material they'd read the previous day?'

Their response shocked him. They didn't have one. They just wanted someone to go on doing exactly the same thing as they'd always done, get quotes from the press conference and write a story for the next day's paper. Even though they knew it would be almost 24 hours old by the time it appeared.

There was no hint of how they might overcome this damaging scenario. No questions to him along the lines of, 'Right, that is what happens now and we cannot go on like this. We must find another way. What would you do to solve the problem?'

Nothing of the sort. They had neither the wit nor imagination even to see the problem, let alone start exploring ways of getting round it.

He went home totally disillusioned, a feeling confirmed by a glance at the circulation figures of that paper. At the start of 2000, they were selling around 100,000 copies daily. Today, only 15 years later, they sell less than half that number. They are facing a continuing downward drift without the first idea of what to do about it.

Should the general public be concerned about this? Well, someone fairly high up in British society clearly is. During his March 2015 Budget speech to the House of Commons in London, the British Chancellor George Osborne announced inquiries into the state of the UK's newspaper business to see how the Government could help.

Osborne said, 'Local newspapers are a vital part of community life – but they've had a tough time in recent years – so today we announce a consultation on how we can provide them with tax support too.'

I have focused in part on the UK national newspapers but a story of similar decline can be found around the world. In response to the crisis, many papers have not only dumped expensive staff but greatly trimmed the size of their product, often by very significant numbers of pages. Some have offered customers that highly unappealing combination of a reduced-sized newspaper at an increased cost with many former supplements dropped. Another example of the lunatics running the asylum.

In Britain, the provincial newspapers, both mornings and evenings, have been battered. In some cases, such as the *Bath Evening Chronicle*, it seemed as though it hardly took five minutes from the start of the recession to a major cutback.

First published around 1760, it was changed from an evening paper to a weekly in September 2007, just as the recession was taking hold. But sales had declined well before that.

Further north, the Trinity Mirror group-owned *Liverpool Daily Post* revealed its difficulties in January 2009 when the Saturday edition of the paper was axed. The paper, first published in 1855, made its final appearance as a daily in January 2012, when sales were down to 40,000. It then became a weekly but was finally killed off in December 2013.

A *Sunday Echo* was launched but revealed only the desperation of its bewildered owners. Having chopped the *Post* because of its poor 40,000 daily sales figures, it invested heavily in a Sunday which a year ago was selling only 33,000.

In October 2012, the owners of the *Brighton Argus*, in their infinite wisdom, raised the cover price by 45 per cent. The result? Sales fell alarmingly. A paper that at one time had sold 25,000 crashed to 16,000 inside a year. Last year, it was selling barely 15,000 daily.

But the Brighton paper was really only mirroring a decline in most UK provincial papers. By February 2014, the *Norwich Evening News* sales figure was down to a paltry 11,945 copies daily.

Around the same time, the *Swindon Advertiser*, another evening paper, was selling 12,690 copies daily on average. Surely papers in this plight have to look at following the example of the *London Evening Standard* which is now given away free and relies on advertising revenue from an increased readership.

But this scenario is not something confined to the UK. A similar story is unravelling right across the world. In New Zealand, the last year-on-year sales figures for the Auckland-based *New Zealand Herald* dropped from 147,593 to 142,566. By some standards, a 12-month dip in sales of 3.4 per cent was very acceptable indeed.

But go out into the New Zealand provinces and a very different picture emerges. The *Dominion Post* in the capital city Wellington dropped from 74,954 to 68,912, a year-on-year loss of eight per cent. On that ratio of decline, in just ten years' time, the paper will be selling around 8,000. These are frightening forecasts.

As for the *Waikato Times*, based in Hamilton, sales dipped from 32,162 to 26,610 in a single year, an alarming drop of 17.26 per cent.

What we may be looking at here, ultimately, is the death of an entire industry. Who can believe, given these troubling figures, that any of these papers will still exist in ten years' time? Maybe that is an optimistic timeline. What about in five years? Almost an entire provincial industry wiped out before our eyes? You had better believe it possible.

There is a neat symmetry here between provincial newspapers and the world of rugby. Well, French rugby to be exact. In 2015, an extraordinary number of clubs which had, in their distinguished past, been champions of France, were languishing in Division Two. The likes of Perpignan, Biarritz, Narbonne, Mont-de-Marsan, Montauban, Agen, Tarbes and Beziers were all in the second tier of French rugby.

Yet all were former winners of the prestigious Championnat de France. Truly, the mighty had fallen on hard times.

There was a reason for that. And the clue was to be found in the list of clubs in the prestigious Top 14 of French rugby. Begles from the increasingly prosperous city of Bordeaux, Racing Metro and Stade Francais, both based in Paris, Stade Toulouse, Clermont Ferrand, Toulon and Montpellier were all either based amid prosperous, industrial cities or enjoyed the financial benevolence of multi-millionaires based in them, like Mourad Boujallel at Toulon and Jackie Lorenzetti at Racing Metro. Toulouse is the home city of the mighty Airbus Industrie and in the case of Clermont, they enjoy the enormous financial support of the Michelin tyre empire which is established in the city. Few businesses of that magnitude have their headquarters in Mont-de-Marsan, Narbonne, Beziers, Agen or Tarbes.

In other words, the clubs based in major cities could attract business sponsorship and crowd support in propitious numbers. The clubs out in the provinces, the old power base of French rugby, had withered. It might appear an inane comparison but it's not. Prosperity has flown the provincial nest in light of the world's worst recession since 1929. The money has gone. It is the big city men who now hold the cash.

Those among the elite in French rugby are enjoying unprecedented financial hand-outs as part of the mega-money television deal negotiated by the French Federation de Rugby (FFR) with ambitious TV stations. Basically, it has turned every one of the Top 14 into millionaire clubs.

To misquote Winston Churchill, 'Never, in the history of human endeavour, has so much been enjoyed by so few.' Or something like that.

He might have been talking about English soccer's Premier League clubs, too.

As regards newspapers, it really ought to have been apparent long ago that they needed to work with, not fight against the internet. By judiciously adapting it to their own products, they could have utilised some of the obvious advantages the net has brought.

It should have been clear, too, that modern-day publications have to engage better and more closely with their readers. By inviting them in to the world of journalism, explaining how their papers worked and operated, how editors arrived at certain decisions they could have forged closer liaisons with their customers.

Personalised e-mails, albeit not those sent every hour on the hour thereby driving the recipient crazy, would have been one way to firm up such ties. A regular Saturday morning e-mail offering, in the words of the editor, the three best articles in that day's paper could have been accompanied by a guarantee of publication for any response from the reader to any of those articles.

Competitions run by newspapers, in print and online, should have offered readers the chance to accompany a sports reporter to a match to see how it was all done. You couldn't expect

London's *Times* to offer all this in its limited space. But you can't tell me the *Norwich Evening News* or *Swindon Advertiser* has never had the room for such initiatives. Invitations to special events were another way forward and occasionally inviting a local personality to be a guest editor for a specific day, yet another.

Now before I get deluged with responses telling me that these papers have done all these things for years and they haven't made any difference, I'd point out that some probably have. But too few, I suspect, in reality.

If you want to keep someone on board you have to communicate with them. Companies in the commercial world, like British Airways, fully understand this concept. If you are a member of their Executive Club, you get regular offers in all kinds of fields. They are offering ideas, articles, promotions, fantasies. Why shouldn't newspapers be like this?

How many newspapers have been proactive in arranging special events for their readers? People are warmed by nostalgia. Could not the *Brighton Argus* for example, or the *Leicester Mercury* stage a series of events where sports stars from the past in their region are invited to an evening to speak about their life and times? Surely the newspapers could provide or find a suitable venue. Perhaps general admittance would be free to those readers collecting a specific number of vouchers. Others would pay at the door.

This theme could be developed in all manner of fields: politics, gardening, cookery etc. And I'm willing to bet many of these one-time celebrities would be only too happy to get involved. The point here is that the local paper would be strengthening its ties, cementing its links to the local community. That has to be an essential requirement of this process.

I'm not saying that not a single newspaper in the land has ever done this type of thing. But I don't think anywhere near enough have been sufficiently proactive or innovative in this field.

And I find that strange. For within the world of journalism you will discover some of the most inventive, thoughtful minds it is possible to come across in life. These are people, in the main, of high intelligence, adaptability and vision. Yet it seems like few of those qualities have been used to fight for their newspaper's survival. Curious, very curious.

The plight of newspapers is emphasised by the fact that so few of the younger generation read them. Most, at least those with a brain to use, know exactly what is going on in the world. But they get their information chiefly from the internet. And in their busy, hi-tec lives, few have time to wade through newspapers.

If you accept that statement, then it is hard to see how many newspapers still operating today will actually be around within a decade, or less. I suspect that in that time we will see a regular procession of closures, papers going to the wall and being abandoned by their owners.

It is a deeply depressing scenario.

Brave new world, say the optimists and it's true. For example, where today are the once beloved Hansom cabs, the ubiquitous hats and caps faithfully worn each day by an entire generation or the steam trains of past years?

Life must mean progress and we all have to buy that philosophy, no matter who we are or whatever our personal preferences.

No profession, industry or social trend has a God-given right to immortality. But you surely have to say, the death of such bodies is made an awful lot easier to accept if they had battled gamely to the end.

In the case of newspapers, I don't believe most can say that. Far too many have been brought close to extinction by their own inadequacies, even incompetencies. And they have subsided tamely, without much of a fight.

Faced by the greatest challenge in a generation, they lacked ideas, flexibility and innovation to re-adjust their company's focus in different directions. If indeed that is to be the legacy of large numbers of this profession of journalism, it will make sad carving for their tombstones.

If, on the other hand, all these foreboding thoughts turn out to be needless and, phoenix-like, newspaper journalism rises from the ashes, I shall be the first to applaud. Whichever world I happen to be inhabiting at the time.

But whatever ensues, you have to say one thing. It was a hell of a lot of fun while it lasted.

Or at least, it usually was.

I want to finish with two stories that reveal very different emotions from my life in journalism.

At the Rugby World Cup of 1995 in South Africa, the Ivory Coast wing Max Brito was horribly injured. Brito, playing against Tonga, was tackled and then trapped when a ruck collapsed on him, breaking his vertebrae. An operation at a Pretoria hospital stabilised the fourth and fifth vertebrae but he was left paralysed.

I was editing *Rugby World* magazine at the time and when the tournament was over, I flew to Bordeaux and went out to a hospital in the suburbs to see Brito. With his skin a soft colour and lean body in the supreme shape of an international sportsman, he appeared in one sense the epitome of perfect health. But this was a grand deceit, à great illusion.

For this young man, still only 24, lay in bed on a warm day in a French clinic, unable to move a muscle. The contrast could not have been crueller. He knew then, well enough, this was to be his prison for the remainder of his life. And it tore at your heart to see it. I could hardly get over how fit and well he looked, facially. Yet if a fly came in through the open window and landed on his nose, he could raise not a finger, still less an arm to brush it away. He was paralysed from the neck down.

We talked for an hour before I left. His tone and demeanour was as soft and gentle as a summer breeze on your face. But when I got outside, the emotions simply overwhelmed me.

Twelve years later, by 2007, Max had some limited movement in his chest and arms but remained virtually unable to move. Even more sadly, he and his wife had separated and he rarely saw his young sons.

In an interview that year Brito spoke poignantly about his plight, saying, 'It is now 12 years since I have been in this state. I have come to the end of my tether...If one day I fall seriously ill, and if I have the strength and courage to take my own life, then I will do it…This bloody handicap – it's my curse. It kills me and I will never accept it. I can't live with it and it's going to be with me for the rest of my life.'

There was another disturbing element to the Max Brito story. In the immediate aftermath of the injury, Brito was given compensation which was funded by all sides competing at the 1995 World Cup.

But in 2003, Damian Hopley, who was head of the Professional Rugby Players' Association in the UK, claimed that his organisation had become involved in supporting Brito financially. This was news that raised many eyebrows.

Hopley alleged, 'We became involved in money-raising events for Max. But there was very little support for him from Rugby World Cup.'

But Rugby World Cup denies this allegation. It told me in a statement in May 2015, 'Following Max Brito's accident in 1995, he received substantial financial assistance from World Rugby [or IRB as it was then]. Through the rugby community, not least former RWC director Marcel Martin, World Rugby has remained in touch with Max, assisting him where appropriate. As with previous Rugby World Cups, Max will be invited to RWC 2015 final as a guest of World Rugby and we will continue to help him where possible.'

That has to be right and proper.

World Rugby, as the international game is now known, receives approximately £80m for its coffers from any nation wishing to host a Rugby World Cup.

What is more, the sport's governing body also demands it keeps all the monies arising from sponsorship and hospitality for a World Cup. The only revenue available to a host nation is through ticket sales alone.

Thus, it is axiomatic that the sport's governing body provides the money to support for life one of its own, a player so horribly paralysed by playing the sport as Max Brito has been.

But there are varying degrees of anguish to be experienced in life. Beyond dispute, the most harrowing place I ever visited in my journalistic career was an encampment just outside a small town in Poland named Oswiecim. Since the 1940s, it has been better known as Auschwitz.

I went with my elder daughter, Hannah, who was by then contracted to the Independent News & Media group as a young photographer. I insisted we went in January for two reasons.

Firstly, International Holocaust Remembrance Day is on 27 January and the feature article with photographs was to mark that day for papers throughout the group worldwide. But the second reason was just as relevant.

'I want to try and gain some sort of understanding of the vicious winter conditions they endured in the camp,' I told Hannah. It was of course, a largely fatuous statement since we were not planning to stand outside the barracks at Auschwitz at five in the morning, with snow falling on our bodies clad only in thin striped pyjamas, as guards threatened us with whips and their dogs leapt at us, trying to bite.

However, when we got there amid the snow beneath a slate grey sky with the thermometer registering -15°C, we did begin to understand something about the agonies of such cold. Even with multiple layers of clothing on our bodies.

We took a three-hour tour, with a personal guide, to extract as much information as possible. And we walked into the gas chamber, with its terrifyingly claustrophobic low ceiling and hatches through which the Zyklon B gas canisters had been dropped, trying all the while to imagine how it must have been as the Germans forced hundreds of Soviet prisoners of war inside and sealed their fate.

There was the wall where other prisoners were shot, the piles of human hair that remain, the barracks where they huddled piteously for some protection from the evil elements of winter. And then, halfway through the experience, Hannah's camera, a Canon, packed up. It simply stopped working in the extreme cold.

Watching a simple rugby game as a job never began to compare with this. I found the experience haunting, appalling and yet conversely, somehow a necessary pain.

It is hard to describe this, even for someone who has used words all his life as the tools of his career. But I felt a more rounded person for having been there and seen it. Not a better person, just a more thoughtful, worldly individual who could prioritise better and accept issues of everyday life that seemed at the time to be crises yet were in truth things of little real importance.

When you have seen Auschwitz you have stared into the eyes of human evil. Few run-of-the-mill events merit serious consideration when set alongside what happened at that place.

What did surprise me, sometime later, after the article had been published around the world, was the hate mail I received from the Holocaust deniers who accused me of swallowing Jewish propaganda and extenuating the so-called lies of that generation.

You have to feel pity for such people. To live your life behind glasses labelled distortion must be a sad experience.

You could never go to Auschwitz to write and call it a pleasure. It was torturous, emotionally shattering and an experience I shall never forget. I know my daughter felt the same way.

Yet I was grateful for the chance to go. That the academically distracted schoolkid whose only advantage was that he knew what he wanted to be at seven years of age could one day be sent to write at the shrine of so many brave people, was a humbling thought.

I have been deeply grateful for everything journalism has given me. But maybe, in the most perverse way, writing at Auschwitz was both the zenith and nadir of my entire career.

For once you have been there you have a better grasp of the potential evil that resides in too many human beings. Not, please note, an understanding; just a grasp. Without that, you are intrinsically a lesser person. It is why I would urge anyone to go there, to look at it and think about what happened. The victims deserve nothing less from us.

To my profession, for giving me that chance and so many other experiences, I shall forever be in its debt.

Index

ACT (Australian Capital
  Territory) 97
AS Clermont Auvergne 120-121
Abbott, Tony 88
Aberdeen 152
Adelaide 288
Aer Lingus 215, 217
Africa 165
African National Congress party
  (ANC) 166
Agen 249, 253-254, 263, 266,
  308-309
Aguirre, Jean-Michel 236
Airbus Industrie 309
Air France 230-6, 235
Aix-en-Provence 269
Alcatraz 121
Allen, Dave 85
Allied Irish Banks 225
Alliss, Peter 287
Allsport agency 250
America 299-4
Andes 282
Andrew, Rob 88
Andrew, Rodney 39
Argentina 281
Arlott, John 37, 130, 288
Arlott, Robert 288
Arlott, Tim 288
Arsenal 37, 49-4
Athletic Ground, Richmond 231
Atlanta 287
Atlantic Ocean 210, 227
Auch 152, 242-246, 248
Auckland 11-12, 95, 152, 185,
  250, 272, 308
Augusta National 10, 286-287,
  300
Auschwitz 314-5
Austin, Richard 14-15
Australia 19, 87, 90-91, 94,
  100, 104, 108, 112, 114, 139,
  182, 185, 188-189, 226, 229,
  249, 264
Australian, The 102
Autoroute des Deux Mers 253
Auvergne 120
Avonvale RFC 274

BBC Radio Cleveland 58
BBC Radio Newcastle 58, 60
BBC Wales 72
BMW 269
Bacher, Ali 288
Bagneres de Bigorre 236
Bagshot 44
Ballester, Pierre 261
Ballymena 114
Balmoral Beach (Sydney) 103
Bangalore 165
Bangor 284
Bangor Hospital (North Wales)
  118
Barbarians RFC 93, 237, 251
Barcelona 49, 56
Basingstoke 43-44
Basque XV 249

Bastiat, Jean Pierre 236
Bates, Alan 64
Bath 143, 219, 274, 278
Bath Abbey Girls Choir 287
Bathampton 274
Bath Evening Chronicle 303
Bath RFC 120, 122-123
Batty, Grant 273
Bayern Munich FC 56
Bayonne 265
Beach Boys, The 233
Beatles, The 41
Beaumont, Bill 128-129
Beauvais airport, Paris 230
Beckenbauer, Franz 55-56
Beenhakker, Leo 56
Beer, Ian 77
Begles (Bordeaux) 308
Bekker, Andries 190
Belfast 11
Belfast Telegraph 114, 209
Benazzi, Abdel 109
Berbizier, Pierre 80-81, 108, 253
Berkeley Court Hotel, Dublin 216
Berlin 268
Berlin Olympics 1936, 288
Bertranne, Roland 236
Best, Dick 80, 82
Best, George 51
Betsen, Serge 122
Bevan, Derek 95
Bewleys, Dublin 194
Beziers 236, 263, 267, 308-309
Biarritz 308
Bills, Hannah 102, 142, 314-315
Bills J.A. (Father) 31, 118-119
Bills James 142, 154, 160, 265
Bills, Katie 137, 142, 287
Birmingham 53
Bishops School, Western Cape
  (SA) 142
Bizet, Georges 239
Blackheath RFC 28-30, 195
Blanc, Eric 263
Blanco, Serge 108, 111-112
Bloemfontein 186
Blue Bulls 190
Blue Riband 40
Boet Erasmus stadium (Port
  Elizabeth) 148
Bognor 284
Bohemians RFC (Limerick)
  196, 198
Bolivia 282
Bolt, Usain 198
Bondi Beach (Sydney) 10
Bordeaux 70, 249, 252, 256, 262,
  266, 308, 312
Bordeaux Airport 255
Border, Allan 184
Botany Bay (Australia) 90, 103
Botha, Bakkies 186
Botha, P.W. 129
Bouclier de Brennus 120, 263
Bouet, Dominique 111-112
Boujallel, Mourad 309

Bourse, The (Paris) 264
Bouverie Street (Fleet St.) 46
Boycott, Geoffrey 197
Bradman, Sir Donald 95, 97, 288
Brains Beers (Wales) 75
Brearley, Mike 288-289
Breitner, Paul 56
Brisbane 109, 185
Bristol 57, 72, 223
Bristol Airport 219, 278
British Airways 67, 107, 134,
  253, 310
British Embassy, Montevideo 283
British & Irish Lions 19-20, 128,
  133, 140
British & Irish Lions 1950s 238
British & Irish Lions 1959 tour to
  New Zealand 196
British & Irish Lions 1977 tour to
  New Zealand 276
British & Irish Lions 1983 tour to
  New Zealand 250, 272
British & Irish Lions 1993 tour to
  New Zealand 80
Brito, Max 312-314
Brive 109, 249
Broughton Park RFC 125
Brown, Gordon 16
Brownsword, Andrew 122
Bucharest 53, 198
Buckingham Palace 277
Buenos Aires 281-282
Burge, Josephine (Reed) 64
Burger, Schalk 190
Burton, Richard 85

Calais 20-21, 162, 237
Calcraft, Bill 93
Calder, Finlay 20
California 233
Callas, Maria 239
Camargue 267
Cambridge University 34
Campese, David 93-99, 106, 108,
  131, 184, 251, 289
Camps Bay (Cape Town) 173
Cape Argus 303
Cape Times 166, 303
Cape Town 11, 94, 103, 133,
  138-139, 142-145, 147, 153,
  171-173, 185, 300, 303
Cape Town Airport 173
Cape Town Castle 145
Capello, Fabio 152-153
Capone, Al 121
Carcassonne 267
Cardiff 58, 72, 76, 152, 185, 188,
  199, 237, 282
Cardiff Arms Park 147
Cardiff Blues 275
Cardiff Millennium Stadium 115
Caribbean 189
Carisbrook (Dunedin) 95
Carling, Will 131, 173, 240
Carter, Dan 183, 289
Casino Square (Monte Carlo) 136
Castlemartin (Co. Kildare) 225, 227

316

Index

Index